ALTERNATIVE COMMENTARY COLLECTIVE ALMANACK

ALTERNATIVE COMMENTARY COLLECTIVE

ALMANACK

BY MIKE LANE AND MATT HEATH

with DYLAN CLEAVER

A decade of NZ sport

CONTENTS

FOREWORD

It has been well documented that one of my first acts as captain of the Black Caps was to win the toss and bat first at a test in South Africa, only for us to be bowled out for 45 before lunch on the first day. We'd lose that test by an innings. It has been equally well documented that as a playing and management group, we then made big changes to the way we played the game and carried ourselves, which eventually helped to win back the fans we had lost during our dark years.

I'm bloody glad the Alternative Commentary Collective are writing a 10-year retrospective of their first 11 years, because as a proud cricket nation we have a lot to thank them for. Sure, a few of us might not love our nicknames, but the ACC's passion for cricket and their blind loyalty to the Black Caps has played a vital role in not only re-engaging a lot of those people who had drifted away from cricket, but also bringing a bunch of new fans into the mix.

Although my great mate Daniel Vettori often tries to disown his former schoolmates Jeremy Wells, Mike Lane and Paul Ford, I know he, like so many other Kiwi sportspeople, gets a kick out of their antics.

We even invited a couple of the ACC team members to one of our sacred capping ceremonies. If I'm being honest, I can't remember what they, or we, had to say that day, but I do have vague recollections of Mike Lane turning up to our 2015 Cricket World Cup 'after party' with a full head of steam on and seeming quite surprised that none of us were as keen to kick on as he was after we'd just had our arses handed to us by Australia in the final.

Perhaps that's a lesson we can all take from Mike and the crew. Cricket, even in the big moments, is only a game. Whether you win, lose or draw, there's still the opportunity to have a beer, have a laugh and talk nonsense with your mates.

Here's to many more years of doing just that, lads.

BAZ (NEVER PRINCE BRENDON) MCCULLUM

CAPTAIN'S NOTE

The past 11 years of the ACC has been one hell of a ride. And we've loved every minute — well, maybe not every minute. The time Leigh Hart left me with a £5000 room bill in London wasn't cool, but we have moved on. It's been 11 years of hanging with past and present friends, watching a vast array of sport, doing what we love, connecting with great New Zealanders and sharing untold amounts of Export Ultras with each and every one of you.

Some of what you'll read in this book is 100 per cent accurate. Some of the stories are embellished for your entertainment. Others are mostly untrue.

We hope you enjoy reading about this time as much as we've enjoyed living through it.

G-LANE — ACC HEAD

THE ACC: A TIMELINE OF TROUBLE

The original seven, closer in spirit to the 'Wild Bunch' than the 'Magnificent Seven', is assembled by self-appointed skipper Jeremy Wells: Lee Baker, Paul Ford, Leigh Hart, Matt Heath, Jason Hoyte and Mike Lane.

The ACC commentates live from the momentous Cricket World Cup. A few weeks later, following a hotly disputed incident involving Hart and allegations of potential match-fixing, the ACC is banned from commentating live at the World Cup.

Daily Bhuja, featuring Hart and Hoyte, takes the drive slot on Radio Hauraki. In years to come, it will also include Manaia Stewart, part of the ACC's generation next, as a co-host.

The ACC launches the informative web series *Champagne Rugby*, the feature being a social-media testicle that the likes of Jason Hoyte and Scotty Stevenson report 'live' from.

Several members of the team fly to Amsterdam to film preview content for the Rugby World Cup final between the All Blacks and Australia — a game that took place at Twickenham, in London.

2013   **2014**   **2015**

The Alternative Commentary Collective is launched on iHeartRadio to a sum total of zero listeners from a beige caravan during the first ODI against India at McLean Park, Napier. Within the first 10 minutes the chat had become 'dangerously sexual'. By the end of the match they had about 3000 listeners.

Incidentally, the *Matt & Jerry Show* starts on Radio Hauraki the day after the first ACC broadcast.

Before the fifth and final ODI of that same series, the team hire a helicopter to fly them 200 metres, then land on the playing surface of the Cake Tin minutes before the start of the match.

The first series of *The Late Night Big Breakfast* starring Hart, Wells and Hoyte screens on TVNZ.

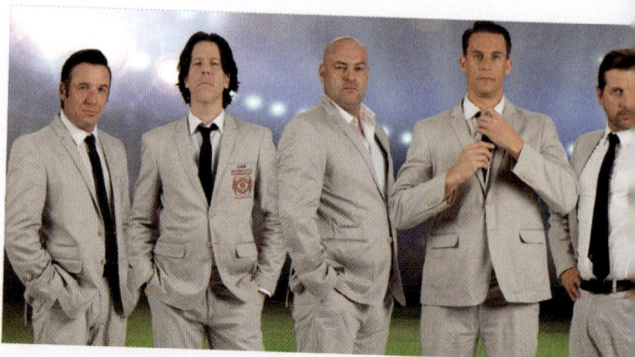

In another world first, Mike Lane sets a little-known world record for commentating cricket live on air while receiving an anaesthetic-less vasectomy.

The British & Irish Lions arrive in New Zealand to much fanfare, but not as much fanfare as the ACC enjoy as they take live commentary shows to Rotorua, Christchurch, Wellington and Auckland.

2016   **2017**   **2018**

The ACC extends its portfolio to include the national game, commentating the Wales tour to New Zealand and also the Rugby Championship.

The burgeoning empire also moves into the world of fantasy with the formation of the ACC Super League, the world's first fantasy cricket league (not fantasy cricket in which players accumulate points for fans based on their performances, but fantasy in that it was completely made up). The league is won by the Hawke's Bay Super Wounders, thanks to a man-of-the-match performance from the late Sir Paul Holmes.

In a very ACC-like happening, Leigh Hart and Jason Hoyte hit the headlines after their 'fishing show' *Screaming Reels* was panned by critics in Australia who were unaware of its parody status.

During the inaugural pink-ball day-night cricket test versus England at Eden Park, the ACC commentary features on Sky TV's yellow-button service for the first time.

Police search the ACC commentary box after a suspicious package was reported. The 'brick of cocaine' turns out to be tightly wrapped icing sugar.

The ACC head to India on an Excellent IPL Adventure. The Bangalore-bound team included Heath, Lane, Joseph Durie and a cardboard cut-out of Jeremy Wells.

The ACC turn their hapless attention to the Commonwealth Games on the Gold Coast with a daily show, *The Moment*, starring Lane and Heath, which screens on TVNZ Duke.

The Agenda podcast is launched, starring Lane, Heath and James McOnie. Manaia Stewart would soon muscle in and has not budged.

We do not like to talk about 2019, but if you insist on reminding us, Lane, aka The Grim Reaper of Sport, travels to London to watch the Cricket World Cup final. New Zealand ties the game.

In late December, Hoyte is spotted on CCTV at numerous airports around the world wearing a small backpack that possibly contained several small vials.

For the first time, the ACC takes on the Dulux Tradies XI in a T20 cricket match. They're still waiting for their first win.

The ACC shocks the media world by winning 'Best Sports Reader, Presenter or Commentator' at the NZ Radio Awards. The named recipients, in a pointer to the growing coterie of talent assembled under the banner, included: Lane, Wells, Heath, James McOnie, Hoyte, Scotty J Stevenson, Mike Minogue, Manaia Stewart, Chris Key, Ben Hurley, Ford, Dylan Cleaver, Hart, Joseph Durie, Joseph Shuker, Tom Harper and Claire Chellew.

The greatest six nights in ACC history, broadcast under the 'No Sleeps 'Til Victory' banner, culminates in Hoyte getting his baps out and being sprayed by champagne while delivering one of the most iconic lines in New Zealand commentary history as the Black Caps become World Test Champions.

2019   2020   2021

Lockdown hits New Zealand. Sport effectively stops. Radio Sport is closed.

The ACC becomes the first commentary team to cover any sport during the Covid-19 crisis with the ACC Super Sevens, a completely made-up rugby competition.

The ACC's rugby commentary starts under the yellow button on Sky for the first time.

Mike Lane gets serious and reveals he has a hole in his head.

The BYC, New Zealand's best-loved specialty cricket podcast, is reignited, starring Ford, Hoyte and Dylan Cleaver.

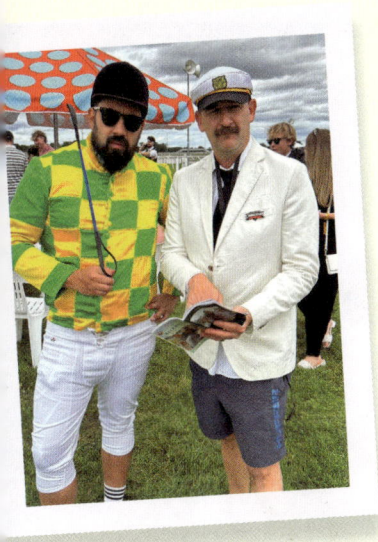

Alternative commentary of Super Rugby, the All Blacks and the Warriors is all carried under the yellow button on Sky, giving the ACC the unofficial title of 'most prolific calling team in New Zealand'.

The *Champagne Rugby* podcast launches, hosted by Tony Lyall (not Tony Ryall).

Heath, Lane, Stewart and Durie don berets, tuck a baguette under their collective arms and take 28 punters to Paris to the world's biggest beer garden. They singularly fail to make it to a Rugby World Cup match.

In one of the most ill-fated ideas in broadcasting history, the ACC pull off a staggeringly unsuccessful 'No Sleep 'Til Victory' rugby/cricket World Cup crossover. The Black Caps lose a thriller to Australia in Dharamshala, and the All Blacks lose the final to South Africa by one bloody measly point in Paris. An absolute shitter of a night/morning.

Adding more strings to their bow, the ACC commentate the Netball World Championships live from a studio in Auckland as the Ferns fall in the semifinals in South Africa.

2022   2023   2024

The ACC starts commentating cricket on the short-lived but celebrated Spark Sport streaming app.

The *Mad Monday* podcast is launched on Tuesdays, starring the Warriors' number-one fan Dai Henwood, along with Chris Key, Manaia Stewart and Ben Hurley.

Boys Get Paid, a podcast from the world of thoroughbred racing, joins the ACC stables.

As the ACC starts its second decade, another brick in the empire is laid with the release of their long-awaited and (potentially) award-winning book . . . which you're reading right now.

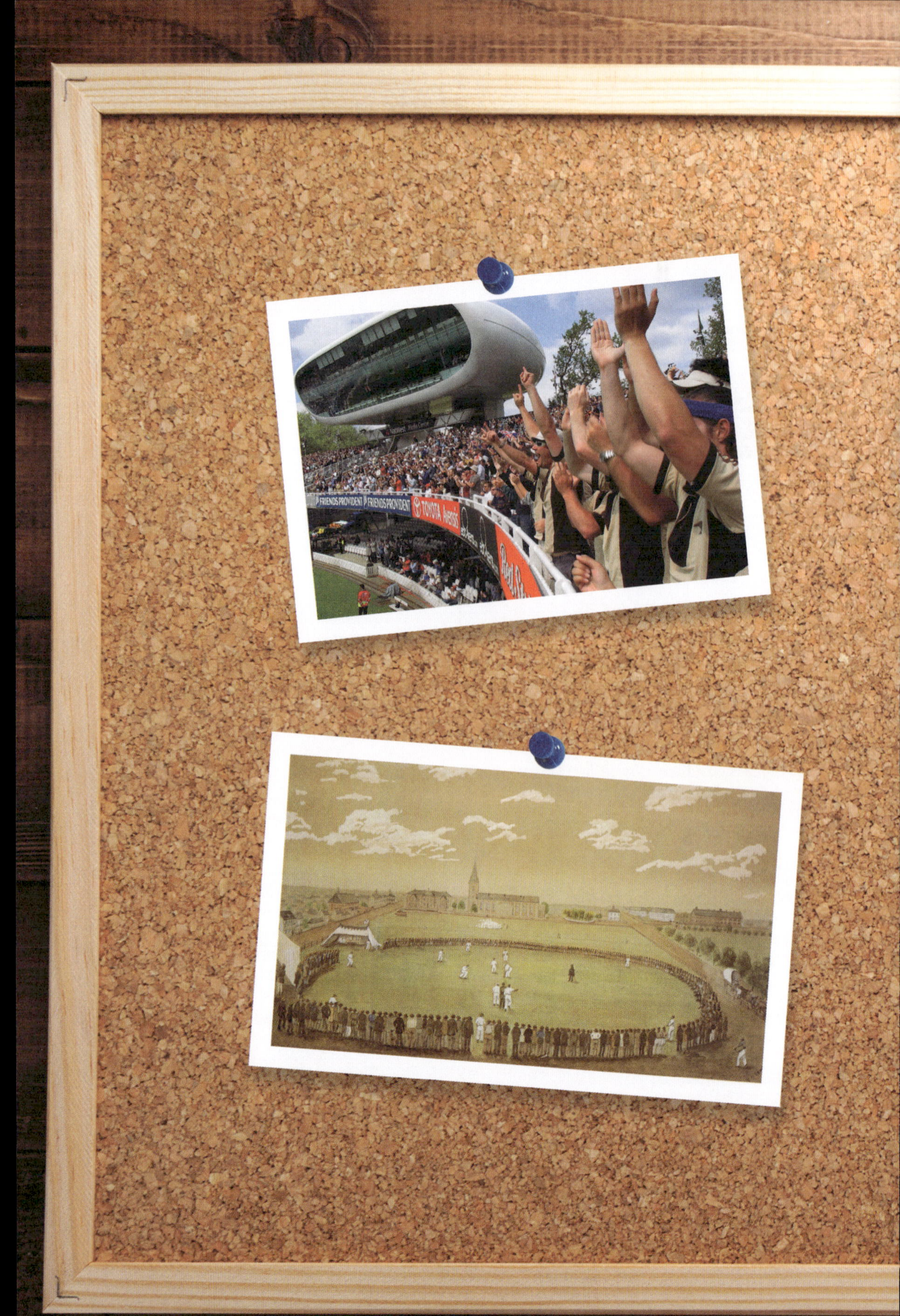
FRIENDS PROVIDENT
FRIENDS PROVIDENT
TOYOTA Avensis

A BRIEF AND UNRELIABLE PRE-HISTORY OF ALTERNATIVE COMMENTARY

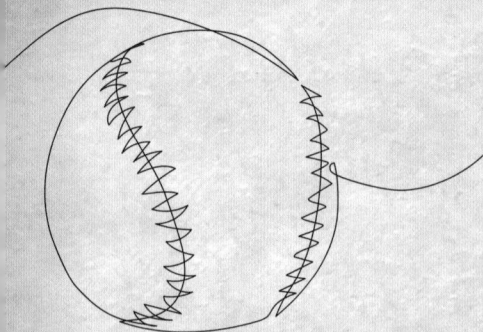

In 1876, Major League Baseball established the first fully professional sports league. For much of the 150 years since, despite the essential premise of pro sports being athletic men and women playing games for the entertainment of the masses, the coverage has been po-faced and earnest. Fun and games have been presented as a deadly serious business.

Of all the sports, perhaps none took itself more seriously than cricket. For more than a century, the only variation on its Persil-white regalia was the cream, the bone, the off-white, the ivory and the beige. This lack of colour on the field also extended to the broadcast, which usually fell to unwieldy state-owned behemoths who inflected (and inflicted) the coverage with dulcet tones and gravitas.

It wasn't until a pugnacious Australian media magnate with a vile temper, a disruptive streak and sacks of his father's cash came along that cricket began to change into something resembling the spectacle we see today. Kerry Packer turned on the floodlights, dressed players in pyjamas and put money in their pockets.

Packer, by many accounts a deeply unpleasant individual, might be 'modern' cricket's most singular figure. He embraced the often-overlooked one-day format of the game, prioritising entertainment and style over textbook and tradition.

He turned his commentary booth over to ex-players, including the famous triumvirate of former Australian captains Richie Benaud, Bill Lawry and Ian Chappell, and a South African–English counterpart in Tony Greig, who brought with him his strong Cape Province brogue.

A new era of commentary and analysis was born. Tactics were explained, decisions were scrutinised, car keys were pronged into pitches. It was . . . 'simply mar-r-r-vellous'.

'You compare it to what we had in New Zealand at the time,' says ACC co-founder Jeremy Wells. 'There were times when we watched cricket from one fixed camera and listened to commentators who had been dragged over from racing or rugby. You couldn't see what the bowler was doing from one end, but it didn't stop Glyn Tucker confidently stating that the ball pitched outside leg every time umpires Fred Goodall or Bob Monteith gave one of our batsmen not out after a vociferous LBW appeal.

'Cricket in Australia looked like a completely different, far more entertaining sport.'

The practice of loading the commentary box full of former stars spread around the world. It was, with some notable exceptions (Mike Lane once called for the RNZAF to un-retire its fleet of Iroquois helicopters to airlift the idiosyncratic Danny Morrison out of India before he caused more national embarrassment), a huge success. While many of cricket's subtleties and nuances remained arcane, the commentators could at least offer penetrative insight into what the batting and fielding sides were trying to achieve at various points in the game. Along with vastly improved camera and audio technology, the coverage improved exponentially.

The fan, it could be said, had at last been put into the heart of the game — but the heart of the fan still remained an unloved and unexplored part of the coverage.

Kerry Packer's revolution also had a spin-off that few anticipated. It was one that would provide a significant landmark in the origins of alternative commentary and the collective that followed.

Billy Birmingham, described by Wikipedia as an 'Australian humourist and sometime sports journalist', achieved a measure of pop culture immortality as the writer of Austen Tayshus's spoken-word hit single 'Australiana'. The comedy sketch, based at a suburban barbecue, contained such gems as: 'Why doesn't Wombat?' and 'Flash your wanger at her'.

The single was never marketed as a threat to Yeats or Tennyson (Alfred, the poet, not Lionel, his grandson and nine-test batsman for England), but the people responded and the record rose to number one in the charts in 1983 and stayed there for seven weeks.

This was just the tip of the iceberg for Birmingham, who turned his attention to cricket in 1984 under the sobriquet 'The Twelfth Man', taking those same sensibilities to his send-ups of the Channel Nine commentary team. He became fond of mangling names from the subcontinent — Areal Muddafarkar and Mohammad Hasabigun to name just two — to the delight of the Australian public, who elevated all of his seven studio albums to number one in the charts. Birmingham was embraced by Kiwis, too, with his penultimate album, *The Final Dig?*, reaching number two on this side of the Tasman. In one memorable scene, Birmingham's Richie Benaud struggles to contain his laughter as he reads out New Zealand's 'shithouse-looking lineup'. To Australian ears, names like Parore, Sinclair, Sulzberger and Tuffey became synonymous with the uselessness of the Black Caps — and many New Zealanders could relate, too.

Birmingham's influence on the genre remains outsized. Not only did he make a name and a lot of money for himself, but he also raised the profile of the Channel

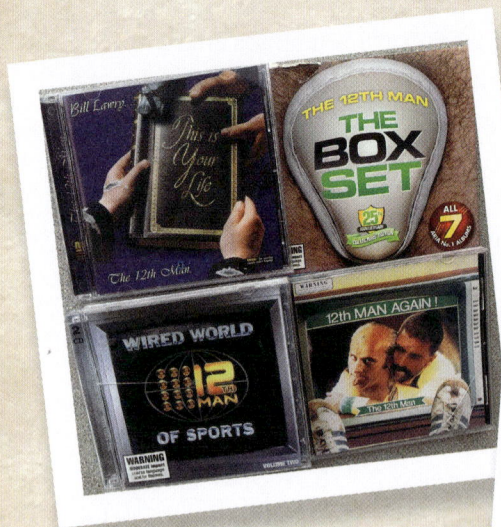

Nine coverage and challenged cricket's comfortable and somewhat cloistered identity by giving it back to the people. For several summers, you couldn't go to a barbecue without somebody trying to impersonate Lawry, Greig, the imitable Benaud, or the hapless Max 'Tangles' Walker.

In The Twelfth Man's wake, Australia became fertile ground for sports satire. John Clarke's mockumentary *The Games* was critically acclaimed, while comedy duo Greig Pickhaver and John Doyle used alter egos Roy and HG to cleverly poke at Australia's obsession with sport while at the same time skewering New Zealand's prowess.

In Britain, Steve Coogan's incompetent and tactless Alan Partridge spent time as a brutally unqualified sports reporter, while *The Fast Show*'s Ron Manager was a television football pundit with a mangled grasp of language and a quixotic view of the sport that occasionally veered into the homoerotic, like when he tried to imagine Gary Lineker's face 'contorted in the throes of sexual ecstasy'.

Despite the cultural cringe element that hovers over New Zealand to this day, sports satire is richly ingrained here. In fact, it pre-dates The Twelfth Man and Alan Partridge.

John Clarke was sending up the All Blacks as the everyman farmer Fred Dagg long before Benaud fell into Billy Birmingham's crosshairs. Around the same time as he emerged in his Red Bands and singlet, so did another cultural icon — Loosehead Len, who was described by his creator, veteran journalist Phil Gifford, as a 'mean-spirited, violent, bigoted, xenophobic, bludging, homophobic, money-hungry, cigarette-sucking, beer-swilling rugby freak'.

There was also Murray Ball's Wal Footrot — a much-loved character whose rugby and cricket dreams and visions were never in sync with his abilities — but perhaps the bravest example of sports parody came from a man who would later go on to become the conscience of the nation.

John Campbell was cutting his teeth in Wellington student radio when he came up with a skit that involved the All Blacks captain naming his team in the showers, with the main selection criteria based on penis size.

MIKE LANE: This was, excuse the pun, a big moment for me. It appealed to my sense of humour. Guessing which All Blacks were running big downstairs operations was exactly the sort of chat I could imagine me and my mates having.

MATT HEATH: Was I influenced by John Campbell's commentaries? I would have to have heard them, or even heard *of* them, which I had not until now. So, no.

These parodies provided sport with a long-overdue laugh track, but it was, for the most part, scripted humour written by professional comics. In the years to come, shows such as the popular *SportsCafe* (featuring a young Leigh Hart as 'That Guy') were looser, performed in front of live audiences with guests, sometimes of dubious quality, but they were at least laughing at sport and everything that comes with it.

The challenge now was to laugh *with* it . . . in real time.

Even with that incomplete history of New Zealand sports satire, it is impossible to draw a straight line from John Campbell to the Alternative Commentary Collective. The lines, as they were, didn't start to take shape until 1999, a pivotal moment in the history of this motley crew.

Here's Beige Brigade co-founder Paul Ford to pick up the story:

'Mike Lane and I were schoolmates with Dan Vettori, and while he was on a youth tour to England he picked up an old 1980s New Zealand kit at a charity auction (Bruce Edgar's according to the label) and gave it to Mike. Then Mike, being the cricket-mad person that he was (and still is), wore it along to sports events, university lectures, while he took his nana out for walks, when he was doing collections for charity, that sort of thing.

'He got a lot of positive feedback — everyone kept asking whether there was anywhere that they could get horrendous retro cricket clothing, too. He pulled the sewing machine out into the lounge of our flat and the construction of a brown-and-tan kit began.'

Back then, Lane and Ford had no designs to permanently shake up the New Zealand sports broadcasting landscape. They simply wanted to show their passionate support for New Zealand cricket by wearing beige, drinking a few beers and generally having a good time. They invited others to join them in the fun. A movement was formed.

Here's Ford again:

'Beige is an iconic colour in New Zealand cricket history: it looks bloody awful, so is quite eye-catching. It's just so uncool, which has made donning Beige Brigade kit emblematic for those calling themselves passionate New Zealand cricket supporters. As we have always said: it's about passion, not fashion.'

While fashion was not the driving factor, Beige Brigade uniforms were crafted with the utmost care.

'The fabric was specially dyed in Christchurch to match the original uniforms, and we found the brown trim and buttons on a scouting mission to a handcraft store,' says Lane. 'We searched high and low for that tan-coloured fabric — it's elusive, but authenticity was important to us.' The brown kiwi logo, also Lane's handiwork, added another badge of honour to these outstanding garments.

'A *New Zealand Herald* article in January 2001 was probably the first time the Beige Bridge were officially recognised as a group,' says Ford. 'Things got wild and crazy at an Owen Delany Park (RIP) ODI between New Zealand and Zimbabwe, and

that coverage attracted interest from other passionate fans. Mike mentioned we were planning to go to Australia for the VB Series at the end of the year, and that set the ball rolling.'

Mike Lane was just three years old when Greg Chappell ordered his little bro Trev to roll one down the wicket Sir Francis Drake style to Brian McKechnie at the MCG in 1981.

'Never forget,' Lane says.

From that moment, Australia and its hallowed grounds had attracted him like dog shit does a fly.

'Our indoor cricket team in Wellington wore the Beige Brigade kit as our inspiration come finals time, and this group became the core of the crew that went on tour to the World Series in Aussie when we slapped the Australians around for most of the summer of 2001–02,' states Ford. 'The series turned into one of New Zealand's most dramatic campaigns in the old three-team format, and we managed to be interesting enough to get on telly a fair bit, which meant even more people started asking for shirts, wanting to join us on tour, wanting to have a few beers, and things continued to escalate from there.'

Ford doesn't mention the police escort into and out of the Adelaide Oval on Australia Day, but there's no debating that the Beige Brigade got noticed. It looked like a hoot.

As this momentum grew, the Beige Brigade saw an opportunity to partner with New Zealand Cricket in a semi-formal manner. But the then CEO Martin Snedden,

Beige is an iconic colour in New Zealand cricket history: it looks bloody awful, so is quite eye-catching.

himself once a wearer of the beige, told Lane and Ford that his organisation had invested too heavily in black branding to turn back the clock. Well, at least until it suited them otherwise.

The beige retro kit continued to gain traction among cricket followers, and NZC spotted an opportunity to make money — the world's first T20 international, a match against Australia at a heaving Eden Park, which saw the Black Caps kitted in brown and NZC selling their own line of replica clothing. The volte-face did not go down well.

'Bastards,' remembers Lane. It wouldn't be the last time he and the sport's governing body would find themselves out of lockstep.

'There has never been a business plan or anything like that for the Beige Brigade,' adds Ford. 'We just dressed up, went to the cricket, had a ball making some noise and having a laugh (and a lot of beers). When people came to us wanting to be a part of it or wanting to help, we made a decision early on that it was not going to be some platform for "extracting value" or "cashing in", so we poured every cent back into the things we love or that we think are funny: a few drinks on the bar, trips to crazy places, ridiculous beige products, match tickets for ourselves and our mates, and accumulating a preposterous amount of cricket-related memorabilia. We even managed to acquire the ball from the Underarm game, increasing our bids on Trade Me well beyond the "upper limit" we had agreed between ourselves and our soon-to-be-wives. It feels bloody awesome to know we have that ball.

'There is something magical about wearing beige to cricket on foreign shores in particular, and having like-minded Kiwi fans come together to help the team out with some rowdy support makes it extra special. I remember being interviewed in the Edrich Stand during a test at Lord's for *Test Match Special* — that was a

There is something magical about wearing beige to cricket on foreign shores in particular, and having like-minded Kiwi fans come together to help the team out with some rowdy support makes it extra special.

pretty surreal moment. Mike was limbering up in a Lycra suit at the time.

'So many more incredible days and nights spring to mind when I think about all the fun had by the Beige Brigade. Beating the Aussies on Waitangi Day at the MCG, Shane Bond ripping their little hearts out on Australia Day, hiring a stretch limousine to drive us around the Gabba and back to our backpackers in Brisbane following a win over South Africa. Mike once took a crowd catch to win $1000 cash at the Basin, which was mad, and the pre-match mayhem we created before the 2015 Cricket World Cup final was awesome, even if the result didn't turn out the way we wanted it to.

'What we've created appeals to the legion of fans who want to be part of something for the fans, and run by the fans, not by the official authorities in their suits and ties and commercial deals. At that time, it felt really disappointing New Zealand Cricket didn't seem to appreciate the positivity and fun the Beige Brigade were bringing to the sport.'

Ford and Lane, however, moved on quickly from any disappointment, and while Lane was doing his OE in London, the Beige Brigade branched out from being the world's smallest clothing manufacturer to become sports tour organisers — including an ill-fated coach convoy to Cardiff for what was meant to be an easy World Cup quarter-final for the All Blacks against a hopelessly out of sorts French team.

It was, instead, a multi-bus calamity.

Lane filled 10 buses with 500 Kiwis. At £149 for a return trip and a match ticket, he had to turn people away. Many of his punters, he noted as they gathered at Paddington Station, had pre-loaded. Many of them, he also noted as a procession of characters went back and forth to the toilet cubicle, were on more than just booze.

'Could be an interesting day,' he thought.

It was. The All Blacks lost, shockingly, 18–20, and Lane's focus turned to shepherding many of his beige-clad flock away from those on more official All Blacks tours, who had outlaid upwards of $20,000 for the knockouts of a tournament New Zealand were expected to win. By the time the buses arrived back in London, he was in the midst of an existential crisis.

'I enlisted ten mates as my tour leaders and they were a liability,' says Lane. 'They were as drunk as the punters, if not more. The Underground had closed for the night. There were no cabs around. Basically I had no choice but to release 500 hammered Kiwis into the London night.'

'Not my proudest moment.'

While Lane was corralling the unwashed and unhinged, Ford was charting a gentler path. Intrigued by the whizz-bang technology that was a compressed audio file, he had a dream.

'Podcasts are *de rigueur* these days,' Ford recalls. 'But in 2006 the distribution of a thirty-minute audio file of three blokes talking cricket nonsense in Kiwi twangs over the internet using syndication technology to allow people to download and listen on mobile devices and personal computers was a pretty futuristic idea.'

The initial dreamer in their universe was former TV3 sports reporter Kevin Sinnott, who had been inspired by his flatmate Jed 'Jedi' Thian, who himself had seen *The Ricky Gervais Show* blaze a podcasting trail in the UK. Thian started a rugby union-focused podcast, *The Rugby Roundtable*, which took off pretty quickly. Cricket was an obvious angle for Ford and company to take.

'For years the Beige Brigade had provided a secondary commentary of the game, just from the embankment (sometimes through a megaphone) rather than over any professional broadcasting channels,' adds Ford. 'This extended to investigating how we could deliver shortwave radio commentary to people in and around the grounds in real time, and morphed into the emergence of the world's longest-running specialty cricketing podcast, *The BYC*. We knew there was an audience — a niche one initially — that was gagging for some not-too-life-and-death chat about cricket.'

And so it came to pass that on Sunday 25 June 2006 the first episode of *The BYC* was recorded.

One might highlight this moment as an official starting point of the Alternative Commentary Collective, a first broadcast as such. In reality this was yet another — albeit significant — thrust towards its conception: hungover, happy and hair-of-the-doggy on a Sunday, talking absolute crap about cricket from various locales in Wellington — including, with the help of a short-lived and ill-fated sponsorship deal, from an Indian restaurant.

'We're surely the first podcast in the history of the world to lose a commercial deal for ordering insufficient naan,' Ford says.

BYC

NZ'S ORIGINAL CRICKET PODCAST

'We're surely the first podcast in the history of the world to lose a commercial deal for ordering insufficient naan.'

People came and went. There were lengthy hiatuses. Then, as the 2000s moved into the 2010s, *The BYC* shifted cities from Wellington to Auckland. Taking over on the mics were Mike Lane, Jeremy Wells and Dylan Cleaver.

'The ACC was born out of *The BYC* podcast,' says Lane. 'First the likes of Paul, Kevin Sinnott, Blair Sayer and Jason Willis, and then me, Dylan and Jeremy talking shit about cricket. It was obvious there was a market for people getting less-than-reliable, less-serious cricket news and views. We weren't ex-internationals, we were just three blokes chatting about cricket in a way that was relatable to both the casual and the committed fan.'

But when the ACC really started to take shape was when True, the advertising agency known for its bold and creative strokemaking, won the New Zealand Cricket account. True's co-founder and chief executive was a bloke named Matt Dickinson, an old friend of Jeremy Wells.

They started chatting . . . and things would never be the same again.

WHAT'S THE WORST THING ANYBODY HAS DONE IN A BEIGE BRIGADE OUTFIT?

PAUL FORD: Mike, in particular, has done some absolutely unspeakably terrible things in his beige kit. Although not all the memorable stories involve him. One we dined out on for ages was when one of the chaps was a sufficiently attractive man to have a young woman accept an invitation to return to his flat after a night out. She liked the Beige Brigade so much she asked him to put his beige kit on before they got into bed. She was only human I guess!

But maybe the worst, and the best perhaps, has to be Mark Richardson racing 100 metres in our 'Slowest-in-the-squad' event wearing a beige Lycra suit. The image of him in a skintight edition of the beige and brown, complete with Cathy Freeman-style hood and a banana inserted you know where is something I'll never forget.

Things got even further off the rails one year when we had an Australian Lycra suit made, too. We couriered it over to Adelaide for Darren Lehmann to use in a race against Mark during a break in a test match. 'We look forward to seeing Boof looking like a weightlifter in it,' we said at the time. We didn't want the Australians whingeing about Mark having an unfair advantage, so in the name of good sportsmanship we had a suit made up for Lehmann. The outfits only came in one size — large.

THE WSTAR SCANDAL EXPLAINED

PAUL FORD: Back in the very early days of the Beige Brigade, we sent our first $100 of revenue to New Zealand Cricket with a note saying we were keen to get the Black Caps back wearing their former brown-and-tan one-day playing strip. The very serious response from NZC CEO Martin Snedden was that they had moved on and had invested a lot of money in 'rebranding' the team and its colours. He wished us luck, but it felt like he effectively kicked us to the kerb.

Then, a few years later, in February 2005 when the inaugural Twenty20 international match was played between New Zealand and Australia, both teams dressed in their retro colours from the 1980s. We felt like this was an amazing opportunity for NZC to acknowledge Kiwi cricket fans and celebrate the amazing support from people who had embraced beige, but instead their commercial clothing partner, Wellfit Limited (Wstar), produced replica beige Twenty20 playing shirts as 'a one-off', with no involvement from the Beige Brigade.

We felt really disappointed, particularly because the Beige Brigade were quite clearly a catalyst for the decision to go retro. We were keen as a bean to co-operate and create some hijinks to help them out, but not prepared to be involved in something that made us look like sellouts.

The extra-annoying part was that the shirts they produced were then passed off as our kit — 'buy the shirt made famous by the Beige Brigade' — and were very much not a one-off but became a regular feature for years to come.

At the time it felt like such a shame NZC could not understand the things we were doing were positive for cricket. Instead, because they couldn't control it through official channels, they regarded two blokes working part-time out of the lounge of their flat as a threat. They really didn't get what the Beige Brigade stood for, particularly our uncommercial view of the cricketing milieu.

MIKE LANE: We weren't going to take this lying down, so we had a chat with our brewery friends, got a pallet of Lion Brown and then put the word out to all the clubs that we would give them the pallet if their player had the best hairdo or moustache. The clubs started harassing their players to get involved. Kaipara Flats started putting pressure on Hamish Marshall to get an Afro and Lancaster Park–Woolston were doing the same to Chris Cairns. They ended up sharing the pallet. It was beautiful — we ended up surreptitiously stealing the limelight from NZC's big night.

FORD: Looking back now, it's amazing to think that an idea we dreamed up in our flat as Mike worked the sewing machine made it all the way to the original T20 international, but it still left a sour taste on what should have been an awesome moment.

BENSON & HEDGES
WORLD CUP 1992
EDEN PARK AUCKLAND
SEMI-FINAL
STARTING AT 10AM
SATURDAY 21ST MARCH
WALTERS ROAD $7.00
GENERAL ADMISSION   CHILD

BENSON & HEDGES
WORLD CUP 1992
EDEN PARK AUCKLAND
NEW ZEALAND V STH AFRICA
STARTING AT 10.30AM
SAT. 29TH FEBRUARY 92
U BLOCK
N   ROW 21 SEAT $0.00
COMP

Black Caps Supporters
Support Group 9th Sept
1) Hurt?
2) Confused?
3) Coping mechanisms

2013

THE IDEA TAKES SHAPE

As 2013 began, the Beige Brigade was trucking along nicely, *The BYC* podcast was finding a niche audience and New Zealand Cricket and the Black Caps themselves were, after sputtering along from scandal to embarrassment, showing the greenest of green shoots of recovery.

Ross Taylor had been 'reintegrated' into the side after missing the disastrous South Africa tour, which he had sat out as he absorbed the disappointment of losing the captaincy, and England arrived for a blue-chip three-T20, three-ODI and three-test tour.

England won both white-ball formats 2–1, but, after the first two tests were drawn, the Black Caps found the unlikeliest of heroes in Peter Fulton. They looked poised for victory as England faltered when chasing 481 on the final two days, but in luck that was typical of the time, the last-wicket pairing of Matt Prior and Monty Panesar clung on.

NEW ZEALAND VS ENGLAND, 3RD TEST
AUCKLAND, 22–26 MARCH 2013
Match drawn

New Zealand	443
P Fulton	136
K Williamson	91
S Finn	6-125

England	204
M Prior	73
T Boult	6-68

New Zealand	241-6 dec
P Fulton	110
B McCullum	67*

England	315-9
M Prior	110*
K Williamson	4-44

An unsatisfying draw was clutched from the jaws of a restorative victory. The pain was prolonged. So, how did all this coalesce into the ACC?

JEREMY WELLS: Geez, that's a hell of a question. The hardest part is digging into the memory and separating fact from fiction. You hear some stories so many times they start to become true, even if they never were to begin with. The way I remember it at the time was that there was a drive to connect a different audience with cricket — not necessarily a traditional audience. We talked through the idea of an alternative view on cricket. It wasn't a fully formed idea. We weren't talking about actual commentary at that point.

MIKE LANE: We were helping Matt Dickinson of True storyboard a few ideas. One of the ideas was providing some sort of fan's view of cricket. The toe-dipping phase of this was Jeremy and I going around the grounds — we actually went to the games, and once an hour we would phone in to Radio Hauraki and give a ludicrous update from a food truck, from the groundsman's shed, basically anything but the cricket. Right at the end we would give the score, but the update was absolute rubbish.

WELLS: What were they? They were reports, slightly different, nothing outrageous, but you have to remember that at the time cricket was very straight. The presentation of cricket was very straight, the commentary of cricket was very straight, whether that be radio or television. We were just trying to add some entertainment to a cricket proposition. I didn't think a lot more of it other than it was getting me into the grounds for free, which I loved.

LANE: These went down really well because at that stage Jeremy wasn't doing a lot of media — he wasn't as ubiquitous as he is now — so it was the only place you could hear him. The following year, NZC went to True and said, 'What else can you do? How can we build on that?' That's when Jeremy, Dicko and I sat down and came up with the Alternative Commentary Collective as a group.

WELLS: If Lane says that he'd be right because, honestly, I have no idea how the long-form commentary idea came about. On the one hand, it's a natural follow-on from what we were doing at the grounds. On the other, it's quite outrageous that we had the audacity to think we could start a commentary team from scratch. I mean, it's not an original idea to do commentary that is slightly different, it's a universal idea, but it actually hasn't been done that often because the barriers are difficult in terms of infrastructure and technology. It's hard to get the rights in the first place, and then to find the drive to put together a team and create a product.

Around this time, the same Jedi Thian, whose podcast mind trick had inspired Kevin Sinnott and Paul Ford to start *The BYC*, was pioneering alternative rugby commentary to live audiences in Wellington bars like the San Francisco Bathhouse and The Loaded Hog, but nobody was thinking longer form — and when it came to sport it didn't get any longer form than cricket — and nobody was thinking of an actual commentary team.

WELLS: Mike, Dicko and I were cricket tragics. We were in love with the game and, I think importantly, in love with the weird parts of the game . . . and there are plenty of weird parts to cricket. Cricket is full of comedy, from the history of it, which is deeply funny, to individual bowling actions that can be quite comical. There's a lot to it. There was a rich mine to be tapped, one that in our view hadn't been explored.

Lane and Wells' timing was serendipitous on two fronts.

In 2013, iHeartRadio New Zealand was launched and became NZME's digital platform. This was a time when many people could not get their collective heads around digital radio or the concept of podcasts. There were a number of heads being scratched among the NZME leadership as they wondered what to do with their new toy. *The BYC* was at this stage still the only sports podcast in the country, and iHeartRadio provided a golden opportunity to launch commentary because there were no associated frequency costs.

The other piece of impeccable timing was the fact that New Zealand cricket was at one of its historic low ebbs. The governing body, NZC, was open to any idea that could help it reconnect with a public that was tiring of the constant negativity.

LANE: In simple terms, they were happy to give us some seed money in the hope we might bring back some of the fans who had given up on cricket.

If you were to pick a point in New Zealand's long and tortured cricket history when you might be able to get away with launching something as countercultural as an alternative commentary stream, it would have been 2012-14.

LANE: They were at the lowest of the low. We had just been through the whole Brendon McCullum–Ross Taylor captaincy saga, which was

immediately followed by a tour to South Africa where we won the toss, chose to bat and were all out for 45. The only interest in cricket was of the car-crash type. Where was the next head-on collision coming from? Fans were so sick of the infighting, the factions. Everyone was sick of the sideshow and cricket fans were wavering. Why bother? Why would they spend their money or their precious time on a team that offered only mild embarrassment in return? There was Team Ross and Team Brendon. It wasn't just selectors and coaches, even the media was forming these factions. It was pathetic.

MATT HEATH: Around this time, Lane, Wells, Joseph Durie and I started the Black Caps Supporters Support Group, because it was so grim.

LANE: It was a safe space, where people didn't judge you for your undying love of the Black Caps. I could stand up in the circle and say how much the Black Caps meant to me.

HEATH: We'd say, 'That's okay, Mike, we still love you.'

LANE: Then I'd rant, 'Ten for fucking three, I mean, Jesus!'

WELLS: It was just nice for me to understand that there were others like me out there. I could safely sit in a room and hold hands with other men who had been hurt by the Black Caps.

HEATH: Then they'd go and win and it would be like welcoming a cheating lover back into your arms. It was like them buying you flowers and taking you out for dinner. All was forgiven.

In terms of commentary, there was no alternative playbook to follow, just a few loose threads to connect.

LANE: Skull, Kerry O'Keeffe, was the only person I listened to who I thought was hilarious, and he provided the inspiration for the use of stings or audio props. The thing he did with *Skippy the Bush Kangaroo* where the theme song was cued up as he was trying to explain its cultural nuances to bemused Indian commentator Harsha Bhogle was wet-your-pants funny. It was the first time I'd ever heard someone bring in audio to fill in a story during commentary, and I thought, 'That's ridiculous, it's got nothing to do with cricket and I love it. There you go, that'll be us.' It was a small thing, but it was so wildly different to anything anybody else was doing.

WELLS: In our mind. No, I'll rephrase that to 'in my mind', because Lane might have a slightly different view on this, a couple of things had to happen. Firstly, if you were going to provide cricket entertainment, it still had to have . . . it had to be almost a parody of cricket commentary. We had to stick to the very strict guideline of calling the game as a commentator would call it. If you were listening on the radio, which is what we wanted people to do, you had to be able to understand what was going on. It couldn't just be a whole lot of people talking, because that is just, well, a whole lot of people talking. It had to be, in effect, a parody of a cricket commentary.

LANE: We thought we could give the fans a different, spectacularly stupid but untainted view on the game, but to be honest we were lucky — we timed our run ridiculously well.

WELLS: The person who was doing ball-by-ball had to be the boss of the moment. They had to know exactly what was going on and had to own the moment. You had to be able to describe the game. The people who were going to be tuning in were going to be cricket fans — maybe of the more casual variety than those opting for traditional commentary, but fans of the sport all the same. They were just cricket fans who wanted to engage with the game, but wanted something different.

So, the commentary had to have some elements of seriousness in it. Elements of genuine information. Infotainment. Mostly light, with just occasional shade. To that end, it needed competent ball-by-ball commentary and respect for the critical moments. That was the sticky stuff that would keep fans glued to the airwaves as the ACC team hit them with the associated nonsense. They wanted to re-engage a demographic who had become increasingly unattractive to sponsors, advertisers and, it seemed, wider society: the drinking-age male.

LANE: People like us, who were starting to look elsewhere for shits and giggles.

There is an anecdote doing the rounds that Leigh Hart was only brought on board by mistake, because he happened to be drinking with one of the others (this part is likely to be true) when they were approached by Wells. In turn, Hart will often take credit for coming up with the concept, claiming that Lane and Wells simply refined his idea.

LEIGH HART: Someone put me on to Mike. I didn't know Mike at the time, but I told him my idea and I can only assume he got hold of Jerry after that and they formed it into something more tangible, I guess. I was more of an ideas guy.

They wanted to re-engage a demographic who had become increasingly unattractive to sponsors, advertisers and, it seemed, wider society: the drinking-age male.

WELLS: Let this lie go no further. It was Lane, Dicko and my idea, and Lane was the one who made it happen. He's a freak like that. I've never met anybody like Mike who can turn an idea into action so quickly. He's like a machine with a list of things and he'll tick them all off so quickly. He's got ten balls in the air and he's not even juggling. His brain operates in both blue sky and details. Both those hemispheres work together; just a very smart guy.

HART: I may not be the most cricket-knowledgeable of the original seven, but I'm the only one with two international wickets. First was Martin Guptill, caught at backward square leg after I tucked him up on his hip and he shovelled it down the fielder's throat. Grant Elliott fell in exactly the same way.

We reached out to confirm this story with the Hairy Jav via WhatsApp. Two blue ticks is a dead giveaway that he read it, but chose not to respond.

HART: He would have said something like, 'I didn't know what was coming next,' which would have set me up perfectly for my pay-off line: 'How the hell could he know, I had no idea myself.' Ha-ha-ha, brilliant.

When Hart wasn't tearing through the New Zealand top order, he was bludgeoning some of Australia's finest bowlers.

HART: I faced Brett Lee in the *SportsCafe* days. That was in his heyday. It might not have been top pace, but a 95 per cent Brett Lee is nothing to sniff at. I wasn't 100 per cent sober either, so we cancelled each other out.

It was time to sound the conch shell and assemble the team.

WELLS: When we thought about a commentary team, the first people we thought about were those we knew who loved cricket and also had a comedic sensibility. I knew Leigh Hart because I'd worked on *The Late Night Big Breakfast* and *Olympico*. I knew he was very funny. I was always a big fan of Leigh. Lee Baker I knew from *Eating Media Lunch*. We were friends as well and all we talked about was cricket. I knew he had a great eye for the absurd. I didn't know Jason Hoyte very well . . .

Nobody does . . .

WELLS: . . . And I know him less now. Lee Baker would always talk about Jason Hoyte and how he'd spend all day shadow batting while on shoots.

I also knew about his comedy act Sugar and Spice and, most importantly, that he was an umpire with great pipes. Mike Lane and I were friends from school. Matt Heath and I were working together in radio, but also had spent time watching cricket together over the years and were both members of the Black Caps Supporters Support Group. Paul Ford was another friend from school, best mates with Lane, one of the funniest people you'll ever meet and knew more about cricket, the history of cricket and the unusual parts of cricket, than anyone I knew. He'd also been to every cricket game that was on in the same town as him. It didn't matter what city or what level, if he was somewhere and there was a cricket game on, he was there. I called everyone up and said, 'What do you think about this . . .?'

LEE BAKER: Jeremy asked me to do it because we had a cricketing relationship outside our working relationship, put it that way. I was very flattered and surprised because I didn't think I was the right person, and still believe that. But no one was going to hear that and not go: 'Oh my god, we're going to go to the games, we're going to commentate as if we're actual commentators who know something about the sport and we're going to get paid to do that, with our friends!' So, it was a definite 'yes' from me.

JASON HOYTE: I'd just been cast in a major American movie*, so it put me in a real dilemma: here's my greatest love, cricket, or a major American film. In the end I chose cricket — probably the worst decision I have ever made in my life.

LANE: Matt Heath said, 'What if you don't know anything about cricket?'

HEATH: I just wanted to raise the issue that I wasn't qualified to do this.

LANE: Jeremy said, 'What do you know about?' and Matt said, 'I know heaps of stuff about animals.'

HEATH: I do know a lot about animals, and I was pleasantly surprised about how much room was afforded to me to talk about animal reproduction and husbandry.

HART: We worked out early on that Matt was going to be doing animal facts. Beyond that, it was fairly loose.

* This is patently untrue.

WELLS: I'll tell you what, if you've got someone who knows something about animals, and they're in a commentary team, that's going to be quite useful. To be fair, for all the talk of Matt's animal facts over the years it's mostly the same fact over and over again. It's about how many vaginas a kangaroo has.

HEATH: A kangaroo has three vaginas.

HART: That's a really strong fact.

LANE: Leigh Hart said, 'Well, I don't know anything.' We said to him, 'Well, you're good with numbers, so you can be the statistician.'

HART: My statistical background and ability to analyse meant I was always going to be doing stats. I mean, there was no two ways about that.

In the background, Lane and Wells were coming up with a loose manifesto of what the product should look and sound like. They decided that even if they weren't going to be immediately ear-catching, they would be eye-catching.

WELLS: If we didn't sound like a commentary team from ball one, I at least wanted us to look like one, so we went to Hallenstein Brothers and chose ourselves a uniform. Mike said, 'Hey, I can get us a caravan,' so we got a commentary caravan like a classic scene from a Shell Trophy game in the days of *Sports Roundup*.

Leigh Hart's Tip for Aspiring Statisticians

I don't think anyone truly understands or appreciates the work that goes into being the key stats man for a commentary team. My colleagues certainly don't. You spend hours getting your head around the latest set of stats and then, bam, just like that they go and change. It's so weird.

It's a constant reordering of your mind, and I don't mind admitting that after a shift with the ACC, I'd go home at night and I wouldn't be able to sleep. I'd shut my eyes and all I'd see was complex combinations of Brendon McCullum's strike rate, old Lotto numbers and discontinued landline numbers for Chinese restaurants. It was starting to really affect my lifestyle. My brain was like a computer hard drive that needed a defrag.

So, my tip for those of you out there striving to be a cricket statistician is this: Never highlight a stat from the most recent 50 years as they are more prone to change. Instead, fascinate your listeners with stats from the distant past. You'll be amazed at the rich seam of stats to mine from the between-the-wars period. For example: Did you know that Bill Ponsford was the first player to notch two first-class quadruple centuries? No, of course you didn't. He was also red-green colourblind, which only adds to his, and my, legend.

A caravan owned by an unsung ACC hero in Paul Silcock was sourced from Thames and reskinned. That was the Trojan horse.

WELLS: The other thing we needed was the ground effects, the stump mics. It needed to sound like a proper commentary.

As they prepared to roll out for the first time, game one of a five-match series against India, it occurred to the team that they really didn't have a plan. What there was remained locked away inside the mind of Wells.

WELLS: We had one meeting before our first game. It was in the hotel on the morning of the match and lasted about twenty minutes.

HOYTE: That was my first experience of Mike Lane's propensity for wandering around nude.

LANE: Jeremy said, 'How about one person does ball-by-ball and everyone else shuts up, but between that, just go for it.'

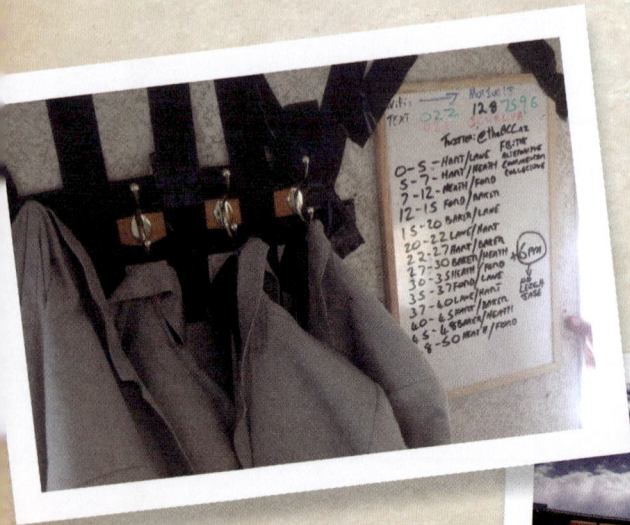

Walking into that caravan for the first time, I felt like Buzz Aldrin, Neil Armstrong and Michael Collins must've felt when they first got into Apollo 11.

HOYTE: It was established early on that Jerry and I would do ball-by-ball.

HART: I was keen to do ball-by-ball as well.

HOYTE: We'd do ball-by-ball and that would be pretty straight, while the likes of Lane and Hart et cetera would provide the filth.

HART: So, we ended up with Jase and Jerry doing ball-by-ball and they still do. They do a good job. I still wouldn't mind doing some ball-by-ball. Mike gets to do some from time to time. Matt's even done some. I've never done ball-by-ball.

BAKER: It was just a dream gig. It could only be fun, and even if it was a disaster it would be a fun disaster.

So, there they were, on the precipice of history, with the secret seven of the ACC readying themselves to enter a caravan and change the course of New Zealand sports broadcasting, right as the rock-star ensemble that was the MS Dhoni-led Indian cricket team prepared to take on the Black Caps.

HART: Walking into that caravan for the first time, I felt like Buzz Aldrin, Neil Armstrong and Michael Collins must've felt when they first got into Apollo 11 . . . actually, maybe more like Apollo 13 because there were so many fuck-ups with it.

One way or another, the ACC were ready for liftoff.

THE 1992 WORLD CUP CHANGED MY LIFE

by Jeremy Wells

In February 1992, I'd just turned 15 and was already a cricket tragic, yet somehow the fact New Zealand was about to host a World Cup opener in my home city had largely escaped me.

Different times.

I was playing cricket on the morning of the 22nd with my mate Simon Dykes, whose father Ross was a Black Caps selector. He said: 'Hey, what are you doing this afternoon? Want to come to the cricket with me?'

It was a life-changing moment.

I'd been to Eden Park to watch cricket before, but it was always with my dad and we'd sit sensibly in the North Stand. This was the first time I went along to the terraces with my mates. It must have been the only place in New Zealand where you didn't get asked for ID when you went to the bar. The assumption must have been made that if you were old enough to go to the bar and ask for a beer, you must be old enough to drink it.

The whole day was intoxicating. New Zealand batted first and Martin Crowe, the most elegant player we have ever produced, scored a magnificent century, but let's face it, 248 was never going to be enough against Australia with Boon, Border, Dean Jones and the Waughs. Dipak Patel opened the bowling and then Crowe the

skipper unleashed the dibbly-dobbly attack on the world. Willie Watson, Gavin Larsen, Chris Harris and even Rod Latham just sucked the life out of opposing batters. What a win. That Eden Park pitch never got enough credit for being New Zealand's player of the tournament.

As for me, I was now committed to going to every game I could.

South Africa were smashed by seven wickets when Mark Greatbatch, elevated to opener in place of the injured John Wright, went Gonzo at the top of the order. What a revelation — I'll never forget him swinging that SS Turbo like a club.

The West Indies were dispatched with five wickets and nine balls to spare. Greatbatch was pinging Malcolm Marshall and Curtly Ambrose over the off side into the stands and staring them down. That sort of stuff just didn't happen.

As a teenager on the terraces, it was so life-affirming. It was a genuine party atmosphere. There was no piped music. The crowd

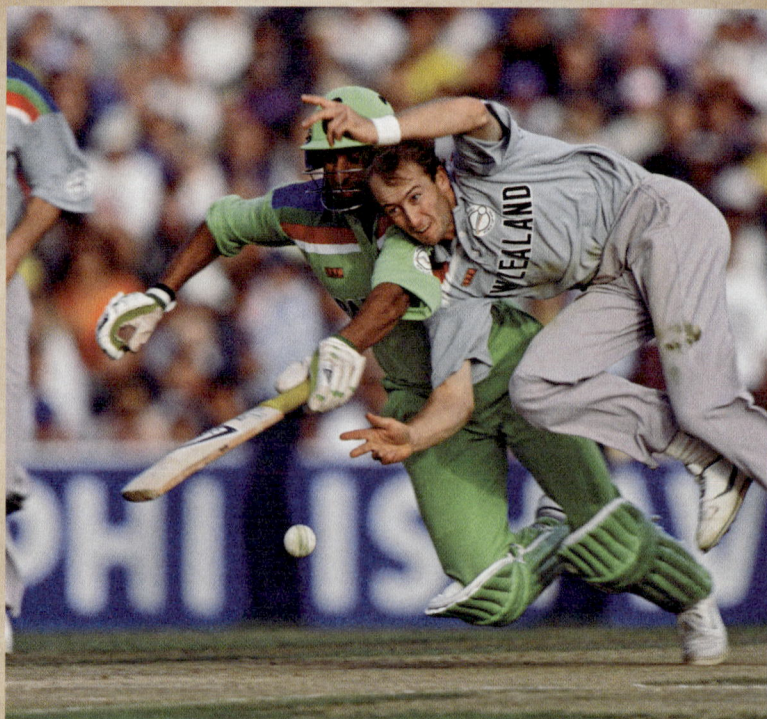

provided the soundtrack to that World Cup and I don't think we experienced anything quite like it again until we beat Australia in that low-scoring thriller at the 2015 World Cup.

Then came Pakistan . . .

That was crushing. We scored enough on that track. Crowe was brilliant again, but he couldn't take the field and John Wright had to captain via hastily scrawled paper notes. We looked certainties to win, though. The crowd was chanting, 'We're in the final', as Imran Khan and Javed Miandad were crawling along and the run rate pushed above the mythical six runs per over mark.

Inzamam-ul-Haq was the first to take on our dibblies, especially Harris, and he embarrassed them in ways that other teams should have. We choked, really, and the loss was reflected on the terraces. Our friend group started to lose numbers. One was evicted for shouting, 'It's sausage time!' and throwing a snarler at a cop. Another for urinating on somebody else.

It all fell to bits on and off the field.

Still, the tournament had a profound effect on me. My love of cricket was elevating just as New Zealand's fortunes were declining. You could look at that post-Hadlee landscape as pretty bleak (Crowe, by now, was also playing on one leg), and some of those bowling attacks we cobbled together were pure comedy, but geez the '90s were interesting. They threw up some unique characters.

Even in our darkest years we were strangely watchable.

Cricket, you can't beat it.

2014

THE INDIAN SUMMER

It is not exaggerating to say that 2014 was a deeply weird year in New Zealand sport, which means there was probably no better time to officially start the Alternative Commentary Collective.

As the year began, there were signs that the Black Caps were starting to head in the right direction under the Mike Hesson–Brendon McCullum leadership axis, with McCullum's record-breaking 302 against India giving the Black Caps Supporters Support Group plenty to celebrate. However, as 2014 progressed, most of the headlines involving New Zealand cricket centred around allegations that Chris Cairns was 'Player X' and accused of involvement in a match-fixing scandal that would end up seeing Lou Vincent receive a life ban from the sport. Cairns would later be cleared of perjury in the High Court in London in a trial that saw McCullum testify for the prosecution.

The All Blacks were defeated just once in the year, a 25–27 defeat at the hands of the Springboks in Johannesburg, but the most-read rugby story of the year focused on first five-eighth Aaron Cruden missing the plane to Argentina after getting on the gas at The Zookeeper's Son pub in Auckland. According to reports at the time: 'He had joined teammates for a meal and drinks on Saturday night, but his movements after that are unclear.'

In other big rugby news, All Blacks coach Steve Hansen described streakers as a 'pain in the backside' after Rose Kupa made a dash for glory in the Rugby Championship match against Argentina at McLean Park, Napier. In doing so, she fulfilled most aspects of Manaia Stewart's Guide to Streaking (see page 144).

'The question is, how do they get on?' Hansen rhetorically asked the assembled press. 'There were enough of them [Red Badge security guards] in the jackets, you'd think they'd be able to stop them. They did really good tackles at the end of it, but they probably should have done something before she went on. I think we've got to have a better plan to prevent them from getting on. And we don't have to smash them over either once we finally catch up with them.'

As for Kupa, the Flaxmere resident was just pleased to have ticked one thing off her bucket list, adding that her next goal was to cycle the length of New Zealand. It is unclear how far she went towards completing that challenge.

Speaking of cycling, 2014 saw Glasgow host the Commonwealth Games, at which New Zealand won 45 medals, including 14 golds, with a third of the haul coming on two wheels.

All things, however, took a back seat to the ACC, as the team pushed the button marked 'GO' in time for the first of five ODIs against India at McLean Park on 19 January 2014.

NEW ZEALAND VS INDIA, 1ST ODI
NAPIER, 19 JAN 2014
New Zealand won by 24 runs

New Zealand	292-7	India	268
K Williamson	71	V Kohli	123
C Anderson	68*	M McClenaghan	4-68

MIKE LANE: Within the first ten minutes of the first broadcast, the subject matter had become dangerously sexual.

JASON HOYTE: It was very exciting.

JEREMY WELLS: Almost immediately we were embroiled in virginity stories and I thought to myself, 'If this is where it starts, where are we going to finish up?'

MATT HEATH: It was a bit frosty from other members of the media initially. I remember one member of the internal NZC media operation setting up two giant speakers next to our caravan, saying, 'Nobody's going to hear your broadcast' and laughing as he walked away.

LEIGH HART: I certainly felt, and I know the rest of the guys did too, a negativity from the rest of the media. Not just cricket media. All media.

LANE: Cricket is a very traditional sport. Its coverage is often quite boring. It's usually older, middle-aged dudes who had been covering cricket for years, and then they see a bunch of fuckwits turn up in Hallensteins suits in a caravan that was basically laden with booze . . .

HOYTE: I don't know if they were massively aware of us at that point, but that certainly changed over a short period of time.

WELLS: They thought this was a novel idea that might last one game and then we'd get sick of it. Little did they know we would bed in for eternity.

HART: We said, 'Once we get in there we're not getting out.'

HOYTE: Quite genuinely, once I'd done that first game, I thought, 'I've finally come home, I've found the thing I'm going to do for the rest of my life.'

LANE: We knew within the first day that we were a dangerous combo that had the potential to take off.

And they did.

WELLS: We didn't have one listener. There's nothing better than starting without a listener. There's no pressure. I remember chatting to everybody and saying, 'Right, we're going to have one ball-by-ball commentator and two making comments.' Everyone had listened to cricket on the radio before and knew how the rhythm works. When the bowler comes in, at a

certain point, whatever you were talking about, you stop, allow the ball-by-ball guy to call the game, then you pick up from where you left off. I was very clear about how that was going to work, the structure and the sound of it.

From the first ball we called in that game, I knew the sound was right. Straight away, I knew it sounded like a commentary. We were in this caravan, it was thirty-five degrees, but after that first over I remember thinking to myself, 'This is totally going to work.' The technical part all worked. How? I'm not quite sure. We had no idea what we were doing and we had no listeners, yet I was super-confident we had something that was going to work.

By the end of the first game, they had a couple of thousand listeners. The next game, the audience doubled, and the game after that it doubled again.

LANE: We didn't market it very well, but we definitely started with zero and might have got to a few thousand by the end of the day. With the iHeart platform we could literally see the listeners logging on. By the end of the series we might have got to 10,000.

We were building an audience incrementally and somewhat organically . . . until the drinks trolley incident at the 2015 World Cup (see page 70). Things went bananas after that.

COMMENTARY AGENDA

* Jim Hickey Pool Party
* DJ A-Hole's Greatest Hits
* World Dictators XI
* Terry Salamanderman's legacy

WELLS: When things are hard, it's usually a sign that there's something wrong, but this was so easy. In the world of entertainment, if it's hard and a graft, then it's wrong. In that sweltering caravan, the chemistry was obvious.

LEE BAKER: Because we never took ourselves or the idea too seriously, we could afford to be authentic. We were unburdened by expectations. It was a wonderful experiment.

We all defaulted to our natural personalities and sense of humour, and there was almost no safety net between us and what was going out. We really did say whatever we wanted. We didn't stop to think, 'Is that appropriate? Is that what we should say?' I certainly didn't. Sometimes I'd feel slightly panicked because I wasn't a broadcaster but knew I had to come up with something, so I'd just say something that was quite revealing, or embarrassing, or incendiary, or ill-conceived or whatever. You just went for it because you knew you had to come up with something.

That gave the team a certain flavour of authenticity.

WELLS: I also realised very early on that this whole thing was just an extension of the best part of my life, which was to go to the cricket and spend the day talking with my friends. These were people I enjoyed spending time with. It wasn't work. We all got on very well. There was a real lack of ego. Nobody wanted to hog the microphone. We were all very generous when it came to giving each other time.

We all defaulted to our natural personalities and sense of humour and there was almost no safety net between us and what was going out. We really did say whatever we wanted.

HART: My biggest issue early on was Wells and Hoyte monopolising the microphone when they were on. I had a lot of amazing stuff to say back then, but hardly any of it went to air. I was doing hours of prep and most of it went unused.

WELLS: Nobody was preparing information. Actually, I think Matt Heath was putting together animal facts to share, but other than that we were turning up with an open mind and seeing where things went. There were no rules around what we could and couldn't say because we were on a digital platform. There were no broadcasting standards that applied to us. It was the Wild West, really.

HART: We knew we were making history.

They were making history, certainly, charting a new course through life like their heroes Shackleton, Lewis, Clark, Hillary, Burke and Wills before them. They were also, from day one onwards, making enemies — enemies who accused them of committing all number of crimes.

CHARGE 1:	Hiring a helicopter to fly a commentary team onto the Cake Tin minutes before the 5th ODI v India.
CHARGE 2:	Hiring a cocktail barman for the caravan.
VERDICTS:	Guilty

GUILTY

BLACK CAPS V INDIA, 5TH ODI
Wellington, 31 January 2014

On the field and on the mic, things were going pretty bloody swimmingly for the ACC in their first series. The Black Caps were unbeaten against the rock-star Indians, winning the first two games before a dramatic tie in game three at Eden Park was followed by a seven-wicket win in Hamilton.

Mike Lane: It was the last game of our first series as commentators. We'd had a little bit of feedback by then.

Jeremy Wells: We'd had word that commentator Bryan Waddle was not happy about the ACC.

Dallas Gurney was general manager of Newstalk ZB and the now-defunct Radio Sport. All editorial decisions and discord across the network tended to end up at his door.

Dallas Gurney: I don't think hatred is too strong a word. At one end of the spectrum you had the traditional commentators. Bryan was the captain of that team. At the other end you had these clowns turning up trying to have some fun with the sport. The traditional guys definitely hated the ACC, which I always found quite sad, because I think a lot of the ACC boys actually revered those traditional commentators.

Gurney is right in his last point. The very fact that the ACC's ball-by-ball commentary mimicked cricket commentary was evidence of this reverence.

Wells: We looked up to Wads. We loved Wads.

Lee Baker: Early on, Ian Smith shouted us beers one night. It was fantastic. We were in heaven as he was sharing these really candid stories about Sir Richard Hadlee and that fantastic team of the '80s.

The good times would not last.

Matt Heath: Wads felt that we, the ACC, were a blight on the game and had no right to be there.

Lane: It was a bone of contention about how much money was being spent on the ACC because we all had suits.

Wells: He wasn't happy about the suits we were wearing.

Lane: It was said that it couldn't be cheap to fly the likes of Leigh Hart, Jeremy Wells and Matt Heath around the country. Ironically, it was paid for by New Zealand Cricket at that time.

Gurney: I had regular conversations with Bryan that started with, 'You won't believe what they've gone and done now...' I don't know, maybe it was always going to be that way.

Wells: He wasn't happy about the special attention we were getting, and he certainly wasn't happy that we were invited to the media lunchroom.

Lane: Through all of this, we still love Wads and his team. They're still all welcome round to mine for Sunday lunch.

Ah yes, eating media lunch. What a strangely delicate, ego-ridden, ferociously political playground the lunchroom can be. As a bite-sized explainer, the stadium operators, in conjunction with New Zealand Cricket, provide lunch for the working media. This is a single-site buffet operation. At the Basin Reserve, for example, it is under the RA Vance Stand in the indoor nets — where the different branches of the cricket media gather awkwardly together.
   There was a hierarchy which generally went something like this: ex-internationals in TV were the big fish, long-time radio commentators were somewhere behind them, then came camera operators and technical staff, followed by print media, the Dalits of the lunchroom. These various branches of the media would line up, spoon chicken curry onto rice next to a green salad, then shuffle off to their preordained spots, only rarely mixing with those from a different branch.
   There really was no place in the natural order of things for an alternative commentary crew.

Jason Hoyte: If looks could kill. Yeah, it's fair to say they really hated us having the temerity to eat food.

Lunchroom politics aside, the ACC decision-makers were left with a choice: come up with a plan of appeasement with Waddle and co., or come up with a plan of maximum provocation.
   They opted for the latter.

Wells: G-Lane thought to himself, 'What is the one thing we could do to annoy Bryan Waddle more than anything else in the world? More than even the suits and Oakley sunglasses. More than even eating their specially reserved desserts.'

Heath: Yeah, so to hammer the point home that we weren't spending too much money, we hired a helicopter to land at the ground minutes before game five was due to start.

Leigh Hart: It wasn't an ego thing. It wasn't our way of saying, 'Hey, we're here.' But if we did want to do that, it was a great way of going about it.

This of course begs the question: how did the ACC, already pushing at the seams of New Zealand Cricket's conservative comfort level, get the okay to land a helicopter in the middle of the Cake Tin moments before a one-day international?

The short answer is indifference. At every level somebody had the power to stop this outrage, but it was pushed up the chain with the assumption by all parties that someone else would be the one to say 'no'. In the end, while nobody actually said yes, nobody said no, so that was permission enough.

Lane: I rang NZC and they said they were cool with it if the stadium was cool with it. I rang the stadium and they said they were cool with it if New Zealand Cricket were cool with it. That's the green light.

Heath: I can't believe we were allowed to do that actually.

Hart: You're better off just doing it and apologising later, so that's what we did...although I don't think we apologised.

Adding to the audacity of the scheme, the helicopter company was located 200 metres from the stadium. It would have been quicker for the team to have walked from their hotel rooms to the ground than the rigmarole they went through to land on the field.

But the stunt had the desired effect. Cups of tea were spluttered in other media boxes up in the ramparts of the stadium. Later on, in the ACC caravan, tea was the furthest thing from the commentators' minds, unless it was a Long Island Iced Tea.

Hart: Everyone was talking about the helicopter on the pitch, but nobody was talking about the cocktail barman in the back of the caravan.

Heath: The ACC caravan has often been referred to by officials and stadium staff as a Trojan horse.

Bench seats under which camping gear would have been stored back when the caravan was a genuine holiday vehicle were instead used to smuggle bottles of Canadian Club, rum and white spirits into the ground. A mixologist was hired to keep the team's spirits up as New Zealand asserted their dominance in the match. Nobody needed to leave the cramped confines for refreshments.

Wells: We were living the dream.

Hart: The cocktails certainly took the edge off, especially after a big flight like that.

Heath: I thought it was taking the piss having a bartender in the caravan. At this point, I was getting sick of all the rule-breaking, so I only had seven or eight, ten drinks max. That was my protest about us going too far.

Hoyte: As team leader I spoke out against that. I thought it was a dangerous game for the ACC to be playing, but weirdly it seemed to improve the commentary performance.

Lane: Jason Hoyte is in no way, shape or form the leader. Nobody is following him into battle.

New Zealand duly wrapped up the match and a 4-0 series win. The commentators, both traditional and alternative, made their way back to their homes and hotels. The helicopter was not required.

Hart: I don't know how we left. I don't think we left in a chopper, did we? No, no, I don't recall leaving at all actually.

The ACC were here to stay, but, due to the crimes of the opening series, they were never to have it so easy with the game's administrators again.

Lane: New Zealand Cricket didn't need us any more after they beat a strong Indian team comprehensively. They won 4-0 and that led into the World Cup in 2015, which was a barnstormer and fed into a golden period for the game in this country, and we just happened to ride that wave at the same time.

Paul Ford's Guide to
SMUGGLING ALCOHOL

The Beige Brigade cult and its experiences navigating Aotearoa's cricketing universe have been an influential feeder for the ACC, and this includes mastering the art of smuggling booze into cricket grounds using a mix of glorious innovation, superb risk management, Trojan horses and trial by unmitigated disaster. Here are the most valuable lessons we have learned.

Player coffin

Literally an elite-level hack is getting a mate selected into a domestic or international cricket team and then commandeering one of their cricket coffins with your jungle juice of choice. There is a level of ability required in conveying the liquor from the player to the practice nets or dressing room to the embankment, but it can certainly be done. Arrive early and choose your friends wisely.

Couch

This stunning Trojan horse was a magnificent option when marketing managers for cricket were trying to get lots of students into cricket grounds instead of families with kids who just play cricket out the back of the stands, returning intermittently to punish players for autographs. 'BYO couch' was a brilliant initiative, providing the opportunity to fill the base of an expendable couch with beer cans to match the in-ground supplier. Be very careful if the couch tips over or if you are required to move its one-tonne weight at pace.

Small child

Find a mate — or hire one — with a cute kid, deck them out in some low-level Black Caps merch and a patriotic homemade banner. Furnish the kid with a lunchbox comprised of snacks, an apple, ham sandwiches and a little bottle of water packed with 40 per cent proof vodka.

The advanced version is to impregnate someone and wait until the small child is old enough to require a hefty transportation device. Simply send the mum in

with the buggy, ideally with her in a frazzled state of mind to ensure no security guard would dare stand in her way, and pack the bottom of the buggy with drinks stashed in multiple boxes of (clean) baby wipes.

The sump

Another Trojan-esque embankment option with a long history of success and associated collateral damage to relationships and reputations. You will need a ground where the joy of a chilly bin and the ability to bring in your own food is not prohibited, and ensure your bin has a tap. Load up on bachelors' handbags (aka supermarket chickens), bread, salads and maybe a crayfish or two. Fill the base of the chilly bin with a layer of ice and pour in copious amounts of white spirits: iced cocktails on tap all day.

The pallet

This is a real Occam's razor option with voluminous rewards given a pallet holds 200 dozen beers. Get a pallet and dress as a member of the catering staff, then thunder straight through the tradesman's entrance with authority, preferably accompanied by a couple of genuine catering staff. High-risk given it was infamously activated and filmed by the *Pulp Sport* TV show during an Eden Park test match.

A caravan

Surely nobody would have the audacity to transform a 1970s Ōtorohanga-made caravan into a mobile drinks trolley: parking it up on the boundary rope and filling it with a smorgasbord of liquids aimed at delivering elevated levels of serotonin, a bartender, much banter and a commentary team in white suits, black ties and Birkenstocks? Surely . . .?

Honourable mentions

- Dressing as a massive beer can and entering the gate wearing 36 beers strapped to your abdomen. Audacious.
- Getting your leg amputated, then getting a custom artificial leg and filling it with the liquid of choice. Not worth it, and the faux leg has a pungency not easily forgotten.
- Hollowing out a book, a Bible or a loaf of bread and stashing within. You need to look like a librarian, a God-botherer or a baker.
- Dig a hole in advance and bury your booze. Everyone knows someone who says they did this in the 1970s. Not successfully deployed for 50 years, although apparently, and possibly apocryphally, the practice is still a big part of the Bathurst 1000 carnage.
- Cars at the cricket is not really a thing, but we love the idea of filling the window-washer reservoir with gin or vodka.
- Catheter bag. Bad taste, but sometimes you gotta do what you gotta do. Get a tear-inducing back story prepped up, too.
- Injected fruit. It's an oldie but a goldie, with oranges and watermelons the most common pulpy vessel of choice, but there is also a niche smuggling industry involving coconuts.

Dear NZME

Of all the innovations in cricket, from increased use of video technology in umpiring decisions, through to reverse sweeps and carrom balls, by far the worst has been the inexorable rise of the Alternative Commentary Collective. What a truly appalling product, delivered, unsurprisingly, by a wretched group of individuals.

If you like the sacred sound of leather on willow being served with a side of toilet humour and washed down with a six-pack of stupid, this might be for you, but for those of us who prefer analysts to anal lists it's a desecration of the sport we love. It's such a terrible combination that I find it hard to say who and what I hate the most.

Is it the supercilious Jeremy Wells and his honeyed tones that can descend in an instant from a florid description of a square drive to a story about a friend's Grindr hook-up? Maybe.

Or is it Mike Lane's bro chat that far too often circles back to the state of his testicles? Likely.

Yet it could easily be Leigh Hart or Matt Heath and the near-constant dribble of inanities about the mating habits of giraffes and the tenderest cut of meat to take when barbecuing a domestic cat.

I think about the childhood psychological trauma that must have created a twisted mind like Lee Baker's, and Paul Ford's straight-man sidekick ruse might fool some, but not me.

If I'm being totally honest, I don't mind Jason Hoyte. Always immaculately prepared and attired, his knowledge of cricket and the intricacies of umpiring is first class. It's more than that, however. His rich baritone fills me with a sense of wonder — sometimes late at night I find myself imagining him appearing on my balcony dressed in double-denim to sing *bel canto*, with a cigarillo clutched between his long, elegant fingers.

Anyway, where was I? Yes, that's right, it's a terrible business this ACC nonsense.

Time and again I've felt like complaining to the highest authorities, only to be sideswiped by something even more contumacious than the previous outrage. So, I keep listening, hoping for insight, and time and again I'm left bereft, soiled and slightly ashamed of myself. I listen for hour after hour after hour.

Just dreadful.

Bryn Waddell (chartered accountant, Seatoun)

If 2014 was a throat-clearing exercise, then 2015 promised to be full noise. On Valentine's Day, the eyes of the cricket world turned to New Zealand for the opening of the 11th Cricket World Cup, which the Black Caps were approaching with newfound confidence after establishing a pedal-to-the-metal style under Brendon McCullum.

Cricket wasn't the only sport played in 2015 — a very good Silver Ferns team tripped up 55–58 against Australia in the final of the Netball World Cup, and there was a rugby tournament we'll get to shortly — but for the early part of the year it certainly felt like it.

The Black Caps' campaign captured the imagination of New Zealanders everywhere, including a skinned-up caravan full of ACC commentators. Whether it was McCullum knocking the leather off the new ball against Sri Lanka in the opener, Tim Southee running through the English in Wellington, Kane Williamson pumping Pat Cummins for six to beat Australia, or Martin Guptill hitting his way to a match-winning century against Bangladesh in Hamilton, the Black Caps quickly established themselves as the most watchable team at the tournament.

Cricket was enjoying a rebirth in this country and the ACC had a ringside seat. Some might even say they captured the zeitgeist and contributed to it, but that's not a theory you would have wanted to posit at NZC or ICC headquarters around that time.

Rather than being patted on their Collective back for recapturing a latent fanbase who had become alienated by the straitjacketed nature of much of the sport, the ACC increasingly found themselves persona non grata.

Rather than the red carpet being rolled out for them at grounds, electric fences patrolled by cattle-prod-carrying officials were being erected instead. The ACC's media accreditation and ground passes might have looked good around their necks, but they weren't cutting the mustard with increasingly officious venue operators.

MIKE LANE: Even before the World Cup things started to become rocky around in-stadium broadcasting. We were creating so much chaos at the grounds that New Zealand Cricket decided they couldn't be seen to be supporting us, even if we thought it was the kind of chaos fans were enjoying, so operationally things started to get niggly. The disconnect with NZC spread to commercial. They started to get pissy when brands who were in competition with their suite of partners wanted to sponsor us.

The ACC had a backer at NZC in James Wear, the general manager of commercial and marketing. He had joined NZC at the height of the turbulence in 2012.

JAMES WEAR: I told my mate that I was taking a job at NZC and he said, 'Why the hell are you going there? You won't be able to sell a thing.' That was a pretty common reaction. People my age thought the sport had lost its way, especially with the youth market. I saw the ACC as a way of getting a new audience that we weren't hitting with Sky TV or Radio Sport.

I think we gave them $20,000 to get them up and running. It wasn't a huge amount, but it was probably too much if you asked some people. David White, the CEO, was always pretty supportive of it, but there were others who hated it and they were probably getting in his ear. I always had to say that it was never intended to be for everyone and Whitey, to his credit, never told us to try to shut it down.

But it didn't take long before the double-edged nature of NZC's investment started to show itself.

LANE: We had all these nicknames for the players and they started to tell us there were rights issues around that. We were like, 'What the fuck are you talking about?' Like Kane Williamson as 'Steady the Ship'. We had talked to Kane and he was absolutely fine with it.

WEAR: That issue probably sat with the Players Association rather than us. The ACC started selling these pieces of memorabilia with the players' nicknames and likenesses, but no rebates were coming back to the players.

LANE: Some people just hated the thought that we might be making a profit with the captain's hats. 'Okay, so why didn't you come up with the idea, or any idea, then?'

Nicknames became a big part of the ACC oeuvre (see glossary on page 278) for both rugby and cricket. Steady the Ship, the Hairy Jav (Grant Elliott), the Sexy Camel (Tim Southee) and Lovely Trenty (Trent Boult) quickly became part of the cricket vernacular. Some, like Elliott, embraced the moniker and have come to use it as a quasi-marketing tool. Others less so.

WEAR: It's my understanding that Ross Taylor was not keen on his at all.

We ruffled people's feathers at the grounds. We were playing loud music and singing and dancing in the caravan, catching choppers to the game, doing heaps of filming, having a lot of fun and just rarking everyone up.

LANE: Yeah, Ross Taylor, Sir Lingus. He didn't complain about it directly, but he made sure it got back to us. It was because he stuck out his tongue extravagantly every time he got a century, and he was getting a lot of centuries back then. If you take the Latin 'cunni' off the front of it, there's nothing sexual about it. Some people just need to get their minds out of the gutter.

George Worker we called the Sex Worker. I got a call from a sheepish comms staffer at NZC who started by saying, 'We don't normally do this . . .' They went on to acknowledge our creative licence, but asked politely if we could change George's nickname.

I replied, 'Why, is he actually a sex worker? You know there's nothing illegal about being a sex worker, right?'

There was a long silence, then, 'No, but if you change it then we'd be very thankful.'

It was a bit annoying, and normally we'd tell them, also politely, to fuck off, but they seemed fairly committed to following this through so we changed it to George Not a Sex Worker. I received a one-word text from the comms guy: 'Thanks.'

I assumed it was ironic.

Sponsors, too, were starting to get edgy about what they saw as encroachment, but Wear was normally able to smooth things out by noting that Sky TV also had their own sponsors that clashed with NZC's and that was just the nature of the media beast.

WORLD CUP DRINKING GAME			
TAKE A SWIG WHEN . . .	TAKE A SHOT WHEN . . .	BOTTOMS UP WHEN . . .	SCULL A SWAPPA IF . . .
Jason Hoyte announces a batter 'LAAAUNCHES into this one!'	Reference is made to an animal's genitalia or sexual behaviour.	A guest commentator is pitched a dubious investment opportunity.	Bryan Waddle graces the caravan with his presence.
Any caravan commentator mentions the word 'certainly'.	Leigh Hart enters the field of play by method of drinks cart or otherwise.	A discussion about the actual game at hand continues for more than thirty seconds.	Any member of the Commentary Collective is forcefully ejected from the stadium.
A new nickname, song or animal comparison is made about a player.	A sponsor's product is consumed or used in an unorthodox manner.	You miraculously sync your TV feed with the ACC commentary.	Any player salutes a milestone with a mangina.
DJ A-Hole ruins a moment of celebration.	A spurious claim or statistic is made about the opposing team.	A Jim Hickey Pool Party is announced.	Any commentator announces that New Zealand has won the World Cup.

WEAR: There were a few awkward conversations had with some of our key sponsors. Everyone likes to protect their own turf.

At ACC Towers, Lane and Wells were starting to get a bit wary of and weary with the conflict. They knew the 'official' relationship with NZC had a shelf life.

JEREMY WELLS: To be fair to them, they started us. We couldn't have got off the ground without them fully funding the first year. They knew they had to re-engage the fans, especially young males who were starting to look elsewhere, and find new fans. We think we delivered that.

LANE: We ruffled people's feathers at the grounds. We were playing loud music and singing and dancing in the caravan, catching choppers to the game, doing heaps of filming, having a lot of fun and just rarking everyone up.

There was one guy who hated us and would try to make our lives as uncomfortable as possible by placing our caravan in places where the public would be constantly going past. They then got shitty when we turned this to our advantage and engaged with the punters. They'd wonder why there was

a ruckus when someone would pass a beer through the window and Leigh Hart skolled it, or someone would poke their head in and yell obscenities about copulating straight into the microphone.

I mean, Jesus Christ, would they put Ian Smith or Mark Richardson right in the middle of the embankment? No. They fed us to the wolves and then got hurt and offended when we found a way to survive and thrive.

The ACC embraced the challenge of making this particular jobsworth's life a misery. They found it fun at first, but after a while the novelty of being placed somewhere that they couldn't see the cricket, of being told they couldn't do this and that by the various stadium operators, and of their behaviour becoming more and more risqué and dangerous, wore off. They decided to retreat to the safety of the studio, where they could continue to behave badly and not get in trouble.

LANE: Actually, we still did get in trouble.

The Cricket World Cup would prove critical in the rise of the ACC, with them on the mics for two of the more momentous days and nights in New Zealand cricket history. But, before we get to that, we have to traverse their biggest crime — the one that, ironically, put them on the map.

CHARGE:	Illegally entering the field of play during the 2015 Cricket World Cup *aka* 'The Infamous Drinks Trolley Incident'.
VERDICT:	Massive stitch-up (although they may have got away with a blatant crime just one week earlier)

**BLACK CAPS V AFGHANISTAN,
CRICKET WORLD CUP ROUND-ROBIN**
Napier, 8 March 2015

As with most things in life, context is everything.

The ACC's most infamous crime, the one that had them in the news pages and bulletins, was to their eyes not even worthy of a misdemeanour charge, but such was the tinderbox nature of their caravan at cricket grounds, this proved to be the spark that set it on fire.

As had become the norm, the ACC broadcast caravan was placed in an area where they had an obstructed view of the game. In this case, the obstruction was the main stand at McLean Park, a brutalist-era concrete edifice that cast an ugly shadow over every event at the ground. To make it even clearer how they were regarded, the caravan was facing away from the stand, so even if the crew had x-ray vision, they wouldn't have been able to see a single ball being bowled. If it wasn't for the ambient crowd noise and the constant waft of cheap cooking oil and propane gas coming through their windows, the only difference between broadcasting from McLean Park and McLean Street, Wairoa, was that there were far fewer people who hated them in Wairoa.

Matt Heath: I remember seeing the back of numerous things, but there was no cricket in our direct line of vision.

Jeremy Wells: No view of the field at all. In fact, I don't remember this game very well because I'd been up for two days and hadn't landed the plane, so I wasn't seeing anything particularly well that day.

Leigh Hart: This was starting to become a habit. The not-seeing-the-ground bit, not Jeremy turning up hungover, but come to think of it...

Jason Hoyte: It was interesting, actually. The caravan positioning became more and more fraught. We started the World Cup right on the boundary, and we went further and further back as our atrocities got worse and worse. Or our supposed atrocities.

Some of those 'atrocities' included the social media hits that came to be known as Manginagate, Guess the Perineum and Milk of the Japsie — all fairly questionable concepts but not, however, the greatest scandal in the ACC's short history.

   They are important to mention here only in that they demonstrate how the ACC were nudging up to and possibly over the line of good taste.

Mike Lane: New Zealand won by six wickets — another win — the World Cup campaign was going great. We were flying back to Auckland and I must have had about ten missed calls from head office, from the GM of talk radio. I rang him back and his opening line was, 'Please tell me you haven't fucking done it?'

Dallas Gurney (GM talk radio): I don't remember specifically how I started the conversation, but yes, that sounds like something I would say.

Lane: I'm thinking, 'What does he mean? We've done a lot of bad shit.'

Gurney: I probably should have narrowed it down, but there was only one thing I was getting terse emails from IMG — the broadcast rights brokers for the ICC — about, so it was obvious to me if not to Mike what the issue was.

Lane: So, I asked Dallas, 'What one? Guess the Perineum, or the Milk of the Japsie, the love mucus?'

Hoyte: Was I involved in Guess the Perineum or Milk of the Japsie? I think I might have been involved in both.

Wells: We'd take a photograph of one of the commentators' perineum, that bit between your testicles and the anus, then we'd put it out on social media and if you guessed whose it was, you could win a prize.

Milk of the Japsie was a similarly cock-and-balls-based competition, but this time you had to guess whose...well, the clue is in the name.

Gurney: It was my turn to say, 'What are you talking about?'

An awkward impasse had been reached, where Lane's inventory of crimes was not marrying up to the offence that was front and centre in Gurney's mind. Finally, the long-suffering radio executive laid out the charges: the ACC had stolen a drinks trolley, then they had driven it onto the field where they proceeded to interview players in an unsanctioned manner, opening the door to allegations of match-fixing. They were being thrown out of the World Cup.

Fortunately, Dallas Gurney was well equipped to handle this dilemma. For a while in 2010, he was arguably the most unpopular man in modern New Zealand cricket history. He knew first-hand how passionate cricket fans can be.

Gurney: I have spent most of my life in radio and managed the likes of Paul Holmes and Mike Hosking, but the most complaints I've had, and it's not even close, was when I made the call to cut Plunket Shield commentary from Radio Sport. I have to confess to being surprised by how fanatical some of the cricket support was. I was the devil in 2010. There was this hardcore, traditionalist fanbase that wanted my head on a pike.

If there's one thing I've heard a thousand times that I never want to hear again it is: 'The Plunket Shield is what I listen to when I paint my house.' I mean, seriously, how often are you painting your bloody house?

That's not to say that Gurney was anxious to worm his way back into the affections of the cricket cognoscenti, but he was desperate to avoid a scenario where his NZME brands would be stripped of the commentary rights for the World Cup — and to his mind, that was what was at stake on 8 March 2015.

Gurney: The thing I was most worried about was protecting our rights arrangement. There were all these different dynamics playing out in the background regarding the ACC, but that was the crux.

Some of those dynamics have been previously discussed, namely the disdain the ACC was held in by traditional media, in particular the Radio Sport commentary team, but there was also anxiety on the part of New Zealand Cricket, who had initially funded the ACC and welcomed them into the fold.

James Wear (former GM of commercial and marketing, NZC): Thankfully we had nothing to do with the whole drinks trolley incident. That wasn't our remit. It was all the ICC. The ACC did go through phases of getting banned from grounds, though, and I'd have to try to help smooth things over. Eden Park under its previous leadership was particularly officious, and I remember on one occasion having to try to rustle up a hospitality box for them to operate out of.

The ICC had made it pretty clear that they hated having to indulge the ACC at the grounds.

Lane: Where they put us, we were better off out of the grounds. They put us, literally, in the car parks. In Wellington, we were outside the stadium and facing the railway tracks. We could have commentated on the 12:10 from Melling more effectively than the cricket.

Perhaps wary of looking out of touch, the suspicion is that the ICC looked to their rights brokers, IMG, to be the blunt instrument to force the ACC out. As IMG themselves state on their website: 'Our global team develops bespoke packages of media rights from over 70 rightsholders and creates multi-channel distribution strategies that are optimised for both traditional broadcasters and emerging media platforms.' In this case, their 'distribution strategy' was to threaten NZME with the prospect of redistributing their bought-and-paid-for rights elsewhere.

Gurney: I received a terse email from my contact at IMG saying our rights were at risk, hence why I was pretty keen to get in touch with Mike and get to the bottom of the issue.

Heath: There were so many things we thought might get us kicked out of the World Cup, but not Leigh Hart on a drinks trolley. Leigh didn't want to be out there, and we didn't want him to be out there. We'd been pressured into it.

Hoyte: It was a total set-up. The authorities didn't like us because we were going great guns and they hated that.

So, what actually happened?

It's a tale with a murky background that involved a shadowy network of multinational soft-drink brands, but in many ways it was rather straightforward. Pepsi-Cola were sponsoring the ACC during the World Cup, essentially covering all their costs. Gatorade, a Pepsi-owned brand, was sponsoring the World Cup itself. Members of the ACC had been approached on numerous occasions to help serve the drinks by going onto the field of play with the ICC-approved company rep in a golf cart that was adorned by a phallic-shaped giant Gatorade bottle on top. This in itself has always been somewhat farcical since the players only drink what is provided to them in individualised bottles by their own sports medicine operations.

In each World Cup one-day international, there was the potential for four drinks breaks, two in each innings. The 'spare seat' on the golf cart in the first three were taken up by competition winners, but Pepsi/Gatorade wanted an ACC presence on the fourth break. By pure circumstance, at this point in the tournament New Zealand was playing such dominating cricket that no matches had reached the fourth drinks break. But a somewhat sloppy New Zealand performance allied to some fight from the Afghanis pushed their World Cup match in Napier into the late afternoon, opening the door to trouble.

Hart: There was a sponsor that wanted us to go out with the drinks and it was that simple. It could have been Matt Heath that went out there. It just fell to me because I wasn't commentating at the time. I had no desire to go onto the field. It wasn't like I was trying to be a fanboy and get near the players.

Heath: I distinctly remember Leigh Hart saying, 'I really don't want to do this.'

Wells: We might have even done paper, rock and scissors to see who'd go out there, but then it was decided by others that it would be Leigh because he was the most instantly recognisable. He wasn't that keen on the idea, but he was bald, he was large and he was liked by the players. The idea was that he would drive the drinks trolley out there, give the players some drinks, then turn around and come back again . . . and I'm pretty sure that's exactly what happened.

Hart: So, I went out there at the request of Powerade [*ed. It was Gatorade*], and I was having a yarn to a couple of the players. I didn't even initiate the conversation. I think the Hairy Jav did. The International Cricket Council complained about it, saying it was match-fixing or something. What a joke. If you were going to get serious about match-fixing, the last person you're going to listen to is me. Can you imagine Daniel Vettori listening to anything I would have to say about cricket?

Lane: It might not have helped that the ground announcer recognised him and started playing the Hamsterman from Amsterdam theme song.

Colin, the Hamsterman from Amsterdam, was an alcoholic, moustachioed, yoghurt-eating, wildly incompetent pet-store owner introduced to the world by Leigh Hart via *Moon TV*.

Heath: There was some complaint that we had violated our rights agreement by interviewing the players on the field. Leigh didn't want to talk to anyone. He doesn't know anything about cricket.

Hart: I wouldn't go quite that far.

Heath: He certainly wasn't looking for an interview. He was looking to get back to the caravan and have another drink, primarily. It was entrapment.

Wells: I don't know what happened between him driving the trolley out there and coming back, but between the moment he drove back and the next day, someone spoke to someone who spoke to someone who got freaked out about something and the next thing you know it was a headline in the paper.

'Alternative Commentary Collective silenced by ICC after drinks appearance' screamed the headline in the *Herald*. Veteran cricket writer David Leggat, an astute and measured observer of the game but never a noted newshound, broke the story to a 'shocked' public. It read:

'An ICC spokesman has told the *Herald*: "An individual went outside the agreed boundaries of an activation and appropriate action has been taken..."'
    The story also included these gems:
    'The umpires, Johan Cloete and Marais Erasmus, commented on Hart's

attire and they engaged in small talk for a matter of seconds.

'As the drinks break was wrapping up, Grant Elliott wandered past and asked Hart how he was going and he replied. None of the conversations were recorded.'

It was good, solid reporting from Leggat. Not at all sensationalised, though the story was accompanied by a screen grab of a shadowy Hart behind the wheel of the trolley like it was a big 'gotcha' moment, even though nobody, especially not Hart, was trying to deny that he was the driver.

Wells: When we got done for the trolley I wasn't that concerned, but I was starting to get pissed off that we were not allowed to tell our side of the story. The 'official' version was taken as gospel. Pepsi ran for the hills, Gatorade ran for the hills, NZME ran for the hills, New Zealand Cricket ran for the hills.

Lane: Well, we eventually managed to get our message out. Those of us at NZME were not allowed to talk, but others could get our message out.

Paul Ford: No comment.

Lane: My bosses were getting shitty that someone was leaking the real story to the press and were telling me to tell Paul to shut up. I was like, 'What can I do? I can't control him.'

Ford: No comment.

Lane: The thing was we had done some terrible things, some really immature shit, but we'd got away with a lot of it, or we thought we had. And then that happened and we genuinely, for the first time, could put our hand on heart and say, 'Hey, we weren't out to make any trouble here.' There was no malice in what we had done.

Hart: I would liken it to Al Capone being done for tax evasion.

A list of all the 'really immature' shit they'd done during the World Cup could fill every page of this book. It's a bacchanalian tale that goes right back to the opening match of CWC15, when a nervous New Zealand watched their side lose the toss and get inserted against Sri Lanka under grey skies that would soon give way to a bluebird day in Christchurch. The atmosphere in the city was, by all accounts, electric. Well, most accounts.

Hoyte: I wouldn't know. I was well into my prep. I like to do six or seven hours of prep before each game, so I left the others to it.

Any nerves quickly dissipated when Brendon McCullum, now firmly establishing himself as a fearless leader after a rocky start to his tenure, and Martin Guptill blitzed an opening partnership of 111 in 95 balls. McCullum's contribution was a thudding 65 from 49. The Black Caps rode that momentum all the way to 331 for 6 — a massive total in those more innocent days — and Sri Lanka never had a look-in as their chase faltered to 233 all out in 46.1 overs.

Drunk on a cocktail of the Black Caps' heady performance, the ACC team were in celebration mode well before the end of the match. They were at the ground, covering the sport they loved, in full flight singing their 'Ronchi Donkey' song when an ICC delegation, including then-president Mustafa Kamal, walked past.

'Who in god's name are they?' exclaimed a suit-and-tied member of the delegation as the caravan shook under the weight of the all-singing, all-dancing troupe.

Lane: Right at that exact moment, a caterer who happened to be a fan of ours passed a dozen Steinlagers through the window.

Wells: Rightfully, I think, questions were asked.

Heath: Maybe if we had been put in a part of the ground where we could actually see the game we might have acted a bit differently, but I doubt it. There's no doubt though that we were living down to our lowly status.

Christchurch was also the scene of the often-referenced, best-forgotten Manginagate episode. Again, placement of the caravan played a part. This time, they were in an area where the caterers changed for their shifts, near some portable toilets and a couple of broadcast production trucks. They couldn't see the ground and, more worryingly, hadn't been cabled to a monitor or the ground-effects mics.

Hart: For Matt and I, it was no problem. We can do animal facts and stats from anywhere, but we were slightly concerned that not having any idea of what was happening could really affect the ball-by-ball coverage.

Lane: We had no cable and the nearest camera we could plug into was 150 metres away up a tower behind the bowler's arm.

Mike Lane used his work credit card to buy 200 metres of cable, ran it from the caravan to the camera and hastily negotiated with the operator to let him plug into his output. All this was happening 10 minutes before the first ball was about to be bowled.

Wells: Because we were right next to the toilets, there was a lot of foot traffic. Every person who was getting drunk on the bank had to pass by us. They all had something to say.

The passers-by included Sir Richard Hadlee of Christchurch, but the knight made a wise decision not to stop for a chat. Gerry Brownlee, at that stage the Minister of Defence, Minister Supporting Greater Christchurch Regeneration and the Member of Parliament for Ilam, was not so well advised. During his time in the caravan, Brownlee was harangued mercilessly by Jeremy Wells and Lee Baker as to when and where he lost his virginity (see page 90). He steadfastly refused to divulge, saying it wasn't an area he had a great deal of expertise in, with Wells uttering the infamous line: 'That's not what I've heard. I've heard you're great in the sack.'

And then there was Manginagate.

Hoyte: That was an interesting one. That was Leigh Hart and I. We were stopped for a photo and in the background of the photo there were some guys doing the old mangina.

As much as it pains me to have to explain it, the mangina involves tucking your penis between your legs and squeezing your thighs together to keep it out of sight, thus giving the appearance of a male having a vagina. It was made infamous by the Buffalo Bill character in *Silence of the Lambs.*

Hart: They, the guys, were half nude at the time. The lower half. We probably should have noticed that.

Hoyte: The cops came around to the caravan to discuss some lewd activity that had been going on. We put our hands up straight away. If there was anything lewd going on it was bound to involve us.

Lane: The cops said we couldn't be inciting nudity and that there were manginas being pulled in front of kids.

Hart: Back then you couldn't encourage people to do manginas. It was a different time.

The incident would become the 'inspiration' for their Manginas of Summer wall planner, created after various punters started sending in pics of themselves playing cricket with a mangina. It was a qualified success.

Lane: Yeah, it didn't sell a lot...but our web numbers went through the roof.

After a quick detour in Wellington — it was literally quick, with New Zealand chasing down England's 123 in the thirteenth over — the scene was set for a blockbuster clash against Australia at Eden Park.

Wells: Eden Park — shit. A lot happened that day.

Hart: I was red carded. Yeah, I think I'm probably the only commentator to be evicted from a ground before play had even started.

Lane: To make it clear, we evicted him, not the officials, but it would have only been a matter of time.

Hart: I think building up to that game we had quite a big day at the sponsors' lunch before entering the caravan — obviously in those days the caravan was on site.

Lane: That's a nice story, but Leigh was drunk before breakfast. Any sponsors' lunch was incidental to his state. He'd had a big night and didn't land the plane, so we told him to go home and get some sleep. We had enough people and he could come back when he was sober-*ish*.

The full extent of Hart's Big Night Out was fairly obvious, but complicating matters was a live interview they had prearranged with Fox Sports Australia's Neroli Meadows, which went something like this:

Meadows: What does New Zealand have that Australia doesn't?

Heath: We're a better-looking team, more sexually potent, we're better players and we're better guys across the board. There are very few boxes that Australia tick that the Black Caps don't tick with a bigger tick.

Meadows: That is brutal. Now Brendon McCullum, how much do you love him?

Wells: I love Brendon McCullum dearly, and I have to say that on paper this has to be the worst Australian team that they've ever produced, probably since Kim Hughes, or probably since Brendon Julian was brought into the team to bolster the bowling line-up... New Zealand is anticipating a big victory here against what is a very weak Australian team on paper.

Meadows: What about David Warner?

Lane: Davey Warner is like that little, annoying, red-headed cousin that you always beat up...

The clip cuts off after Lane excoriates Warner, but in the full-length interview, Hart, who had been visible at the back of the shot, beer in hand, nodding along to Wells' pearls of wisdom, starts to reveal more of his state, and himself.

Lane: Thankfully he didn't say anything. He was just in the background rubbing his nipples. There's a great photo of him somewhere with his shirt down and his nipple out.

Baker: I quite enjoyed it when Leigh went off the rails. We did that interview with Neroli live from a bar in Kingsland. She loved us, but I can't remember what Leigh was saying. All I can remember was that he was struggling to stand. I looked at my watch and it was 11am and I thought, 'This is going to be a crazy day.'

It was.

Hart: I was fairly hammered and it was in everybody's best interests that I exit stage left. I do remember playing cricket with some kids outside. I only lived a block away from Eden Park, so once I was red carded it was a fairly easy stumble home. It turned out to be an amazing game that I now wish I'd been there for, but at the time I was like, 'Thank god, I can go home and watch the game on TV.'

  I even saw some other loser who had been kicked out of the ground as well, so he came back and watched it with me. What a pair.

Hart's insobriety was not the only concern that day.

Wells: We had a run-in with another ICC official around our access.

Lane: The caravan was not allowed in the ground, but our access allowed us boundary-side. So, when we weren't commentating we'd grab a couple of chairs and sit in the tunnel and watch the game. This guy, he was a school principal I think, doing this shit job so he had someone to boss around on the weekends, told us we couldn't be there.

  'Well, our access pass says we can,' we proudly said.

  It was unambiguous. His worst mistake was arguing with Paul and Jeremy. If there are two guys you don't want to take on in an argument about due process it's those two because a) they're smarter than you and, b) they have no respect for petty bureaucrats. They tore him a new one, but this guy was nothing if not resourceful. He went away and reprinted the accreditation board, came back, set it up in front of us and said, 'You can't come here now because I've changed it.'

  He was so laser-focused on us that a terrorist with plastic explosives strapped to his chest could have walked onto the middle of Eden Park and he would have been none the wiser, but at least he got rid of the ACC from the boundary, so I guess he felt important.

Heath: Didn't we also carjack the groundsman's tractor?

Lane: Yeah, this same bloke wanted to move our caravan back even further and promised to bring somebody back to do it. I spotted the tractor and moved it in front of the caravan and kept the keys so nobody could access our towbar.

Hoyte: Chalk that up as a win for the good guys.

Hart: When I found out about all this the next day, I immediately felt better about life because I wasn't the only focus of their debrief.

When the ICC used the drinks trolley as a battering ram to remove the ACC from the grounds, there was righteous anger, but there was also relief.

Lane: Because we'd done such terrible things beforehand, I didn't feel like I had any room to move. That was the straw that broke the camel's back. Everyone had just had enough by then. It was just a collective, 'Fuck these guys, no more.'
   In hindsight, it was the best thing that ever happened to us. We got kicked out for a bullshit reason, and our notoriety and audience soared. We liked going to the games and it was a hit to the ego, but we were better off from a broadcast point of view, and long term it massively played into our countercultural personas.

A meeting with their bosses at NZME confirmed the decision to take the venue ban on the chin.

Hart: We got called into the old NZME office like kids being made to see the headmaster. The strange thing was I couldn't give a shit about the drinks trolley thing. That didn't bother me at all. I thought I was going to get a bollocking for the week before at Eden Park. I deserved one for that.

The World Cup didn't end with the ACC ban. The Black Caps continued to charge through the tournament, with friend of the ACC Martin Guptill lighting up the quarter-final with an incredible 237 not out against the West Indies, before Lane, Wells and Ford's old schoolmate Daniel Vettori took a sensational one-handed catch on the boundary to remove Marlon Samuels during the chase.
   The semifinal was arguably the greatest ODI in New Zealand history, thanks to an extraordinary final-over finish that saw Vettori eke out a boundary to third man then watch on as the Hairy Jav hit a six into the stands off the penultimate ball to seal a famous victory.
   When the commentary team finally stopped shouting 'Jav! Jav! Jav! Jav!' half of them upped sticks for a trip to Melbourne and a seat at the final.
   Except nothing much happened that day. The Black Caps got crushed in the final and Mike Lane got steamed and made a bit of a dick of himself when invited to the team's after-party, which really wasn't much of a party at all.

NEW ZEALAND VS SOUTH AFRICA, CRICKET WORLD CUP SEMIFINAL
AUCKLAND, 24 MARCH 2015
New Zealand won by 4 wickets (D/L method)

South Africa (43 overs)		R	BF
H Amla	b Boult	10	(14)
Q de Kock	c Southee b Boult	14	(17)
F du Plessis	c Ronchi b Anderson	82	(107)
R Rossouw	c Guptill b Anderson	39	(53)
AB de Villiers	not out	65	(45)
D Miller	c Ronchi b Anderson	49	(18)
JP Duminy	not out	8	(4)
Extras		14	
Total		281-5	

Bowling	O	M	R	W
T Southee	9	1	55	0
T Boult	9	0	53	2
M Henry	8	2	40	0
D Vettori	9	0	46	0
K Williamson	1	0	5	0
G Elliott	1	0	9	0
C Anderson	6	0	72	3

On 24 March 2015, the day dawned like any other day . . .

Except that it was World Cup semifinal day, at home. It was the exact opposite of 'any other day'.

Especially for Paul Ford. As he sat in Wellington Airport waiting on his flight to Auckland, he kept anxiously refreshing the weather app, while contemplating the logistics required that day to keep the two loves of his life happy — his wife Tracy and his ACC buddies.

MIKE LANE: Paul Ford choosing to take his lovely wife Tracy to the actual game rather than calling the game with us was romantic and lovely, and good on him . . . but it was also a massive stab in the back for us that won't be forgotten any time soon.

New Zealand (target 298 from 43 overs)		R	BF
M Guptill	run out (Amla/de Kock)	34	(38)
B McCullum	c Steyn b Morkel	59	(26)
K Williamson	b Morkel	6	(11)
R Taylor	c de Kock b Duminy	30	(39)
G Elliott	not out	84	(73)
C Anderson	c du Plessis b Morkel	58	(57)
L Ronchi	c Rossouw b Steyn	8	(7)
D Vettori	not out	7	(6)
Extras		13	
Total (42.5 overs)		299-6	

Bowling	O	M	R	W
D Steyn	8.5	0	76	1
V Philander	8	0	52	0
M Morkel	9	0	59	3
I Tahir	9	1	40	0
JP Duminy	5	0	43	1
AB de Villiers	3	0	21	0

PAUL FORD: Tracy and I met at the Basin, and on 24 March 2012 we got married at Tarureka in the Wairarapa. I remember the date, which is good for a guy, let's be honest. We postponed our honeymoon because there was a test match on. We went to that straight after our wedding, so it's fair to say cricket and love have intertwined for me for many years.

JASON HOYTE: We all had the sense it was going to fall over. The Black Caps, that is, not Paul and Tracy's marriage. We were going to drop the ball on the tryline.

JEREMY WELLS: The story of New Zealand cricket was always the same. It was of tragedy, of disappointment, of unfulfilled promise.

Paul and Tracy had tickets for the game. One problem. The ACC no longer did. So, Paul used a rain delay to ditch Tracy and join his colleagues at their cave in downtown Auckland.

FORD: Thanks to the incident involving Leigh Hart in Napier, we had been, I don't know what the word would be, censured? We were allowed to keep doing the commentary, but we certainly weren't allowed at the ground. The boys were in a studio set up specifically to commentate cricket, with food arriving, a few beers, a big screen. It had been a great campaign. I wanted to be a part of it.

LEE BAKER: I was still in shock. I was outraged that we weren't allowed to be at the game. We were the victims of a conspiracy. People saw us as a threat and wanted to kill us off, and that was the dagger to the heart. I still haven't forgiven the nefarious forces behind that.

MATT HEATH: When I think back on that game I always picture us at the ground, but we weren't there, were we?

WELLS: I picture us in some form of bunker.

HOYTE: It was a foul, stinking bunker.

BAKER: It felt like the sort of place where you'd find used condoms and tampons . . . and needles.

HOYTE: If I recall, it had none of that. It did have Britney Spears posters though.

We're going to fast-forward here, right past South Africa's 281 for 5 in 43 overs that, due to the vagaries of Duckworth–Lewis, left New Zealand chasing 298 to win in the same amount of overs. We'll skip right past Brendon McCullum's pyrotechnic 59 from 26 balls and Corey Anderson's 58 from 57.

We'll join the ACC commentary team with eight balls remaining. New Zealand are 280 for 6 chasing 298. Grant Elliott, unbeaten on 71, is on strike to Morne Morkel. Dan Vettori is at the other end on 3. The game has tilted in South Africa's favour, but where there is hope there is life.

MIKE LANE: Here we go.

HOYTE: Morkel comes in to Elliott . . . and he smashes this over cover for four!

LANE: (*Unintelligible, but something about being unshaven.*)

HOYTE: That was a great shot. Full, and he smashed it over cover for four.

HEATH: It's down to two runs a ball now. Two runs a freakin' ball, ladies and gentlemen!

HOYTE: Fourteen off seven.

WELLS: We can do this.

LANE: If you know anybody at the ground just text them and tell them to yell as loud as they can.

HEATH: Don't even get them to form words. Just urghhhhhhhhhhhhhhh.

LANE: South Africa are the ones under pressure, they're the chokers, not us. Come on, come on.

HEATH: This one's going over the boundary.

LANE: Come on you hairy, erectile pole.

HOYTE: Morkel pulls out of his run-up, the tension is with him now and he comes in and it's PULLED, high, high in the air and . . . it's a COLLISION!

There is a lot of screaming in the background as JP Duminy and Farhaan Behardien make an absolute mess of a regulation catch on the boundary by colliding with each other. Likewise, Elliott and Vettori make a bit of a mess of their running between the wickets as they watch the collision, missing the opportunity to take three and get Elliott, the established batter, on strike for the final over.

HOYTE: Two runs. The ball went right up in the air and the two South African fielders collided. What a disaster! Twelve off six, the last over in store. Steyn will bowl it.

As the last over starts, a remarkably restrained Wells can be heard muttering 'this is it', while a jacked-up Heath, for reasons known only to himself, starts a *Sesame Street*-style numbers-based chant.

HEATH: Twelve off six, twelve off six, twelve off six . . . come on. Twelve off six.

WELLS: This is their moment, this is their hour. Vettori will be facing.

HOYTE: What a match!

HEATH: Absolute scenes!

HOYTE: We're standing on the precipice of history for New Zealand cricket.

More idle chatter, including Lane telling the WAGs of South Africa to stick something in their 'a-holes, because you've got nothing'.

HEATH: Whoa, that's spicy!

LANE: That's a spicy emotional meatball.

HOYTE: Here comes Steyn to Vettori, a swing and a miss, but they run a bye and they'll get away with it, eleven from five. Technically ten from five.

The countback rules determined that if the scores were tied, New Zealand would win by virtue of carrying more pool-play wins into the semifinal.

HEATH: Two hits of the ball, over the boundary.

WELLS: I'm terrible in this situation and I am going to have to pass you on to someone else, because I am useless.

HEATH: You look horrendous.

WELLS: I am going to pass you on to Leigh Hart.

Wells' predicament was contagious. Few had the constitution to call the match. Heath's bowel was playing up, Baker was a quivering wreck. Even Hart, usually four sheets to the wind and devoid of an emotional quotient at that hour of the night, was struggling with the enormity of it all.

HOYTE: Eleven from five, it comes down to this. The final over of an extraordinary match — 287 for six in the forty-third, everyone looks terrified out there. Who is going to seize the moment? Goodness gracious me, Steyn looks relatively composed actually, an experienced campaigner.

HART: Taking their time to set the field, as you would.

HEATH: This one's going over the boundary.

HOYTE: Steyn to Elliott, full toss. Driven just in front of the man at cover and they'll only get the one run.

HEATH: Urghh, urghh. Should have gone over the boundary.

HOYTE: Elliott should have done better with that one. The New Zealand camp looks extraordinarily tense.

HEATH: Coulda, shoulda, woulda. Ten from four. Dale Steyn's blown a hammy. Too much Fanta can do that.

More mindless chatter, until Heath pulls this out of his commentary pocket.

HEATH: There is no past, there is no future, just here and now. The here and now is just four balls and ten runs.

HOYTE: Listen to the crowd chanting Vettori's name . . . could it have any more drama this match?

The team runs through some pointless mathematical scenarios while a 'drunk-looking' physio tends to Steyn.

HEATH: Remember when Kane Williamson won that game with a six.

HART: Oh yes indeed . . . I don't actually. When was that?

HEATH: Oh yeah, you were drunk. You're familiar with the situation though, right?

Finally the action resumes . . .

HOYTE: Crowd in full voice as Steyn comes in to Vettori. Full and wide and chopped by Vettori to the third man boundary! Six off three. Five off three in fact. It's carnage in the caravan, chairs are being thrown, it's out of control. It's got to be possible, you've got to believe it!

Cue more bedlam, some very dodgy maths, a few sotto voce exhortations and then a bye to New Zealand after Vettori misses a wild swing.

HOYTE: Five off two to win, but also four off two to win. Oh my Lord. Oh Jesus.

HEATH: Hairy Jav-e-lin, Hairy Jav-e-lin, Hairy Jav-e-lin.

HOYTE: Elliott is facing. The crowd in full voice.

HEATH: Come on Grant Elliott. He takes a deep, deep breath. Is he going to try to hit it for six? Is that what he has to do here?

HOYTE: Here we go. Here we go. Steyn to Elliott. He pulls it . . .

In 20 years' time, audio specialists on behalf of Te Papa might be called upon to try to separate the different contributors to the noise that ensued in the studio immediately following that moment, until from the depths of their diaphragms you hear the crescendo build.

'Jav! Jav! Jav! Jav! Jav! . . .'

LANE: I've taken the earphones off Lee Baker because he was there hugging Jeremy Wells sexually behind me, but this is easily the best moment of my life.

BAKER: This is going to set this little country of ours on fire.

The match was won. There was beer and bubbles to be drunk, but it was a time to let the moment sink in rather than to let loose.

FORD: Walking around outside the stadium you'd run into people you knew or worked with who were just so amped. Then you hit the Auckland traffic and we had to wait twenty-five minutes for a taxi. Tracy and I did go into town to meet the rest of the guys and we found a pretty dingy bar that was open. We said, 'Bring us your finest bottle of champagne.' The lukewarm Lindauer tasted pretty good.

LANE: Yeah, we found a bar where the most expensive champagne was about $15 a bottle, had a couple of sips and went home.

WELLS: That whole experience was a crystallisation of what I meant when I said the ACC was an extension of the best part of my life. I was watching cricket with my mates and we were just having the best time.

BAKER: That was an amazing time. Every now and then those memories of that tournament and that night in particular will creep back in and it just fills me with so much fucking joy. How cool was that?

> **That whole experience was a crystallisation of what I meant when I said the ACC was an extension of the best part of my life. I was watching cricket with my mates and we were just having the best time.**

CHARGE:	Inappropriate dialogue with a government official.
VERDICT:	Guilty

**BLACK CAPS V SRI LANKA,
CRICKET WORLD CUP 2015**
Christchurch, 14 February 2015

With the joy of that epic semifinal coursing through our veins, let's return to the Cricket World Cup 2015 opener for a wince-inducing recreation of the time the Right Honourable Gerry Brownlee, then the Minister for Canterbury Earthquake Recovery, joined Jeremy Wells and the Right Dishonourable Lee Baker in the caravan for a commentary stint.

Sit back and marvel at the nonchalant pivoting from ball-by-ball commentary to questions about dogging. [The commentary has been lightly abridged for clarity and length.]

Jeremy Wells: We are welcoming into the commentary position, Gerry Brownlee.

Lee Baker: This will be the closest we get to real power, Jeremy.

Wells: Gerry, you're enjoying the cricket today?

Rt. Hon. Gerry Brownlee: So far.

Baker: You sound nervous. Are you worried about how the match is going?

Brownlee: I'm more worried about the interview and the opportunities that presents by being here as a commentator. I think New Zealand have this match under control.

Wells: You must be very pleased by the way Hagley Oval has shaped up? A great facility for Christchurch...and with these extra stands we have a capacity of 20,000. It looks a picture to me.

Brownlee: It does look a picture and is a kick in the backside to all the naysayers who said you couldn't do it. It derails the argument of all those who say if you've got a park, the best thing to do is not to use it.

So far, so benign. It wouldn't last.

Wells: Here comes Boult to Sangakkara and he pushes forward to mid-on and there's no run. Mr Brownlee, we've been discussing virginity stories this afternoon and it would be remiss of us not to ask about yours. Mine was actually at the back of the Northerner train from Marton to Auckland. It happened around Taihape, when I was sixteen in 1993, under the back table in the caboose. Here comes Trenty again, he's bowling to Sangakkara who comes forward and gets a leading edge to cover and there's no run.

Baker: He's talking about loss of virginity, Minister.

Wells: Yes, it was around Taihape, on the overnight train in the middle of winter, and I'm just wondering if you could share your first time with us.

Brownlee: Well, nobody's going to believe yours, that's not even out of the mould.

Wells: It's absolutely true.

Brownlee: Nah, come on, that's a total cliche. The midnight train from Taihape — come on.

The Minister does have a point here. Jeremy's virginity story sounds like a mash-up of Journey's 'Don't Stop Believin' and a *Penthouse Forum* letter.

Wells: The train wasn't actually from Taihape. It was from Wellington. It was the Northerner.

Brownlee: If you were writing that story, you'd really have to sell it wouldn't you? Important occasions on the midnight train from Taihape. It's in that zone, isn't. Here we go...

The Minister desperately tries to move attention to the cricket where there is a close call for a run out. He will soon learn he is not out of the woods yet.

Wells: The Central Plateau is a sexy zone, I've always thought that.

Brownlee: I've never driven over the Central Plateau as it happens. I've never travelled extensively in that part of the country.

Wells: You've never driven over the Desert Road?

Brownlee: I was probably genuinely asleep in the back of the car.

Wells: Trent bowls again, this time to Thirimanne, who pushes the ball into the off side and there's no run. So, back to your virginity story as we didn't quite get there...

Brownlee: I wasn't telling the story, I was listening with some fascination to yours and coming to the conclusion you were paraphrasing or projecting, perhaps from some novel you were reading at the same age.

Baker: You're doing what ministers do. You're avoiding the question expertly while respecting the issue itself.

Brownlee: With all due respect, there have been no questions so far.

Baker: Well, if it's that simple, Mr Brownlee, how did you lose your virginity?

Brownlee: You can tell by looking at me that I'm approaching pension age. At that stage of life, you start to lose a lot of things, including your memory, and as much as I want to recall that experience, it's going back a bit.

Baker: Surely it was a formative experience for you? You look like the type of man who enjoys his sex.

Brownlee: That's an interesting observation, and I'm a little concerned about how you managed to make that assessment.

Wells: Elliott bowls to Thirimanne, who drives through the covers and it's a single — 98 for one, Sri Lanka. I have heard amazing stories about you Mr Brownlee, your exploits in the Christchurch social scene. The sex scene.

Baker: A happy hunting ground?

Wells: Elliott again and he looks to guide this to third man but it's not there...a very happy hunting ground I hear, particularly in the late seventies. As a single man, I heard you were very popular with the ladies.

Baker: Before you were burdened with ministerial responsibilities.

Brownlee: Yeah, well, you have to be careful about the circles you move in...I'm always very reticent to respond to stories that try to puff up the ego.

Wells: As Elliott bowls again to Sangakkara, who this time turns it on the on side. He looks for two but it's not there.

Baker: See, you're giving hints there, you're giving subtle hints.

Brownlee: I'm not at all, I'm just concerned about the susceptibility for some journalist to, um, [muffled] a minister and use it to blow up someone's ego. As soon as your ego gets blown up, you're close to blowing up completely.

Wells: Can we nail you down to an age?

Brownlee: Don't talk about nailing me down.

Wells: Elliott bowling to Thirimanne and there's no run. Just an age, just throw an age at us.

Baker: Late teens I'm guessing.

Wells: A lot of guys out there, a lot of young men, are going through that phase of wondering whether or not to [have sex] and it's good to know if a minister...here comes Elliott and Thirimanne lofts him over mid off. It's a good shot. Thirimanne moves on to fifty-six and Sri Lanka are 103 for one after nineteen overs.

Wells: Even a location, Mr Brownlee, would be quite nice.

Baker: What about a province? North or South Island?

Brownlee: Firstly, it's not something I really should be giving advice on because, despite Jeremy's assertions earlier, it's not something I have great expertise in.

Wells: That's not what I've heard; I've heard you're a demon in the sack.

Brownlee: (awkward laughter)

Baker: Devastating is the word I've heard used.

Wells: A generous lover...

Brownlee: You've heard from someone who has had the covers pulled over them. You have been victimised by whomever is telling you these things.

Wells: I've heard from a number of sources both inside and outside of Parliament.

Brownlee: Oh well, there you go...

Wells: Some people in the private sector, some people in the public sector.

Baker: Both sectors.

Brownlee: There really are only two.

There is a brief interlude from locker-room talk as Brownlee informs our intrepid commentators that he was never Minister for Sport and that it didn't matter if they read that on Wikipedia, it's still wrong.

Wells: A lot of people use Hagley Park as a spot for dogging, and as the Minister for Earthquake Recovery are you finding post-quake there's still a lot of dogging or is there less now? As Trent Boult bowls to Thirimanne, who drives through the off side for one.

Brownlee: I'm not sure what you're referring to. You'll need to explain that.

Wells: Dogging...I'll leave that up to Lee.

Baker: Dogging is, well, basically it's sex in public. People who enjoy having sex in the great outdoors meet up to indulge in that mutual hobby. In places like Hagley Park.

Wells: It's Trent again. He bowls to Sangakkara, who drives and runs with the shot. Good running from Sangakkara. It's 112 for one at the end of the twentieth over.

Baker: Particularly popular in Canterbury, I'm told.

Brownlee: Not something I'm familiar with or have witnessed.

Wells: We're being told you have to go. It's been absolutely fascinating.

Brownlee: I haven't said a word about the cricket.

Wells: We weren't that interested in that. We wanted to get a good virginity story out of you and you dodged that question superbly.

Brownlee: I've said enough to go away feeling worried, so you've had some effect.

Wells: Gerry Brownlee, thank you so much for joining us on the Alternative Commentary Collective.

Brownlee: Did you ever get New Zealand on Air funding?

Wells: No, that was stripped away from us.

Brownlee: There will be no change there.

CHARGE:	Taking money to cover the 2015 Rugby World Cup in London, spending most of it in Amsterdam.
VERDICT:	It's complicated

IT'S COMPLICATED

ALL BLACKS V AUSTRALIA, RUGBY WORLD CUP FINAL
London, 31 October 2015

The year 2015 was perhaps the most pivotal year in the ACC's history. While 2014 might have been Year Dot, 2015 was the Big Bang, when the nichest of niche products exploded through fair means and foul into the national sporting consciousness during the Cricket World Cup.

By the time that tournament finished at the end of March, the ACC had moved from niche to known. So much so, that, in a media environment that was all about slashing costs, between NZME, V Energy drinks and All Blacks Tours, the money was found to send seven ACCers whose passion was cricket to the Rugby World Cup.

Jason Hoyte: I'll be honest with you, I had no idea what we were doing at the Rugby World Cup. None at all.

Mike Lane: We were originally invited by All Blacks Tours to help do the entertainment for their tour groups in England. They had two charter planes full of absolute, pure nutter All Blacks fans, who were going over for two weeks of rugby. They offered us seven seats, accommodation and tickets for the semi and the final. So of course we said, 'Shit, yeah.'

Leigh Hart: I saw our role as much the same as the Glenn Miller band playing in the UK during World War Two, or Marilyn Monroe singing for the troops in Korea. We were a way of keeping morale up, except, I guess you could say, we weren't so much playing for the troops as for cashed-up dairy farmers and small-business accountants. Apart from that, exactly the same.

If the intention was to raise morale, the trip got off to a rocky start. On the Los Angeles to London leg of the journey, Lane and Heath's schtick on the intercom fell flat as the passengers' morale was being boosted just fine by Reese Witherspoon's performance in *The Good Lie*. They did not need two clowns interrupting their movie, or sleep.

Lane: Leigh and Jeremy struck when the iron was hot. Everybody was excited and receptive. By the time Matt and I came on, all they wanted to do was watch their movie and fall asleep. A dangerously drunk boomer came up and started yelling in Matt's face. 'You're not funny, you're not funny...'

Matt Heath: '...You're boring, you're boring.'

The irate tourist proceeded to mistake one of the galley cupboards for a toilet, but by then Heath's confidence had been shattered.

Heath: Lane and I retired to a corner of the plane near the galley. We stole some champagne and started drinking straight from the bottle. After that things calmed down a lot.

Lane: After the champagne things actually spiralled dangerously out of control. An impromptu game of rugby started. One thing led to another and we packed down a scrum. We noticed a weakness and when Heath popped up out of the front row, we drove him right back into row seventy-two, much to the chagrin of the passengers who had paid good money to be there and the Air New Zealand staff.

Once safely landed in London, the boys had another of Europe's great cities in their sights.

Lane: V Energy drinks came to us with some ideas around the Rugby World Cup. We said, 'How about you sponsor the build-up to the Rugby World Cup final and we'll do it from Amsterdam, the home of rugby.' So, it was all planned before we went, it just might not have been communicated with all interested parties, namely our employers at NZME. On Wednesday, I think, we flew out from Gatwick at 6am, which meant an outrageous early wake-up call to get there.

Heath: It might have been two days before the final, I'm not sure. Time was an abstract concept by then.

Hart: Yeah, that was horrendous. Mike and I were sharing a room in London and we had this world-record bar tab on our mini fridge. So

I'm already in suboptimal condition by the time I get to Amsterdam for a very important Rugby World Cup preview.

Lane: We flew into Amsterdam and the idea was that we were going to film a bunch of content 'live' from Amsterdam in the build-up to the final, and we were going to release it in New Zealand in the twelve hours before the match, so it would look like we spent the whole week in Amsterdam and were going to miss the final. We had ten hours to film all this content, so my idea was to smash out six hours of non-stop work, then go and see some 'sights'. I'd booked a van and a driver at great expense and I'd lined up to film at the Heineken factory tour, the Van Gogh Museum and Anne Frank's house.

Heath: We had a whole lot of wholesome stuff planned, but we got off the plane and the first thing Leigh Hart said was, 'We're going to the Red Light District.'

Lane: We got the minivan from the airport and realised that because it was so early, none of our tourist destinations were open yet. We found the nearest cafe in town and stopped for coffee and a pastry. We were adjacent to the Red Light District, so there was a suggestion from one of the team that we should just go and have a look.

Heath: Leigh Hart, just like that, erased all our tourist activities for the day.

Hart: If I remember rightly, it was Matt Heath who suggested we go to the Red Light District. He was adamant. I said, 'Hold on, Matt, that's all well and good, but would you mind if I went to the Anne Frank Museum first?'

Hoyte: Generally speaking, I think we behaved ourselves.

Hart: I think it was me and Jerry first who went to the local shop with all the gummies and other perfectly legal stuff. We were hammered, but probably not as bad as the others said we were. Having said that, I don't remember a whole lot about the trip.

Lane: No sooner had we arrived than a barge cruised past on the canal. It was a cocktail barge and I don't think I'm overstating it to say a smoking-hot Dutch girl came out and said, 'Would you guys like to hop aboard and cruise the canals?'
  'Fucking A, we do.'

  We piled on to this barge, having morning cocktails poured for us. It certainly took the edge off. We must have been on it for about an hour when we realised our driver, who had all our bags, passports and equipment, was chasing us down the street that follows the canal, shouting at us that we needed to get off if we wanted to fit in all these activities. An executive decision was made that we were pretty happy with where we were, so he basically found somewhere to park and guarded our passports for ten hours. It definitely would have been cheaper to get a locker at the airport.

Heath: I took a whole lot of mushrooms. Actually, they were truffles, but whatever, it was a psilocybin situation and I started hallucinating. There was a castle with babies manning the walls; the pub was a ship on the ocean, crashing over monstrous waves; there were various World War Two scenarios.

Lane: We had a perfectly innocent mushroom omelette that had a disastrous effect. The next thing I can really remember was we were heading back to the airport with a lot of unusable content that will never, ever, see the light of day. We did, however, manage to get something in the can that was usable. Thank god for Jason Hoyte.

He didn't have any omelette, steered clear of the cocktails and basically saved our arses by starring in our piece to cams.

Hoyte: I stayed pretty clean, which wasn't easy when we spent most of our time in a pub.

In Hoyte's final piece to camera, filmed inside a drinking establishment, you can see some damaged individuals in the background as Hoyte, staring intently into Joe Durie's camera, intones: 'Well, thanks so much for joining us from the marvellous city of Amsterdam as we build up to this magnificent World Cup final, New Zealand versus the All Blacks [*sic*]. It's been an absolute joy being in such a magnificent city where rugby is on everybody's lips. Now it's been left to me to get these reprobates on the plane and make sure they get to Twickenham for game time.' He wasn't exaggerating, getting the reprobates on the plane was no straightforward task. For one in particular, the journey back to London was when it all started to go horribly wrong.

Heath: On my way to the airport I had convinced myself that we were in a land occupied by Nazis, which I guess it once had been. We were driving through bush and I was pretty sure we were coming up upon a checkpoint. I was terrified. It was one of those situations where the more I tried to gather myself, the deeper I fell into this hallucinogenic black hole. We had to stop for a toilet break. Joe Durie was with me and he said, 'Do you think the driver is about to kill us?' I could only reply, 'Do *you* think he's going to kill us?'
   Thankfully we managed to get on the plane. I was sitting in the front row, right by the stewards. They're looking right at you, eyeballing you, because you're so close. I was still in a bad way when we took off, but I managed to fall asleep. Fast asleep.
   Until we landed at Stansted.

Lane: We landed with a thud at Gatwick.

Heath: Was it Gatwick? It was one of those ones that is miles away from London. It didn't really matter, all I knew was that we hit the ground and I thought we were in an accident and screamed in this poor stewardess's face. 'AAAAARRRRGGGGHHH! WE'RE ALL GOING TO FUCKIN' DIE, AAAARRRRGGGGHHHH!'

Hart: I do remember the flight back. I was a bit of a mess, but a peaceful mess. Matt Heath was asleep and when he woke up as we were landing he started screaming, which when you think about it, is probably not what a plane full of nervous fliers wants to hear.

Heath: I just kept screaming and looked around and saw Jeremy and G-Lane cracking up. They could not stop laughing. There was no sympathy at all.
   It was like being in a film. I always wondered what it would be like in a plane crash and how I'd react. Now at least I know. I was quite vulnerable, but Lane suggested to the stewards that I should be cable-tied. They were actively trying to get me arrested, or sectioned, whereas all I wanted was a reassuring cuddle.

Hart: I remember thinking that Amsterdam wasn't a bad place, somewhere I wouldn't mind visiting again. As it happened, Hellers booked me in to do a shoot there after the World Cup final. I ended up having a huge night in London and didn't quite manage to get to bed, so the state I was flying to Amsterdam in was a bit of rinse and repeat really.

The pay-off line to these particular hijinks was the timing of the release, which the ACC started to do on their social channels in the 12 hours leading into the final, by which time they were largely recovered and looking forward to the excursion to Twickenham.

Heath: Lane thought it would be funny to trick everybody back home that we hadn't turned up to the final that we were over there to cover. We started releasing social media of us in Amsterdam. I don't know why. The ACC had already started attracting problems for our content, but here we were trying to actively piss people off for no other reason than for the sport of it; to get an outsized reaction from people.

Lane: When we released the acceptable footage, I got a text message from either the COO or the CEO of NZME, I can't remember which, and it was: 'WHAT THE FUCK ARE YOU DOING? THIS WASN'T PART OF THE DEAL. WHY ARE YOU IN AMSTERDAM?!'
  I had great pleasure in replying, 'We're not.'

Jason Winstanley (Dallas Gurney's replacement at NZME): Yes, it did trigger many. It caught me by surprise especially given the Rugby World Cup was in London. I was pretty quick on the phone to Mike to ask what the hell was going on. He gave me an explanation, although I'm still not sure it was legit.

In a story that has played out time and again in media organisations around the world, budgets that once afforded sports journalists the opportunity to cover events on the ground were being slashed. Seeing seven idiots in off-white suits parading around London and continental Europe getting drunk on the company dime was bound to trigger many. On this occasion it was another company's dime, but the mud stuck.

Lane: I think what really pissed people off back in New Zealand was that the *Herald* had only sent two or three people over to cover the entire tournament, and we had seven dudes over there doing nothing except getting hammered and causing chaos.

Which is probably a good time to mention we all went to the final as pure spectators. We had no work commitments whatsoever. It was great fun.

Heath: We managed to piece ourselves together and went along to the final, and after that there was an incident that probably won't make it into this book.

Ah yes, the incident after the final. A mystery shrouded in a secret and encased in an enigma. The final was, as we all know now, a triumph for the men in black, who beat the Wallabies 34–17. It was a heady occasion for the ACC, beers were drunk in and under the stands at Twickenham, and the party continued back at the Edgware Road Hilton...sans one member.

[Redacted]: Ha ha. We all got home okay except for one of us, who became separated from the pack. Some great New Zealanders had latched on to him, I believe, and somehow convinced him to carry on to a pub with them somewhere in suburban South London. A general state of dishevelment turned into a state of disrobement, and then his clothes either got nicked or he forgot where he put them. Either one was entirely possible.

It is not like the ACC to protect their own. In fact, for six years running, they have been voted 'Commentary Team Most Likely to Turn on Themselves' at the *Manawatu Evening Standard* TV and Radio Awards*, but just this once they have circled the wagons, kind of. From this point forward, all names have been redacted and some details have been fudged or slightly exaggerated. The rest is true, however.

[Redacted]: Ah yes, the incident. My recollection of that night is that I had just retired to my room at the Hilton when [redacted] borrowed a phone and rang me. I had just nodded off from a rather large night and thought I must have arranged a wake-up call. I picked up the phone and heard: 'It's not good. It's not good. I'm lost, I haven't got my phone and I'm relying on the kindness of strangers.' I wasn't sure what to do, but the call was worrying enough to prompt me to ring [redacted]. He was calm and he took

* This is a made-up awards ceremony to protect the identity of the real awards.

control immediately. He said, 'Don't worry about it, I'll take care of it. I'll sort it out.' Of course, he did nothing of the sort. In fact, I think he went straight back to working his way through the bucket of beers he'd had delivered to his room at 4am, but it was still reassuring to hear that.

[Redacted]: It was the morning after Halloween and [redacted] had the huge fortune of catching the attention of a couple returning home from a party. As luck would have it, they gave him a pirate costume to wear, so Captain Jack Sparrow returned to the Hilton in a puffy shirt, some velvet pantaloons and jacket and in what can only be described as a state of disarray.

[Redacted]: We never talk about this. I don't even feel comfortable mentioning that the only thing that would have made the scene any more perfect would have been a parrot on [Redacted]'s shoulder.

The ACC have never been big believers in the mantra of 'what goes on tour stays on tour', which is maybe why they don't tour that often.

Wells: Have we ever travelled overseas together as a large group since the 2015 Rugby World Cup in Holland and the UK? The answer to that is no.

Heath: To clarify, Wells hasn't been on any trips since, but G-Lane and I have gone on to commit ACC atrocities in a number of countries — France, India and I think we might have even been in Japan at one point.

RUGBY WORLD CUP FINAL
TWICKENHAM STADIUM, LONDON, 31 OCTOBER 2015
Man of the match: Dan Carter

All Blacks 34 — 17 Australia

All Blacks		Australia	
Milner-Skudder	(39)	Pocock	(53)
Nonu	(42)	Kuridrani	(64)
Barrett	(79)	Conversions: Foley	2/2 (54, 65)
Conversions: Carter	2/3 (40, 80)	Penalties: Foley	1/1 (14)
Penalties: Carter	4/4 (8, 27, 36, 75)		
Drop goals: Carter	(70)		

2016

THE NATIONAL GAME

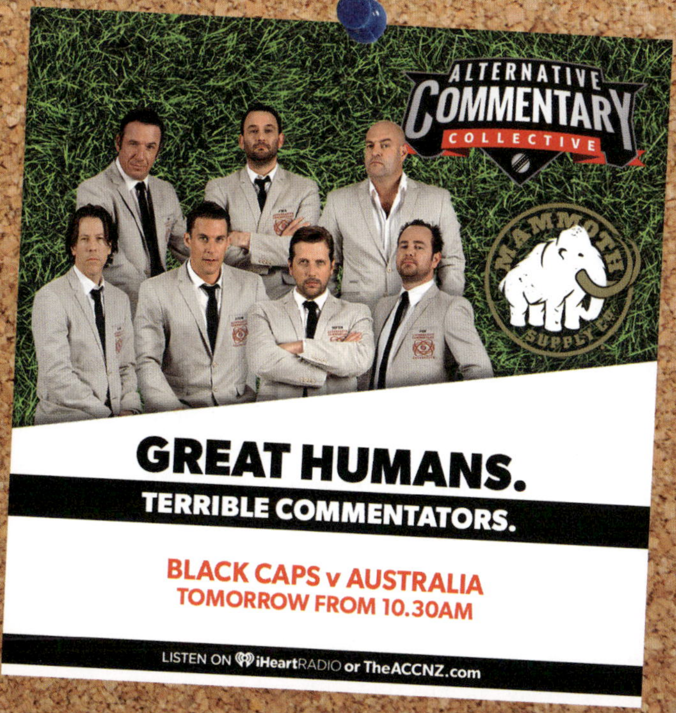

Ah yes, Rio de Janeiro, or to translate, the River of January. Turns out that, although it was definitely January when Gaspar de Lemos cruised in during that hot summer of 1502, it wasn't a river at all, but Guanabara Bay. The Portuguese, as was in keeping with the empire builders of the day, weren't that keen on admitting their mistake and so the name has stuck. Just think, if James Cook and the mapmakers of the 18th century had taken such a hard-and-fast attitude, New Zealanders would still be visiting Banks Island and Stewart Peninsula.

Anyway, where were we? That's right, 2016's main event was Rio and the sporting carnival that was the 31st Olympiad. During that August fortnight, New Zealanders proved they were very good on water, with all four of the team's gold medals coming by way of floating vehicle.

RIO 2016 OLYMPIC MEDAL TABLE

COUNTRY	GOLD	SILVER	BRONZE	TOTAL
New Zealand	4	9	5	18

The cricketing summer of 2015–16 ended on a bittersweet note as Brendon McCullum retired from international cricket with a 0–2 test series loss to, as Jason Hoyte refers to them, 'the dirty, filthy, cheating Australians'. Still, he did so in a style that would become the template for Bazball, smiting 145, bringing up his century in a world-record fast 54 balls.

'It would be nice to be remembered as a guy who played for the right reasons and who, if in doubt, was prepared to take the positive option,' McCullum said at the conclusion of his final test.

It is no exaggeration to say that McCullum played a pivotal role in the success of the ACC.

MATT HEATH: Before the ACC, G-Lane and I had started the Black Caps Supporters Support Group. Joseph Durie, the ACC's Mr Fix-It, was part of it as well and we'd call fellow supporters in and have a roundtable discussion because the Black Caps had been hurting us for so long.

We'd stand up one by one and say, 'I was hurt last night by Scotty Styris because . . .' and then just get everything off our chest about why he'd hurt us and how it made us feel. We lived through such a period of pain. To grow up being such a fan of cricket, to feel such regular pain and to have that low emotional base as a fan of cricket puts you in such a great position to really enjoy the successful years.

We started at the beginning of a golden era and we rode that. The 2015 World Cup saw cricket embraced by the nation in a way it hadn't been for a long time — not since the Underarm, probably.

Because there was no history of success like the All Blacks, it had always been controversy that had driven interest from the casual fan. You think of the Sour Summer of 1980 and the Underarm ball a year later. It was the controversy allied to a pretty good team. In some ways, 2014 onwards was a lot purer and we were lucky enough to ride that.

JEREMY WELLS: Or to put it another way, would the ACC have taken off in an era where the new ball was shared by Richard de Groen and Willie Watson? I don't think so.

Drawing on their experiences scoring free tickets to the Rugby World Cup, 2016 was to be another watershed year for the ACC as they scythed off the excess love they had for the summer game and transplanted it to the national sport, rugby.

MIKE LANE: It wasn't money. It was purely because we wanted something to do in winter. Most of us, not all but most, loved the game, not to the same extent as cricket, but enough so we weren't frauds.

When we pitched it we were targeting the Lions because the tickets were ludicrously expensive and everybody we knew was struggling to get hold of any. We saw it as an opportunity to run our own events, doing live commentary for great New Zealanders who had been priced out of the tour.

The Lions were a year down the track, though, and Lane and company knew they couldn't just rock up and commentate rugby like it was second nature. Sure, there are traditional commentators who have done both sports to a high standard, Grant Nisbett and Scotty J Stevenson to name but two, but there's a different rhythm and sensibility to calling rugby. There were some in the original crew, admittedly, who didn't want a bar of it and didn't think it could be done.

LEIGH HART: I love rugby, but I'm not a big fan of doing the alternative rugby stuff. Others are great at it, but I struggle. I think cricket is perfectly suited to this shit, my shit, because you have the space to talk crap and that's what makes it.

LEE BAKER: Cricket is so rich in idiosyncrasies, in magic and intrigue — and psychology. It's a deeply psychological game. To have all that in a team environment, I found that brilliant. To feel like you're part of something so unpredictable and potentially quite big. It's a team game, but it's not like rugby. The individual can express themselves and their personality in a way that rugby players, for example, can't. It's quite unique and we carry that culture into the commentary. I wouldn't know how to do that in rugby.

LANE: It took us a while to be honest. I don't think the first few years of our rugby coverage were that good. I don't think we quite knew where to dial in and dial out because you just can't sit there and talk shit like the cricket.

We didn't know the rugby players as well as the cricketers. When we used to tour with the cricket, we'd see them every day and gradually start chatting to them. Good guys. We only knew Kieran Read, who'd been on the ACC a few times. He was captain, so a good one to know and such a good dude — the epitome of a great New Zealander.

How about rugby — was the sport ready for an ACC take?

LANE: When you think about it, rugby was actually in dire need of an injection of counterculturalism, much more so than cricket. There were a lot of rugby fans, myself included, who had got to the point where we only engaged with the All Blacks and that was it. There were so many fence-sitters in rugby — people who wanted to like the game but were sick of it being taken so seriously. They were desperate for a laugh.

We'd seen Jed Thian, Jedi, carve himself out a nice little niche from it, so we knew the audience was there. It's our national sport, and we knew they wanted something less life and death. There will always be the passionate rugby heads who will tune into Nisbo and Tony Johnson, and that's totally cool because that product is actually good, but there's also a massive audience who can give or take rugby. The idea was that we could put an alternative take on it that might engage a latent audience.

After cutting their teeth in Super Rugby, won for the first time by the Hurricanes (these were the days before the Crusaders won every year), the team prepared to call their first test against Wales (the second of the series) at an event live from the iHeart Lounge at NZME headquarters in central Auckland.

LANE: With nothing to do during the winter, it was logical to give rugby commentary a bit of a shake-up. So we targeted an All Blacks game, organised a party in and around it, and didn't really think past that.

HEATH: We bullied Wells into doing the play-by-play for this as it looked quite hard and we felt sure his skills were transferable from calling ball-by-ball in the cricket all summer. Turns out we were wrong.

WELLS: I played for the 2nd XV at school. I was dangerously skinny, slow and could never get my stiff frame low enough at rucks or scrums to be of any use. Turns out that's not the only thing I wasn't any good at. Compared to cricket, rugby was like a hamster on amphetamines.

LANE: We had about 150 people crammed into the iHeart Lounge ready for a big night. For some reason, we thought it was a good idea to bring the caravan into the lounge and commentate while inside it.

HEATH: Why did we have the caravan inside? It was like one of those Russian dolls. We were inside NZME HQ, inside the iHeart Lounge and then inside a caravan.

WELLS: When we saw the punters turn up and flock to the caravan like moths to a flame, I realised Lane was just using it as a giant theatre prop, and it worked. People were getting photos in front of it, in it and even on it.

LANE: The audience was febrile. It was complimentary beer and pizzas, so I'm not sure why I was surprised. We managed to get into the caravan and then Jeremy turned to me and said, 'I actually don't know that much about rugby.'

WELLS: It's true. At a pinch I could bluff my way through an Andrew Mehrtens double-around, or a wipers kick, but modern rugby trends had largely passed me by.

HEATH: Alarms were ringing, briefly, but it's at moments like this the ACC step up as a team. We had enough time through the anthems and haka to bury four shots of tequila, slap Jerry on the back and say, 'Good luck.'

WELLS: Turns out rugby is quite different to cricket.

LANE: I thought he did a pretty good job — as the effects of the mezcal hit, I couldn't even read the text machine.

HEATH: In Jeremy's defence, he had to cope with a lot of distractions being pressed up against the windscreen of the caravan. From my recollection, three male bums (one that looked like it belonged to a possum) and a set of breasts. I can't tell you definitively if they were male or female breasts, but they were certainly a distraction.

WELLS: I think the All Blacks won that game? Did they?

Yes, 36–22.

WELLS: I enjoy watching rugby, but certainly didn't enjoy calling play-by-play. I was very happy when Lane offered to take those reins. He played a lot of rugby as an undersized flanker with sociopathic tendencies. He knew way more than me about the dark arts — seemed to thrive on them, actually.

HEATH: To the point where he only seemed truly happy when somebody was bleeding or seriously injured.

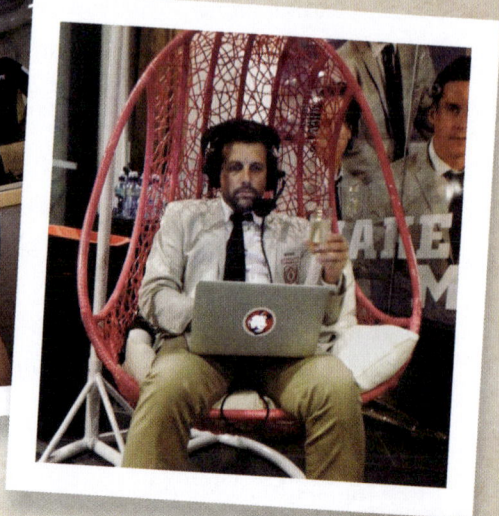

HART: I don't think there's any question that out of all the ACC original crew, I knew the most about rugby, but for one reason or another, I was never asked to participate. I guess the thinking was that with my encyclopaedic knowledge of All Blacks history from the 1885 Originals through to the World Cup-winning 1996 side, I was probably a bit too 'rugby establishment'.

LANE: We asked all of the cricket guys if they were interested. Leigh Hart was an especially hard no.

WELLS: I was more comfortable offering my skills elsewhere on the coverage. Mainly extracurricular.

LANE: I could tell Jeremy wasn't enjoying calling the rugby. It has an intensity that doesn't suit his rhythm. He loves a yarn, to build up a long-winded narrative at a more gentle pace. Rugby was just a bit frantic.

FIRST TEST
11 JUNE 2016, AUCKLAND

All Blacks **39**   **21** Wales

SECOND TEST
18 JUNE 2016, WELLINGTON

All Blacks **36**   **22** Wales

THIRD TEST
25 JUNE 2016, DUNEDIN

All Blacks **46**   **6** Wales

HEATH: I have no idea who won that game, but I do remember stepping out of the caravan and being mobbed. Punters loved it . . . or maybe they just loved the free beers?

LANE: After the game we had to hide in the boardroom until the place calmed down a bit. Can't say it was our best work, but it was suitably ludicrous and offensive, so job done. Bring on the Lions.

Rugby might have been a burgeoning part of the portfolio — Scotty J Stevenson even joined the ACC team around this time — but cricket was still the beating heart of the ACC operation.

In another gutsy innovation that may or may not have expedited the fraying nature of the relationship, NZC okayed an ACC sports ears venture.

LANE: We bankrolled it through a third party. We sorted the technology and it only had our commentary on it. NZC okayed it, but insisted it had their branding on the packaging. I recommended they didn't, but they said anything sold at the grounds needed their imprimatur. They later wished they'd listened to me.

JAMES WEAR (NZC): We had a lot of people ringing up. We learned a valuable lesson that day (ha ha). If nothing else, make sure you let people know there's some R18 content on there.

BAKER: Someone wrote an absolutely beautiful letter to us. I've still got it because the care he took with it and the way he covered off our sins in such a wonderful style still makes me smile. It reads:

Enquiry

I attended the NZ V Australia game at Eden Park on 3 February and we enjoyed the occasion.

I thought I should give you some feedback on a product which came with New [Zealand] Cricket endorsement 'official Product'[.] It was what I believed to be a cricket commentary earpiece so I purchased two at a total cost of $30.

There was no or very little commentary on the cricket and instead there was a general babbling by lightweights who mistakenly considered themselves to be funny.

There was a 10-15 minute slot where one commentator was obsessed with the different types of protective cricket boxes and continued to talk about the intricate details of the part of the male anatomy protected.

Then there was an account of taking a cat to Eden Park with the suggestion by another commentator that this could have been useful to smuggle a bottle of vodka up its anus. That led on to a desription [*sic*] of how the cat was buried under the Eden Park turf and opened up into a full discussion of how to dispose of human remains with an account of how one commentator disposed of his step-father's ashes. Listeners were then invited to talk about how they had disposed of ashes.

Then there were comments on the smallness of Trent Boult's mouth with a suggestion that his mother probably had small nipples, followed by discussion on one of the Australian players being a lesbian.

A product like this which is officially sponsored by New Zealand Cricket brings your organistaion [*sic*] and the game into serious disrepute.

Apart from the content of the commentary I did not receive any commentary on the cricket and that is what I paid my $30 for.

I would therefore like to receive a refund of my $30[.]

Yours sincerely

Barry [name withheld]

BAKER: Isn't that amazing. It's not just the care he has taken in writing it, but the obvious care he took in listening and making mental notes of everything we talked about that day. And he was bang on, Leigh did lead us down a dark path with the dead-cat chat.

It wouldn't be the last carefully crafted complaint the ACC received, and it should also be noted that this particular match was probably the highlight of the one-day summer, with the Black Caps beating an understrength but hardly weak Australia by 159 runs in close to a perfect performance.

Martin Guptill (90) and Henry Nicholls (61) were the only ones to go past 50, but there were contributions all down the order as New Zealand piled on 307. Trent Boult and Matt Henry then knocked the top off Australia with three wickets each as they stumbled to 148 all out.

A week later, New Zealand won the series 2–1 with a 55-run win at Seddon Park.

At the end of the year, New Zealand toured Australia and in the three ODIs lost by 68 runs, 116 runs and 117 runs, but nobody really needs to hear that.

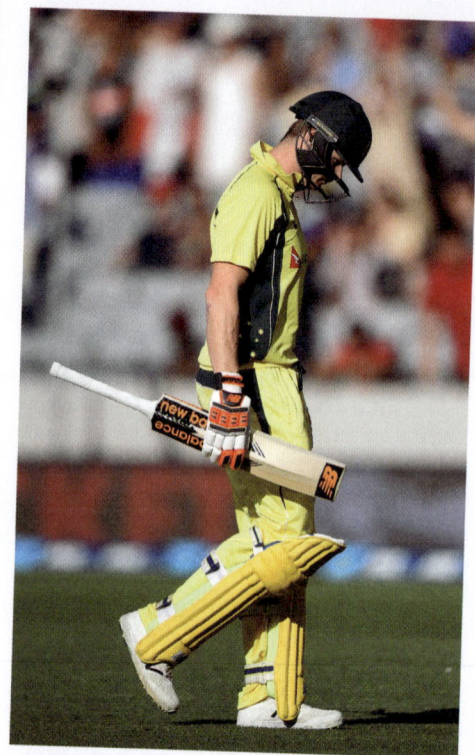

NEW ZEALAND VS AUSTRALIA, 1ST ODI
AUCKLAND, 3 FEBRUARY 2016
New Zealand won by 159 runs

New Zealand	307-8		Australia	148 (24.2 overs)
M Guptill	90		M Wade	37
H Nicholls	61		T Boult	3-38
			M Henry	3-41

THE ACC SUPER LEAGUE

While those series were very much based in the real world, the ACC Super League occupied a fantasy world largely untapped. But it paid not to have an urban dictionary on hand when the team announcements were made.

The Super League had a draft system with players and celebrities from past and present all featuring, while commentary highlights were produced for each game.

MATT HEATH: There was a point when T20 cricket leagues were popping up all over the place with ridiculous names and even worse franchise names. And we wanted to be part of the action.

JASON HOYTE: I mean, the Chennai Super Kings, the Sydney Sixers, the Auckland Aces — what five-year-olds with crayons are coming up with these names?

HEATH: Hoytey loves T20.

JEREMY WELLS: There was the Big Bash, the IPL, the Super Smash and the Blast, and every franchise seemed to have a 'super' in and around it, so we thought: 'Let's start our own ACC Super League.' The key difference was that this was a made-up league. We took fantasy sport to a new (and very niche) level.

MIKE LANE: We checked our joint account and came to the conclusion that we didn't quite have the resources to start a proper cricket league, so we went full satire. We believe this is the first league in the world to have fantasy teams and players, but 100 per cent legitimate commentary, team logos and even team merchandise.

HEATH: Given my southern roots, I bought the Dunedin Power Bottoms franchise and immediately recruited some hometown names in the draft. I'm talking about the likes of Robbie Burns, Stu McCullum and the hard-hitting Robin Bain. It was my way of giving back to the community. Having said that, I knew I needed some bigger international names to help attract sponsors. That's where the likes of Lorde and Richie Benaud came into their own.

BROWNS BAY—RED BEACH UNITED

Kane Williamson (c)

Willie Apiata (vc)

Lance Armstrong

The Mad Butcher

TV psychic Sue Nicholson

David Tua

David Bowie

David Bain (wk)

Fred Goodall

Stu Gillespie

Richard de Groen

Wider Squad: The Prophet Muhammad (peace be upon him), Tammy the Briscoes Lady

Owner: Lee Baker

THE DANNEVIRKE DUTCH RUDDERS

Steve Crowe (c)

Morgan 'Fingers' Fahey

Hitro Okesene

Brendon Tuuta

Chic Littlewood

Suzanne Paul (wk)

Annelise Coberger

Simon Wi Rutene

Richard Reid

Neal Parlane

Michael Parlane

Wider Squad: Barry Cooper, Steve Randell, Peter Plumley-Walker

Owner: G-Lane

THE WAIRARAPA BUSH

Richard Reid (c)

Ewen Chatfield

Michael Mason

Marty Berry

Luke Ronchi

Ladyhawke (wk)

Georgina Beyer

Tim Boyer

Ross Taylor

Jesse Ryder

Bob Charles

Wider Squad: Jemaine Clement, Zac Guildford (former owner of the Buckhorn Bar & Grill in Carterton)

Owner: Paul Ford

HAWKE'S BAY SUPER WOUNDERS

Phil Horne (c)

David Halls

Peter Hudson

Peter Sinclair

Sarah Ingham

Joanne Ingham (wk)

Jock Edwards

Gary Robertson

Derek Stirling

Sir Paul Holmes

Richard Reid

Wider Squad: Chubb Tangaroa, Olly Ohlson, Peter Pokai

Owner: Jeremy Wells

MATAMATA SUPER FIXERS

Richard Reid (c)

Former seam bowler with name suppression

Mohammad Asif

Mohammad Amir

Danish Kaneria

Maurice Odumbe

Hansie Cronje

Saleem Malik

Mohammad Azharuddin

Herschelle Gibbs

Lou Vincent (wk)

Wider Squad: Chris Cairns, Sachin Tendulkar, Mark Waugh

Owner: Joseph Durie

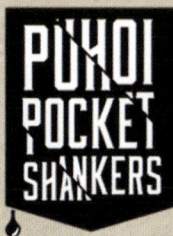

PUHOI POCKET SHANKERS

Richard Reid (c)

Heath Davis

Abdul Qadir

Richard de Groen

Gladstone Small

Rod Latham (wk)

Brian Turner, poet

Greg Turner

Glenn Turner

Blair Hartland

Gavin Greenidge (lesser-known cousin of Gordon)

Wider Squad: Shane Thomson, Susan Devoy, Trevor Franklin

Owner: Jason Hoyte

CANTERBURY LOG SPLITTERS

Mike Pero (c)

A woodwork teacher with name suppression

Ben Harris

Dipak Patel

Neil Ensuite

Chad Chewbaccaman

Dan Chiznell

Richard Petrie

Leigh Hart (owner, player-coach)

Fergie McCormick (wk)

Terry Salamanderman

Wider Squad: The Christchurch Wizard, Robbie Deans, Jason Gunn

Owner: Leigh Hart

DUNEDIN POWER BOTTOMS

Robin Bain (c)

Gary McCormick

Callum Procter

Vin Scully

Metiria Turei

Greg O'Connor

Roger Hall

Robbie Burns

Billy Ibadulla

Chase Utley (wk)

Stu McCullum

Wider Squad: Peter Williams, Lorde, Richie Benaud, Colin Craig, Rachel MacGregor

Owner: Matt Heath

WELLS: I purchased the Hawke's Bay Super Wounders and assembled what I believed to be a bloody good squad. Having a deceased opening bowler didn't initially seem to make sense, but I think it's fair to say the late Sir Paul Holmes surprised a lot of teams with his accuracy and, at times, merciless sledging.

LANE: The draft was a total fuck-up. Richard Reid got drafted into five teams! I chose him first for the Dutch Rudders, then he cropped up in the Super Wounders, then as captain of the Pocket Shankers, Bush and the bloody Super Fixers. I was happy to secure the exclusive services of Fingers Fahey, though. He could turn it square.

WELLS: The problem was we had no robust rules around the draft and people took advantage of the loopholes. Richard Reid was going to be a busy, and very well paid, man.

HOYTE: Admittedly, the Richard Reid thing was an issue, but the Puhoi Pocket Shankers was the only team with actual cricket players in it. When I saw the other squad lists I started to question the legitimacy of the league.

LEE BAKER: I was happy with my squad. The right balance of cricketing knowledge, boxing, steroid use and spirituality. The Prophet Muhammad (peace be upon him) was a real coup for Browns Bay–Red Beach United.

PAUL FORD: I had no idea what the fuck was going on. Lane just told me I owned the Wairarapa Bush and sent me some merch. He didn't even explain it was a fantasy T20 league. I was dangerously confused. It wasn't until I saw the draw that I understood what madness was ensuing.

LEIGH HART: I took on a lot being a player-coach-manager-owner of the Log Splitters. Too much, probably. It became hard when I had the likes of Neil Ensuite and even Mike Pero coming to me as a sounding board when they were struggling for form and missing being home. The coach in me wanted to drop them immediately and bring in the likes of the Wizard and Jason Gunn, who were training the house down, yet the owner in me knew exactly how much they were being paid and I really wanted a return on my investment. Overall, I was disappointed in the other ACC members for not taking on a more active role within their teams.

WELLS: When you have Hudson & Halls opening the batting in flamboyant fashion against the likes of Robin Bain, I knew I had the talent and experience to win the whole comp.

LANE: The competition lasted three weeks, with round-robin games being played over the weekends and highlights packages released online and on Radio Hauraki on Monday morning.

HEATH: I seriously started to believe this was a real competition and would hang out for the results and highlights packages on Mondays. I had my Dunedin Power Bottoms merch. I was fully invested. But we lost the semifinal and I immediately fired the entire squad. Except Robin Bain — he was the only one who deserved to stay.

The final was a close-fought affair. Starting in near-darkness at 6.30am, Leigh Hart's Canterbury Log Splitters probably made a mistake when choosing to bat first in front of the largest media contingent seen in the Hawke's Bay since the Jan Molenaar siege (according to match commentator Mike Lane).

The Jeremy Wells-owned Hawke's Bay Super Wounders, who needed 13 off the last two balls of Leigh Hart's final over, won thanks to the late Sir Paul Holmes hitting both deliveries for six, one of which was a no-ball. It was an incredibly dramatic finish to an entertaining tournament, but the ACC Super League did not return for a second season.

MY FIRST SPORTING HERO

by Leigh Hart

It is a huge honour to have been tasked with writing a tribute to my cricketing hero Terry Salamanderman.

Terry, with a batting average of 7.2, was gifted in so many ways, but his career was hobbled by a rare physical condition that resulted in him having webbed feet, no eyelids and reptilian skin that needed to be in a state of 78 per cent moisture at all times.

As a military-medium bowler, he was best suited to the conditions of the humid subcontinent. Much like today, cricket in the late '60s and early '70s meant long periods out in the field. This concept meant Terry was often battling adversity. With skin that had more genetic similarities to a Guatemalan cane toad than Homo sapiens, he often struggled when exposed to direct sunlight.

Terry was a specialist fielder who needed to be placed in the moistest and shadiest parts of the ground. In later years, as his condition worsened, he needed his own irrigation sprinkler system, which he attached to his back in a duffle bag-like contraption.

His controversial backpack moisturising system often came into question when he was batting. The wicket around him was always damp, regardless of the weather, a fact that upset some of his more delicate batting partners. Also, many an umpire argued about whether a batter can be caught behind with a thick edge off of a retrofitted Marley-style irrigation system. In later life, Terry could often be heard complaining that his average would have been much closer to 10, which was considered acceptable for an all-rounder in the '60s, if he hadn't been given out caught off his downpipe so often.

As the game of cricket moved inexorably towards the shorter formats, Terry struggled to keep up; his frog-like skin wasn't suited to the one-day game. The fact he was allergic to flash photography made transitioning to day-night cricket almost impossible. So, Terry retired, six months after he was officially dropped from the team.

Post cricket, Terry's life spiralled into chaos. He abused substances, mainly worm pills and cocaine. Tragically, he was found dead in his spa pool in 1986. An autopsy revealed he had six grams of chlorine in his system. Somewhat ironically, police found 12 grams of high-grade cocaine in the spa-pool filter.

The coroner ruled it death by misadventure.

CHARGE:	Rubbing genitalia upon a revered cricket trophy.
VERDICT:	Guilty as sin

BLACK CAPS V AUSTRALIA, 3RD ODI, CHAPPELL-HADLEE TROPHY
Hamilton, 8 February 2016

The Chappell-Hadlee Trophy series of 2016 was a short, sharp, three-match affair that culminated in the nation's chlamydia capital after the first two ODIs were split in Auckland and Wellington. The nerves were heightened when New Zealand could only post a subpar 246 during their turn at bat.

But that's really no excuse for what happened next . . .

Matt Heath: We witnessed a shocking piece of G-Lane behaviour.

With the series on the line, a white-gloved member of the security team — with an NZC communications person in tow — brought the trophy, named after the respective countries' two most esteemed cricket families, to the ACC caravan, where it was gingerly passed through the window.

Jeremy Wells: Somebody distracted security and G-Lane used the opportunity to take out his testicles and plop them on the large ball/sphere at the top of the trophy.

Jason Hoyte: I have seen Lane's testicles far too often, so when he got them out I wasn't overly surprised. Seeing him molest that trophy was next level, though.

Mike Lane: In my defence, security were asleep at the wheel and it looked highly likely that Australia might win the series, so I was banking a bit of happiness insurance.

Hoyte: He once rested his testicles on my shoulder mid-commentary for no reason other than his sick amusement.

Wells: I thought we were better than that as a team. I thought we could aim higher.

Lane: My rationale was that Australia was going to win the trophy, which would lead to their captain Steve Smith kissing that trophy. So if Australia won and then ran around celebrating like twits, at least we'd know that Smith would be, in effect, kissing my balls. I thought it was a pretty sound plan.

New Zealand won by 55 runs after an inspired bowling performance.

Lane: Baz McCullum, the people's hero, ended up kissing the footprint of my plums. The win was bittersweet.

Heath: Despite Jerry's misgivings, you have to admit they're not just any nuts. They're a cherished set; the Moeraki Boulders of ACC testicles. Any trophy is better for having been rubbed by them.

Wells: I still think we're better than that.

Lane: We're not. By the way, I'm sorry Baz. I hope you didn't get any cold sores.

Matt Heath's Guide to
A GOOD BANNER

Like calligraphy, weaving wool on a loom and building model train sets, making a quality banner at a sporting event is a dying art. Help revive this ancient and revered craft by following my carefully curated plan.

Size matters

Like all things in life, size matters when it comes to banners. In an age of punishing short TikTok videos and mind-shrinking snippets of content, the modern banner has also become infected by the cult of small and often.

The hand-held whiteboard with a pen and duster at a cricket game — piss off!

The tiny A4 piece of paper with a crayoned 'Hi' on it — go fuck yourself!

A good starting point for a worthwhile banner is the single bedsheet. That's your entry-level enterprise, but ideally you should be working on a queen size (top sheet, fitted sheets are relatively niggly).

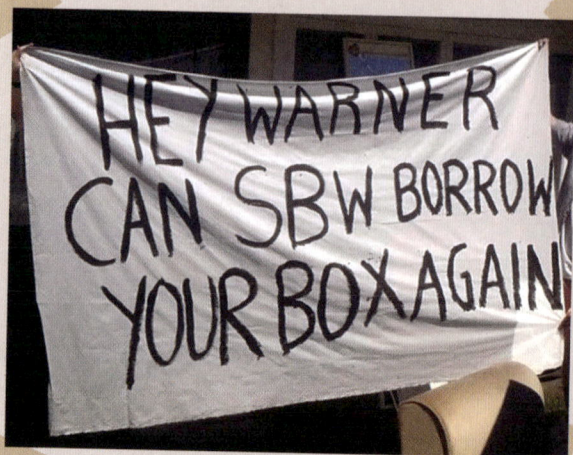

If you're still living with your mum, check down the back of your linen closet, because there's bound to be some cheap sheets going musty that she reserved for when her loser brother Derek came to stay with his ex-girlfriend who had a reputation for testing the tensile strength of manchester from here to the Chatham Islands.

What colour, I hear you ask? Well that's obvious, it needs to be white with a minimum cotton thread count of around 250–300.

Word count

It needs to be punchy, but also needs to tell a story. The balance is crucial.

For example, the copy on the banner on the opposite page is highly effective — no visuals required.

An outstanding example of the ability to mix words with imagery came when Sri Lanka were at the peak of their powers, led by the rotund Arjuna Ranatunga.

Generally speaking, banter has moved on a bit since the days of The Twelfth Man tapes, when the principal source of humour was mangling the names of players from Pakistan, India and Sri Lanka, but there is still a place in the banner game for this sort of carry-on.

Speak truth to power

A brilliant example of this came after beach umbrellas started to dominate the boundary lines of Shell Cup matches during the 1990s. Like Germans marking their territory — something they've been prone to do in different ways throughout history, including laying out their beach towels at Spanish holiday resorts — privileged boomers would get to the cricket early and set up under their giant parasols. At some low-lying grounds, this meant the rest of the crowd could see bugger all.

A simple banner reading 'Fuck the Bomb, Ban The Umbrella' was unfurled at Blake Park (now Bay Oval) and was paraded around the ground to rapturous applause. By the time of the next game, a demarcation line had been drawn, in front of which umbrellas (but unfortunately not boomers) were banned.

Victory for the banner bearers!

Visuals

Sometimes a picture is all that's required.

Never before or since has the travesty of a 'banner competition' — true artists are in it for the laughs, not the prizes — been so gloriously derailed than during the National Bank banner championships, circa 1999. To be in to win, all you had to do was include the National Bank logo on the banner. Some legend used a regulation double sheet to draw a 2.5 x 3 metre logo . . . but with a twist. The rearing black stallion was joined by another black stallion, which was casually entering it from behind.

In another masterstroke, it was hung over the Basin Reserve picket fence at third man in a prime viewing spot the TV cameras could not avoid. Cue blind panic in the New Zealand Cricket commercial team.

Language

In these challenging times, it's often hard to get a banner into a ground that really cuts to the chase and delivers some solid abuse to an individual or team.

The key here is to use a foreign language. It's not foolproof by any stretch, but will give you a window of opportunity to get your message across before the wowser event organisers Google Translate the banner. A prime example is a banner that appeared at Bay Oval in 2019 that read: 'Bryan Waddle é uma batata gorda'. It lasted a full 30 overs before somebody, possibly Bryan himself, realised it was telling him he was a fat potato in Portuguese.

Erection

Given the vomit of commercial signs and messaging around the grounds these days, getting wall space to actually erect your banner is a challenge. Nobody is allowed to cover up signage and poles are banned!

The key here is power in numbers. With four fully grown humans, you can quickly unfurl a banner of most sizes in less than three seconds. Two need to go high, two low and work to a minimal angle of 75 degrees for optimal TV exposure.

Child labour

The dark arts of getting a message across the live broadcast is often the most obvious: kids.

No one would expect a group of small children in Black Caps merchandise to unfurl a banner reading: 'Nothing worries Danny. He loves Cheesy Fanny' live on TV — but they do.

2017

HEAR THE LIONS RAW

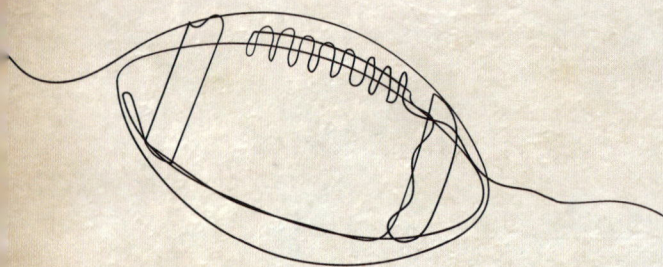

The sporting year of 2017 was another full one. James McOnie and his many talents joined the ACC commentary team, the Crusaders, under the breath-of-fresh-air leadership of Scott Robertson and Sam Whitelock, got back on the winning horse for the first time in eight years and the all-conquering Black Ferns conquered all to reclaim the Rugby World Cup.

In further Cup action, New Zealand played host to the Rugby League World Cup, losing a try-less quarter-final 2–4 to Fiji. It was a little embarrassing.

The year delivered redemption for Grant Dalton, savaged for screwing up an 8–1 lead in San Francisco four years earlier, as the preternatural sailing talent of helmsman Peter Burling and skipper Glenn Ashby guided Team New Zealand to perhaps the biggest triumph of 2017. They well and truly exorcised the ghosts of San Fran as Team New Zealand ran away with the 35th America's Cup, winning 7–1 in the waters of Bermuda that were blue, azure, cobalt, sapphire, cerulean, ultramarine, aquamarine or even lapis lazuli depending on what page of the thesaurus reporters and broadcasters landed upon that day.

Sad news came from the King Country when the mightiest pine tree of them all was toppled. Sir Colin Meads, the never-improved-upon prototype of a modern rugby forward, died of cancer aged 81. Meads would have described the ACC as 'a bunch of stupid clowns', but he would have stopped and had six to eight beers with them anyway because, well, he's Pinetree.

There was also the prospect of a visit from the British & Irish Lions — a tour that happens only once every 12 years and one that had provided the impetus for the ACC's move into rugby the year before. The hype was through the roof, even if, this time, the tourists did not bring with them a PR 'maestro' like Alastair Campbell.

But, before then, there was an ODI series against the old enemy to look forward to. The match at Eden Park turned out to be a hell of a game.

NEW ZEALAND VS AUSTRALIA, 1ST ODI
AUCKLAND, 30 JAN 2017
New Zealand won by 6 runs

New Zealand	286-9		Australia	280 (47 overs)
N Broom	73		M Stoinis	146*
M Guptill	61		M Santner	3-44
M Stoinis	3-49			

For many Aucklanders, 30 January 2017, a Monday, was a day to get the boat out for a sail on the Waitematā. For others, Auckland Anniversary Day served only as a painful reminder that, although the weather remained hot, the summer break was over and that school and work were about to kick in properly the following day.

After a month of friction-free commutes around town, the motorways would regress to their normal gridlocked state, buses would be standing-room only at peak hours and shorts were no longer going to cut it in the office.

PAUL FORD: It was a public holiday, with spirits high in both a metaphorical and a physical sense. The game also coincided with the Laneway Festival, so there was a palpable, rollicking atmosphere in the city.

For a few thousand cricket fans wanting to suck a little more marrow out of their holidays, there was an ODI against Australia at Eden Park to look forward to. It might not have carried the high stakes of the match between the two teams on the same ground in 2015, a game that carried such frenzied expectations that Leigh Hart could only cope by drinking himself into a pre-match stupor, but for pure unadulterated drama, this game had everything.

FORD: There was a feeling of high expectation with it being the first game of the series. There was high emotion in the crowd and the caravan as it seemed like New Zealand had scored too many for Australia to chase down. But, as always against the Aussies, the possibility of a resurrection or a mind-blowing finish lingered.

New Zealand had cobbled together 286 in their 50 overs, thanks to Martin Guptill's 61 and a 73 from Neil Broom, the only one of his six 50-plus ODI scores to come against a team other than Bangladesh or Ireland.

In reply, Australia were dead and buried when Trent Boult, Tim Southee and

Lockie Ferguson knocked the top off Australia's batting.

Marcus Stoinis, aka the Stoinis Infection, was playing just his second ODI for Australia and had entered at 54 for 5 to bat alongside Sam Heazlett. Remember him? No, neither do any of the ACC commentary team.

Shortly after, Australia were 67 for 6, and although Stoinis, who went to school in Perth with Daryl 'Son of a Mitch' Mitchell, glued together some useful partnerships with James Faulkner and Pat Cummins, when the ninth wicket fell at 226 the match felt like it was all over bar the shouting.

Here's where the game got super freaky. The number 11 batter, Josh Hazlewood, was eventually run out without facing a ball, but not before Stoinis had faced all 30 balls of their 54-run partnership to bring them within one more six — he hit 11! — of tying the game.

Let's cross to the commentary team in the caravan, where Australia need seven runs to win thanks to Stoinis's heroics.

JEREMY WELLS: Last ball of the Southee over. What's he going to try to do? I think Stoinis will try to hit it [for six].

MATT HEATH: It's a great supporting role from Hazlewood, remarkable.

WELLS: Here comes Southee, last ball of the over to Stoinis. Stoinis drives . . .

PAUL FORD: Run him out . . .

[unintelligible shouting]

HEATH: Stomp on his head!

FORD: It's going upstairs.

HEATH: Stomp on his head!

LEE BAKER: It hasn't been given, it hasn't been given.

WELLS: It's gone upstairs. What's happened here is Stoinis has driven the ball to Kane Williamson, who cleverly positioned himself at short mid on.

HEATH: Go ball, go ball, yes, he's gone!

WELLS: He's been run out by Kane Williamson.

BAKER: Oh my god!

MULTIPLE VOICES: He's gone, what a game of cricket!

WELLS: God knows how they won that. They nearly lost it. And Stoinis remains not out on 146 and you have to say what an impressive knock, one of the greatest innings of all time, one of the greatest one-day innings you'll ever see.

HEATH: And Hazlewood, one of the worst one-day innings you'll ever see. He didn't face a ball and lost them the game.

FORD: It's a remarkable effort to lose a game by scoring zero off zero.

So, New Zealand won a thriller, but a lot of the ACC's pub talk later that night focused not so much on the end of the game, but the fact Matt Heath had become, as far as records show, the first accredited broadcaster to openly propagate the idea of committing a specific act of violence on a visiting cricketer. For the second time in less than a year, the captain of the ACC was enduring the same existential crisis.

WELLS: I thought we were better than that. I honestly did.

HEATH: That's one of my favourite ACC moments of all time. More than that, it's one of my favourite moments of all time. The Stoinis Infection nearly stole the game from the Black Caps. That was everything a one-day international should be and it was everything a game involving the ACC should be. The caravan was rocking all day. It was utter madness.

Heath had wittingly added to the madness by suggesting that the ACC caravan was a safe haven for streakers.

FORD: Well, that's what he says now and it makes for a good story, but I can't actually remember him encouraging streakers beforehand. Regardless, I could hear this roar rise like a swell from the crowd and looked up to see the streaker near the wicket block and heading in our direction. With Australia under the pump in the run chase, a glorious day overhead, there was a sense that this was a streak of victory and glory — it was the thirty-sixth over and Australia were already seven down. We were already starting to celebrate an unexpected and rare dominant New Zealand win over our big brothers.

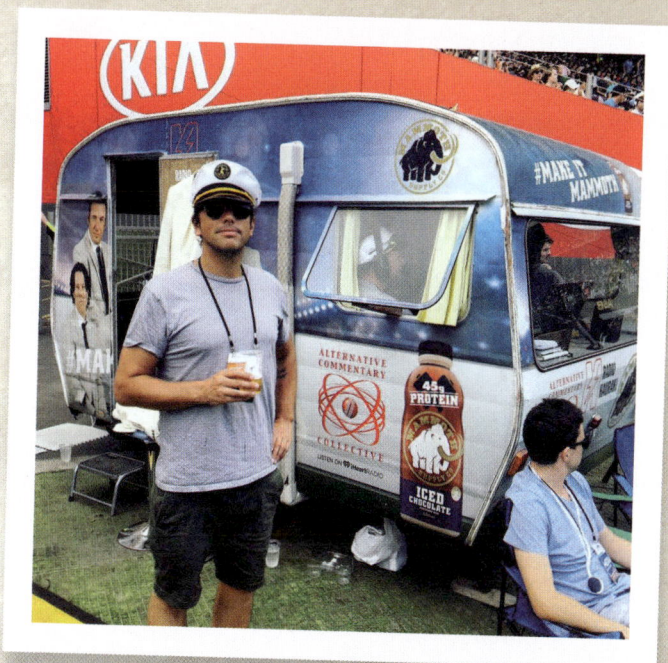

The partially zinced, slightly portly, quite hairy and very sunburnt streaker tumbled over the front of the eastern terraces and set sail towards the ACC caravan beneath the scoreboard at Eden Park, holding only his stained T-shirt for whatever lay ahead.

FORD: I was commentating with one arm out of the side window and saw him as he made his way to square leg at pace. Pat Cummins, Marcus Stoinis and Lockie Ferguson looked on. The streaker sidestepped and delicately fended the first orange-fluoro-clad security guard, who tried to mow him down, and I could see the glee on his face as he approached the boundary rope and leapt over the digital signage.

The footage makes for excruciating viewing as the all-nude male streaker sprints west across the field towards the caravan's position in a slipway between the west and north stands. He has a decent lead on Red Badge security and, to the casual observer, is doing better than most in the shrinkage department (see Manaia Stewart's Guide to Streaking on page 144 for further explanation) as he approaches the boundary edge.

It is here that he makes his critical error. In trying to leap one of the advertising hoardings that encircled the ground he forgot to take half a step of pace off and judge the takeoff. As it turns out, he's carrying slightly too much speed and a fraction too little elevation. His foot clips the top and . . .

FORD: He doesn't stick the landing.

HEATH: He tripped and scraped himself along the gravel like a cheese grater before he got absolutely smashed by security. I just loved the fact that we were running a Julian Assange-like sanctuary. If you could get to our caravan we would let you in the door and keep the security forces out à la the Ecuadorian Embassy in London. I was very proud of coming up with that idea. He was so close. We were by the door yelling at him to get in, but he got munted. Shit, he would have been sore for days, maybe even weeks after that. He landed front first, too, so I don't know about the state of his downstairs operation, but I would suggest it probably needed a conservative rehabilitation programme.

FORD: In the commentary there was also discussion about the technique — good pace, tidy sidestep, nearly excellent vertical leap, BYO T-shirt a nice touch — and also a sense of admiration for the audacity and fully nude spectacle that had been created.

Our reaction was a mix of empathy (this was one of 'our people') and sympathy as he was so close to completing the Eden Park crossing and was hammered twice: once by the combination of his foot and the concrete and then by the crash tackle of the late-arriving security guard.

If Heath was proud of his humanitarian efforts to have the ACC caravan designated as a safe haven — a place of refuge — he was slightly ashamed of a chant he spewed over the airwaves as the match was winding down.

HEATH: I was less proud of chanting 'stomp on his head' on the commentary about Marcus Stoinis. It was a great innings. He didn't deserve that. But it was an awesome day.

To use a sporting cliché, my favourite moments are the games like these. That feeling when we're in the caravan during a big moment and we're jumping around and it's nearly coming off its rocker. To use another cliché, that really is living the dream.

Speaking of downstairs operations, the year 2017 also saw a remarkable demonstration of the commitment the ACC team has to their craft.

'Nothing to see here, just a cricket commentator announcing a match during his vasectomy,'

MASHABLE, 1 FEBRUARY 2017

'Commentator Commentates Cricket Match Live From His Vasectomy,'

HUFFINGTON POST, 2 FEBRUARY 2017

'That's a Bit of a Pinprick: Cricket Commentator Continues Calling Match During His Own Vasectomy,'

VICE, 2 FEBRUARY 2017

'Kiwi broadcaster's on-air vasectomy goes viral,'

NZ HERALD, 3 FEBRUARY 2017

Yeah, that actually happened.

'Not even a vasectomy will stand between this man and the sport of gentlemen,' wrote Jacob Lauing on Mashable, his amazement speaking for pretty much anybody who tuned into the Facebook livestream of Mike Lane, nuts in the palm of his doctor's hands, getting his vas deferens cauterised.

The amazing thing is it worked. Lane has had no new children since that one-dayer.

MATT HEATH: G-Lane had actually been talking about doing that for a while.

JEREMY WELLS: He had three children. He didn't want any more. He had a busy schedule of commentating coming up. It was summer, his busy time and he managed to shoehorn in two things. He didn't let the team down.

JASON HOYTE: It was literally ball-by-ball. I have a confession to make. I have a real affection for Mike's balls. They rested on my head during commentary once.

As the team crossed to Lane a second time, his face was in that weird halfway house that could signify either extreme pleasure or pain. There were momentary concerns that he wasn't getting a vasectomy at all, until the camera panned to a slightly bemused-looking blue-coated man armed with the arc welder that would be used to cauterise the tubes.

HOYTE: I'm almost certain it was a first in international cricket.

LEE BAKER: I'm not even sure it was legal.

LEIGH HART: Originally we wanted it done in the caravan itself, but the medical establishment deemed it an unsafe environment for cricket commentary, let alone a surgery.

HEATH: It definitely wasn't sterile, unlike Lane now.

Spare a thought for the man documenting the journey.

JOSEPH DURIE: I will never forget that burning smell for the rest of my life.

As far as we are aware, Durie remains fertile.

There was a lot going on in the early part of 2017, but as the year progressed focus began to narrow in on the national game. All across the country, it was Lions this, Lions that, Lions, Lions, Lions.

MIKE LANE: We had targeted the Lions tour because we looked at it and the tickets were ludicrously expensive and nobody could get them. We saw it as an opportunity to run our own events, doing live commentary at licensed venues for all those New Zealanders who got priced out of the matches.

The tour would take them from Christchurch to Rotorua to Auckland to Wellington and back to Auckland for the third and final test. It would encompass not just the test matches but matches against the Crusaders and New Zealand Māori as well.

From the very first call, they made an impact, especially in the deep south. Here's Carol Tippett from Waldronville writing to the *Otago Daily Times*:

'As I don't have Sky and Prime was not replaying the Lions–Crusaders game, I thought I would try the old-fashioned way and listen to a radio broadcast. I had no idea what stations would broadcast, couldn't find listings in newspapers so I surfed the FM channels, finding one somewhere around 106.40FM. The game was five minutes in play and I wasn't sure if I was on the correct station as the announcer was in the middle of relating the most bizarre story I have ever heard on radio, let alone during a sports commentary. He was relating a narrative about a rugby player and a businessman, neither of whom I heard by name. I was so disgusted at the ridiculous commentary I switched off and can only say if this is the normal standard of radio broadcast on our national game then long live Sky, even if I don't have it.'

Poor Carol. She got the story slightly wrong. It didn't involve a rugby player, but a businessman and a business sock. She'd happened upon Jeremy Wells talking about a friend of his who, on a work trip out of town, decided to kill an hour or so with a Grindr hookup. It just so happened that his match had a fetish for business socks and proceeded to make love to a hole in the one Wells' friend was wearing, before finishing up and leaving.

And there was Carol, tuning in from Waldronville, expecting to hear about the Lions' prowess in the frigid Christchurch conditions, but instead she was subjected to some X-rated smut flying under the rainbow flag with a bunch of guys purporting to be rugby commentators wondering what you do with a sock that had been ejaculated in.

Carol was far from alone. Another letter of complaint during that ill-fated tour started: 'I was on my launch at the Bay of Islands when I tuned into the official commentary of the rugby and I was disgusted by what was going on . . .'

DEAN BUCHANAN (GROUP DIRECTOR, ENTERTAINMENT, NZME): The boys discovered pretty quickly that radio frequencies were a different beast to the internet. Streaming was the Wild West back then, and you could pretty much say what you wanted to. Not so much on radio.

The boys were pretty smart and soon adjusted to that line in the sand, but the volume of complaints certainly went up during the Lions tour when we were going out over the Hauraki channels.

LANE: We caught a few channel surfers by surprise, yes.

The ACC also had an add-on to their touring team. Journalist Dylan Cleaver was invited along for the ride, embedded if you will, and the blurb to the story that eventually appeared in the *Weekend Herald* read: 'Dylan Cleaver wasn't going to watch the Lions, until he got an offer he could have refused and hitched a lift with the lads of the Alternative Commentary Collective.'

From there, the story went downhill. Here are a few lightly edited excerpts:

There is a slice of New Zealand you may have forgotten existed. While you were busy growing older, growing your debt mountain and growing children, parts of the country carried on as if you didn't exist.

They are the ones who survive Monday to Thursday so they can do all their living on Friday and Saturday nights. They're mainly young men, but not exclusively so. They want people to talk to them how they talk among themselves: giving each other stupid names, recounting sexcapades real or imagined, and getting a massive head of steam on.

I saw these people.

They were in Christchurch, in Rotorua, Hamilton, Auckland and even Wellington, the nation's capital.

They were fizzing. They were doing shots. They were getting tattooed. They were doing brown-eyes on the window. They were getting selfies with the 'stars', one even doing so with his penis out, much to the amusement of his mates.

As a mostly sober observer it's a strange but strangely compelling watch, like *Animal House* meets the BBC's coverage of Wimbledon.

There are all these people and all this mayhem and they're there because, for a couple of hours or so, the Alternative Commentary Collective — Mike Lane, Jeremy Wells and Matt Heath — were talking to them and they liked what they were hearing . . .

MATT HEATH: This was a weird time in the ACC's history. Although we like to play up the whole party-on-the-job thing, doing these commentaries from bars made you realise that there were people on a completely different level to you.

MIKE LANE: There was a lot of drinking in Wellington. It was like a stag party.

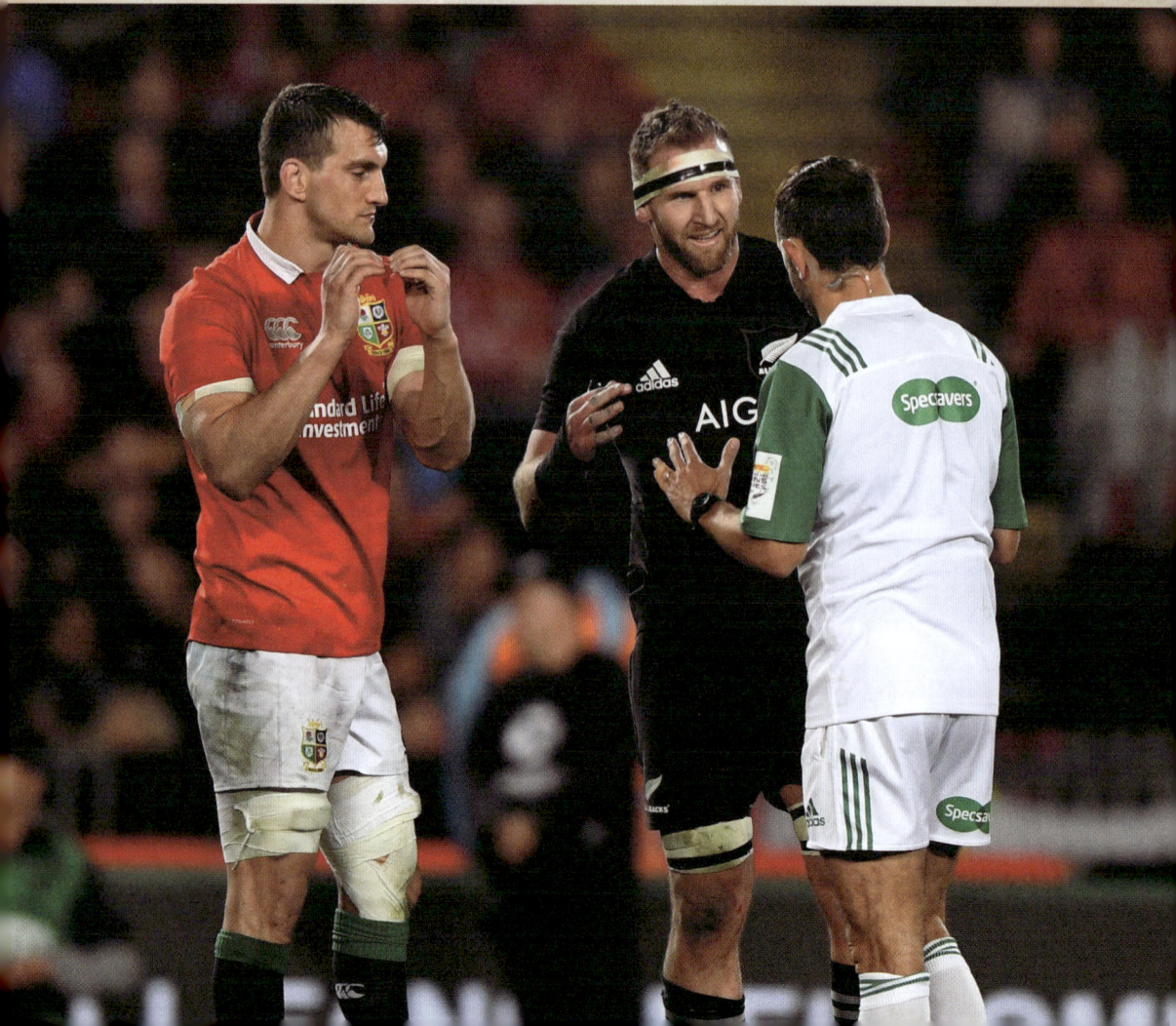

HEATH: Jerry filled the sink of our Airbnb with white spirits, a bag of ice and a splash of mixers, which was quite some move at 10am.

JEREMY WELLS: I thought we came in a bit cold during the first test and we needed a few more looseners before the second.

HEATH: Dylan Cleaver was staying with us in Wellington and I remember him emerging hungover from his bedroom one morning and declaring, 'I have nothing useful to offer the world today,' then turning on his heels and walking straight back into the dark cave that was his bedroom. I didn't see him again.

WELLS: It was like a zombie apocalypse at that bar once we finished commentating, but it only got more intense in Auckland.

The controversy at the end of the Wellington test, when a late Lions penalty led to a win over the 14-man All Blacks, was a mere warm-up for the deciding game in Auckland, which remained undecided after the match ended 15-15. With two minutes to go, referee Romain Poite awarded a kickable penalty to the All Blacks . . . but then changed his mind.

Poite initially deemed Lions hooker Ken Owens to be offside when he touched a restart that had been knocked on by Liam Williams. However, after consultation with his assistants, Poite overturned his decision, deciding Owens had instead committed accidental offside. He awarded a scrum to the All Blacks instead of a penalty, despite strong pleas from the New Zealand skipper, Eye Sockets Read.

The match remained drawn and the series ended 1-1 as a result, much to the frustration of the All Blacks and the anger of New Zealand fans. Some of that negative energy was transmitted to a nearby pub.

HEATH: The scene at the Kings Arms was confirmation of what we all had known for some time — G-Lane's got the worst fans.

WELLS: The absolute worst.

LANE: They are good people. They just had a bad night . . . as did the bloody ref.

In 2021, Poite admitted he made the wrong call. He said he got back to the changing sheds and 'destroyed everything' when he realised the error. Coincidentally, at the same time, everything was getting destroyed at the Kings Arms, the venue for the ACC commentary, as it was the last week of the venerable establishment's existence.

LIONS TOUR 2017, FIRST TEST
24 JUNE 2017, AUCKLAND

All Blacks **30** **15** British & Irish Lions

SECOND TEST
1 JULY 2017, WELLINGTON

All Blacks **21** **24** British & Irish Lions

THIRD TEST
8 JULY 2017, AUCKLAND

All Blacks **15** **15** British & Irish Lions

HEATH: There was a real demo-party vibe to the night.

LANE: I loved these events. We had people getting tattoos, DJs, drink specials and the ACC commentary blaring out over the speakers with big screens everywhere. However, the Kings Arms only had a couple of weeks left before it was due for demolition and that only seemed to embolden the public to expedite the job.

HEATH: The atmosphere when the game finished was odd. The match was a draw. The series was a draw. People were confused. They decided to take out that confusion on the poor old Kings Arms.

LANE: I popped my head out of the back of the stage where we were commentating and saw a barbecue table being dismantled in the garden bar. This was swiftly followed by various bottles hitting a projection screen.

HEATH: I'm pretty sure I saw a bottle smash on someone's head. They were the bloody G-Lane fans.

LANE: Like I said — they are good people. In many ways no different to you and I. Don't pigeonhole them.

WELLS: They were chanting 'G-Lane, G-Lane' and banging on the door to backstage where we were hiding. At one point a fist came through a small hole in the wall. I was waiting for Jack Nicholson to come flying through the wall with an axe screaming, 'Here's Johnny!'

HEATH: The problem was we were stuck backstage with G-Lane fans trying to get in. It was an *Assault on Precinct 13*-type situation. It was a siege. It was Helm's Deep in there. G-Lane fans all over the place and the only way out was through the main bar and into the car park.

LANE: Fuck off. Heath is massively exaggerating. Not all of them were G-Lane fans. There was a smattering of Leigh Hart fans as well. They were just having a good time and letting off some steam.

LEIGH HART: Leigh Hart fans are good people, too. Except maybe for Neville — that guy can be a real arsehole.

HEATH: It was a dire situation. But we couldn't stay in there waiting to be overrun. So we ordered an Uber, waited until it was right outside the pub door, threw a dozen beers and half a bottle of vodka out to the mob and while they ripped the booze to pieces we ran for it. We jumped in, the driver gunned it and amazingly we got out alive. It was a horror show.

LANE: It was a huge success. I immediately saw it as a template for future events.

WELLS: I was on edge for days after that, jumping at shadows, but in hindsight, the whole shocking debacle was a fitting farewell for the Kings Arms.

LANE: That Lions tour was a big moment for us. A big success. We understood that we had a product that could travel. We sold out every venue, including the Kings Arms twice, and could have sold a bunch more tickets had we had more room. We got to see up close and personal how dedicated some people were to the brand as well. I didn't know whether to be alarmed or proud when people came up to show us their 'Punisher' tattoos. Probably a bit of both, which is the sweet spot for the ACC.

Manaia Stewart's Guide to
STREAKING

Manaia Stewart has become a fixture across the ACC's commentary and podcast network. He is best known for being able to connect any global celebrity, dead or alive, to South Canterbury within four degrees of separation. He is highly regarded at the national level for his views on the fine art of streaking.

Quality streaking is fast becoming a lost art. Fully clothed muppets streaming themselves live on TikTok is not the New Zealand I grew up in, nor is it the one I want my grandchildren to call home. In an effort to preserve this fine tradition, I present to you my tips for a good streak.

Appropriate nudity levels

It doesn't matter if we live in a time of wanton disregard for social mores or an age of Presbyterian principles, nudity is *the* defining characteristic of the streak. There is no getting around that. Without being in a state of déshabillé you are a mere pitch invader. If you think about it on an evolutionary scale, the clothed pitch invader is the single-cell amoeba, while the streaker is the beautiful butterfly emerging from its cocoon.

A world-class streak may involve some clothing or accessories, but these must be used for comedic effect rather than self-promotion. For example, the famous '19th Hole' sign pointing to the buttocks of a golf streaker was a nice touch. It's becoming more common to see security wearing sprigs in anticipation of pitch invaders, so to level the playing field, streaking in footwear is perfectly acceptable.

Otherwise, that time-honoured phrase remains applicable: get ya kit off.

Are you a grower or a shower?

If you're male, understand the fact you might start out as John Holmes — spot the vintage '70s porn reference — at one end and as a flashy sports car owner* at the other.

I can't believe I have to spell this out for you, but the penis is not a muscle. Pre-streak manipulation may provide you with a sturdier starting base, but the

* Using the time-honoured scale of men compensating with expensive cars.

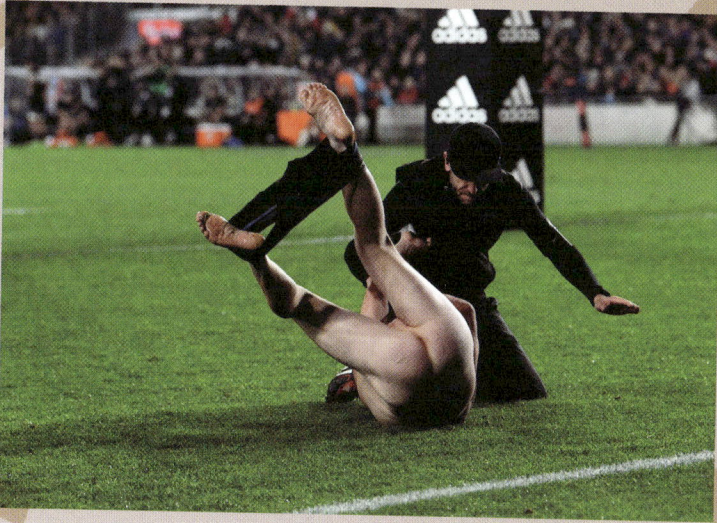

dynamic responses of blood redistribution and thermoregulation will draw blood away from the groinal region to the muscles that are being used for sprinting and to the skin surface for heat dissipation.

The only way this can be counteracted is if you find the mere act of running naked sexually arousing, in which case you might find yourself banned from naturist venues if that was a path you ever wanted to explore.

In any case, just be happy with what you are and what you've got.

Game awareness

A good streak must have no effect on the outcome of the game, or the perpetrator risks turning the crowd against them.

Perhaps no greater example of this came in 1977 — the '70s represented the Golden Age of Streaking — when New Zealand took on Australia in a cricket test at Eden Park. In the midst of Greg Chappell and Rick McCosker compiling a painstaking 115-run third-wicket partnership, the cricket was interrupted not once, not twice, but thrice by sunburned exhibitionists. The third fence-jumper, Leonard Bruce McCauley, tried to add a bit of pizazz to his routine by wearing large earphones with a dangling cord. As he reached the middle and went to shake Chappell's hand, to the amazement and amusement of the crowd, the Australian captain took his revolutionary Gray-Nicolls one-scoop and started thrashing McCauley's lily-white arse, very near another kind of dangling cord.

Narrating a best-selling VHS that highlighted the incident, Sir Richard Hadlee intoned: 'Greg Chappell was visibly distressed at the streaker running onto the field of play and holding up the game. Personally, I cannot condone his actions,' he added ambiguously, for it is not known which of the two actions he wasn't endorsing, 'but concentration had been broken and it helped bring about his dismissal, even though he was unlucky to be given out.'

In an amazing postscript, McCauley unsuccessfully sued Chappell for assault, but was instead fined $25 for disorderly conduct, which is worth $236 in 2024[*].

Again, without wanting to create confusion between a streak and a pitch invasion, the scenes when the Warriors took an NRL game to McLean Park in Napier in 2023 were Exhibit A in terms of complete lack of game awareness from several fence-jumpers.

The ACC is working to introduce designated 'Streaking Lanes' at stadiums around the country to counter this issue. But for now, as a good captain needs to be aware of time and score, so too should a good streaker. Time your run during a pause in play for maximum impact.

Climax

As with any performance, a good streak should build to a crescendo. Notable streaking climaxes include the Andrew Symonds shoulder-charge at the Gabba in '08, and the textbook cheek-to-cheek tackle by Ruben Wiki in 2013. Obviously you can't plan for those, but at least you should have a plan. It can be as simple as making it the full length of the pitch, sidestepping a Red Badge or scoring a fake try, but it's important to have a closing move in your head before hopping the barriers to avoid a fizzle-out.

The grass ceiling

It's a fact — the streaking world has a gender disparity problem. Men are sadly still over-represented in the streaking community and, frankly, we need more women to try to crash through this particular grass ceiling.

Perhaps because it's a relative rarity, female streakers tend to gain more fame and notoriety than their fellow male free-runners. We have already, for want of a better term, touched on Rose Kupa, but think also of Jacqui Salmond on the 18th green at St Andrews when Tiger Woods was set to win the Open Championship; Erika Roe, the godmother of streaking, going topless at Twickenham; and even a bikini-clad Lisa Lewis, who parlayed a semi-streak at an All Blacks test into a run for the Hamilton mayoralty.

---

[*] Manaia is far too young to have any knowledge of this seminal moment in NZ cricket history, but it was too good to leave out.

The ACC envisages a future where streaking opportunities are equally accessible to all, and remains committed to encouraging more women into the sport and narrowing the streaking gap.

Escape plan

The ultimate streak ends without capture. This requires high-level planning and execution, often involving scaling a perimeter fence and outside assistance in the form of clothes and transport. Very rarely does an impromptu, alcohol-assisted decision to streak end in evasion. However, if you're going off the cuff and still have dreams of getting away scot-free, aim for exits, low-slung exterior fences (sans razor wire), stairwells, toilet cubicles or ACC caravans.

Back when the ACC caravan was allowed at grounds, it was viewed, perhaps with some justification, as a refuge for streakers, a safe space.

Just think of the performance at the 2017 Eden Park ODI (see page 132), when one streaker was haring towards the caravan and presumed safety. With just one hoarding, his very own Berlin Wall, between him and asylum, he was spear-tackled by a security brownshirt and had his naked body grated across the concrete for his efforts.

Exit strategy 10/10. Execution 1/10.

To all those who succeed — we salute you.

Financial and legal literacy

The cost of streaking can be high if caught, with fines ranging from $400 to $5000. We suggest setting up a PayPal account or something similar and get your cash up front, rather than relying on the, 'Yeah mate, we'll cover it' pledges from friends who are 10 beers deep at the time.

Although less common these days, there is also a chance you might find yourself in court, like Jordan Wade did when he streaked across Eden Park in just his socks during the Lions series in 2017. But that's not the most remarkable part of his story. He launched a Givealittle page to help fund his costs and, in an interview with Radio Hauraki, made this stunning revelation:

'It was a bit of spur-of-the-moment peer pressure from a few different people, my father being one of them.'

That might be the final tip I have for you: don't streak on the advice of your father.

2018

STUCK IN THE MOMENT

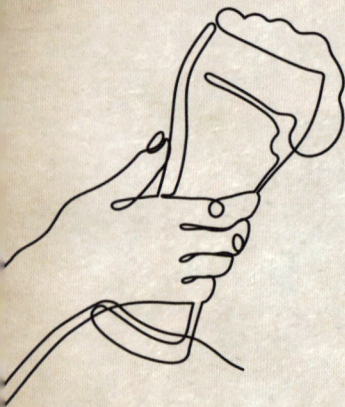

Almost as if mirroring the iconoclasm of the ACC itself, a bold new innovation hit New Zealand shores for the first time in March 2018: day-night test cricket.

Unfortunately, rain would prove to be a real shitter, with days two and three, the Friday and Saturday, completely ruined by the weather. This might have kept the crowds away, but didn't prevent a truly remarkable test match that ended in the final session of day five.

On day one, Kane Williamson won the toss, inserted England into bat and was at the crease himself by the second session of the match. England's innings lasted just 94 minutes and 20.4 overs. New Zealand used just two bowlers, Trent Boult (6-32) and Tim Southee (4-25). Williamson took a worldie to dismiss Stuart Broad for one of the five ducks in the innings. At one point, England was 23 for 8 and challenging New Zealand's world record all out 26, achieved at the same ground against this same opposition in 1955, but Craig Overton slapped a face-saving 33 as England crumbled for 58.

New Zealand's reply of 427 for 8 spread across four days, by which time Williamson had accumulated his 18th test century and Henry Nicholls his second.

It was tremendous dominance, but the foul weather meant it would all count

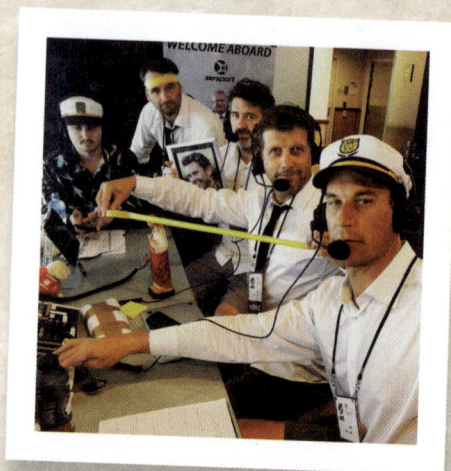

NEW ZEALAND VS ENGLAND, 1ST TEST
AUCKLAND, 22–26 MARCH 2018
New Zealand won by an innings and 49 runs

England	58
C Overton	33*
T Boult	6-32
T Southee	4-25

England	320
B Stokes	66
T Astle	3-39
T Boult	3-67
N Wagner	3-77

New Zealand	427-8 dec
H Nicholls	145*
K Williamson	102

for nought if England manned up in the second dig, which they did — to a point. Mark Stoneman, Joe Root, Ben Stokes and Chris Woakes all scored half centuries, but Neil Wagner bounced three of them out, and then Todd Astle — a future trivia question — took two of the final three wickets as the Black Caps wrapped up a win by an innings and 49 runs.

It was a summer-defining victory and one that was followed by an autumn-defining rearguard, with New Zealand clinging on by the skin of Ish Sodhi's teeth for a draw in Christchurch.

Chasing an improbable 382 to win on the final day, New Zealand still had 30 overs to survive when the Minute Piece, Colin de Grandhomme, was the seventh wicket to fall (for 45 and the total at 219). Enter Wagner to join Sodhi. Together the pair put on 37 runs in 188 nerve-shredding balls, before Wagner was out, caught in close for 7. But by then the light had deteriorated beyond a level deemed playable by the umpires and the game and series was saved.

These were big moments for the ACC, whose commentary had featured on the Sky remote under the yellow button for the first time.

MIKE LANE: That was a big deal for us. The series was the last one the Black Caps played under the command of Big Mikey Hesson, a man who is on record saying that everything he learned about cricket could be telescoped down to afternoons huddled under the blankets with Matt Heath on the terraces of Carisbrook*.

* There is actually a tiny element of truth in this.

ISH THE DISH

What a dish, the dark eyes and dreamy complexion make Ish quite The Dish.

Amateur rapper.

A man who is bucking the trend and still rocking a consistent goatee from 1990s Hamilton.

Rumoured to have invented the Sodhi Stream – the idea was stolen and remarketed as Soda Stream.

Some of the strongest wrists in the game developed not just from self pleasure but a relentless off-field exercise programme.

The only other NZ spinner to have longer legs than Dan Vettori – they go all the way.

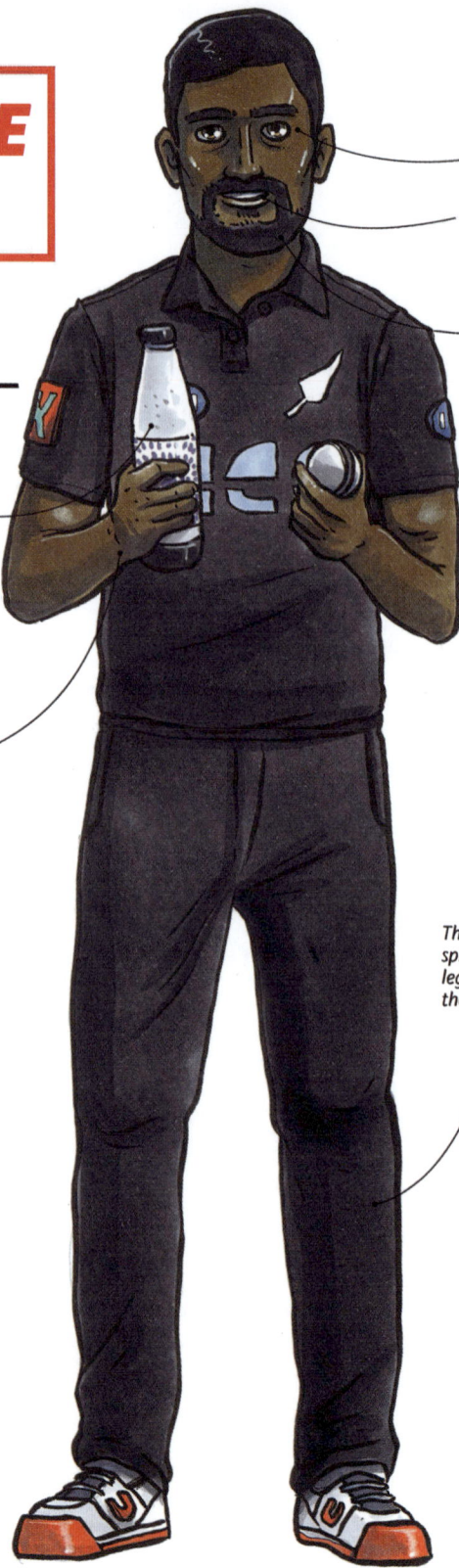

@UGLY_INK

NEW ZEALAND VS ENGLAND, 2ND TEST
CHRISTCHURCH, 30 MARCH–3 APRIL 2018
Match drawn

England	307
J Bairstow	101
T Southee	6-62
T Boult	4-87

England	352-9 dec
J Vince	76
M Stoneman	60
C de Grandhomme	4-94

New Zealand	278
BJ Watling	85
C de Grandhomme	72
T Southee	50
S Broad	6-54
J Anderson	4-76

New Zealand	256-8
T Latham	83
I Sodhi	56*
N Wagner	7

CHARGE:	Buying and smuggling a kilogram of high-grade, uncut cocaine into Eden Park for personal consumption.
VERDICT:	Not guilty

NOT GUILTY

NEW ZEALAND V ENGLAND
FIRST TEST
Eden Park, 22–26 March 2018

The Eden Park pink-ball test was also the scene of the most serious 'alleged' crime in the ACC's felonious history, one that carried the possibility of a prison sentence from the courts.

Joseph Durie (ACC's Mr Fix-It, Mr Big or Mr Nice, depending on circumstances): During the pink-ball test we were broadcasting out of the Beefy Botham box, which was basically a converted hospitality suite.

James Wear (NZC): I had to work pretty hard to get that box for them because they'd worn out their welcome under the old Eden Park management, and it's also fair to say they might have been running out of friends at NZC as well.

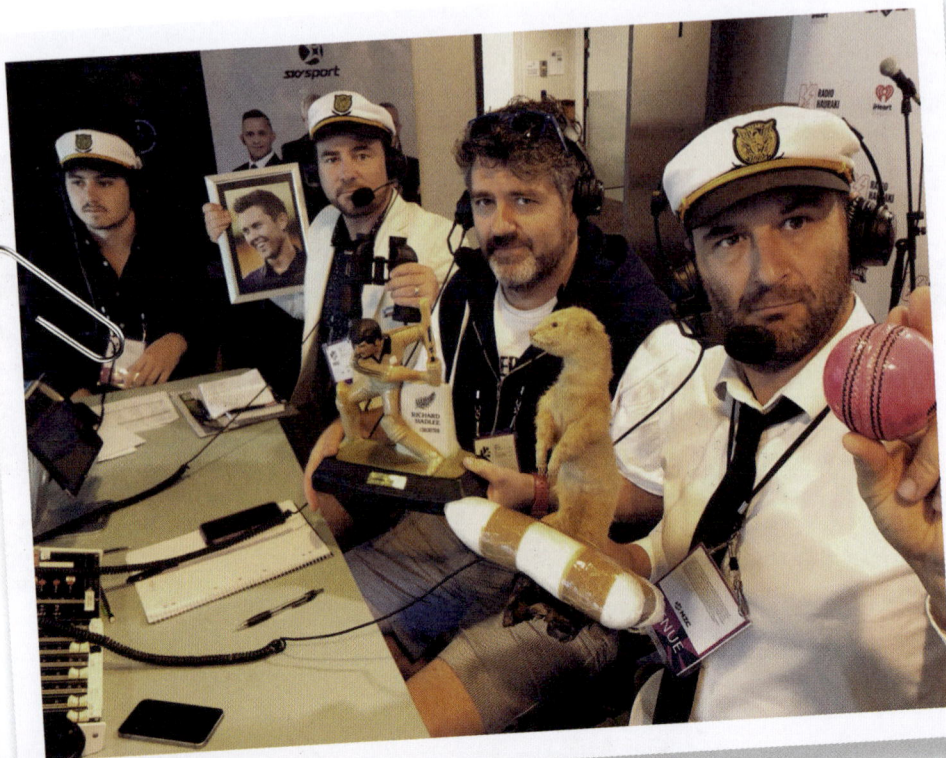

Durie: The day before the test, me and a couple of others went into the box to set it up as a studio for the five days. We took some of the props that we still have today — including what looked like a brick of cocaine from the movie *American Made*. I didn't think anything of it at the time, but I did notice that the police operations for the test were based out of a room across the hall from where we were broadcasting.

The ACC rested up before their big moment, but on returning to the ground the next day to prepare for the opening ball, they noticed some telltale traces of white powder on their studio bench and a cut made in their bag that looked like it came from a box-cutter knife.

Durie: I later learned that somebody at NZC or Eden Park had seen our set-up and panicked, concerned that we had brought a whole lot of drugs onto the premises. I don't think the police actually thought we were dumb enough or ballsy enough to bring more than a quarter of a million dollars' worth of drugs into Eden Park, but I guess they felt obligated to check it out.

It was tightly packed icing sugar.

This was also the match that saw the commentary team retire to a cocktail bar on Ponsonby Road during a rain break and not return to the ground, leaving unpaid intern Jesse 'The Pest' Williamson (not related to Steady the Ship) to provide the rain-delay updates to fulfil their yellow-button commitments. That's a level of professionalism uncommon in other commentary outfits, where trust in the most junior members of the team is implicit.

Williamson (not Kane): I still can't believe they did that to me. I must have had about eight texts from G-Lane saying they were on their way back to the ground. I think I gave up on them around 10pm.

COMMENTARY AGENDA

* Benefits of playing cricket in the nude
* Is Steve Smith the love offspring of the Topp Twins?
* Would you take $10 million but for the rest of your life a snail is trying to get you? (It is immortal and if it touches you, you die.)
* Wagner Roulette (Which delivery isn't short?)
* Greatest umpire in the sack
* All-time cheating XI

Elsewhere in sport, New Zealand secured their first Winter Olympic medals since Annelise Coberger in Albertville, 1992, when Nico Porteous and Zoi Sadowski-Synnott both won bronze medals in PyeongChang. Sadowski-Synnott won her medal in the snowboard big air while Porteous had ACC vibes about him by vomiting three times* at the top of the course before finishing third in the freestyle skiing halfpipe.

The Crusaders won Super Rugby and, to save everyone some time, we won't mention that again because they didn't stop winning until 2024. The All Blacks, possibly still with a Lions hangover, lost twice — once to the Boks in Wellington and once to the Irish in Dublin, but balanced that out with a miraculous comeback win against South Africa in Pretoria. And the Australian cricket team committed a crime of their own — the ball-tampering scandal that became known as Sandpapergate — which has provided countless hours of entertainment for the ACC team ever since.

In addition to joining Sky's yellow-button experience, the ACC added a couple more shows to their portfolio. *The Agenda* podcast launched in 2018 and has been a resounding success, constantly leading the sports podcast charts in New Zealand. *The Moment*, a TVNZ Duke-backed show that involved the ACC turning their hapless attention to the Commonwealth Games on the Gold Coast, possibly less so.

---

* Unlike the ACC, this was through sheer nerves, not overexposure to alcohol.

THE HOME OF SPORTING NONSENSE & CLAPTRAP

LISTEN ON iHeartRADIO

Marvel: "Infinity War is the most ambitious crossover event in history"

Me:

SKY Sport NZ
March 7 at 5:14pm · ☀

Yep, this is happening... 😂

We are nervous/excited to announce that Kiwi cricketing cult heroes The Alternative Commentary Collective will be providing an uninformed alternative audio option for SKY Sport's coverage of the "Pink Ball Test" between the Blackcaps and England starting March 22nd.

ACC JOINS SKY SPORT FOR PINK BALL TEST | SKY

The collective of cricket has-beens and never-wills will graduate from the trusty ACC caravan to an old disused box at Eden Park, making their LIVE ball-by-ball debut as an alternative audio option for SKY Sport viewers.

COMMONWEALTH GAMES 2018

COUNTRY	GOLD	SILVER	BRONZE	TOTAL
🇳🇿 New Zealand	15	16	15	46

MATT HEATH: I had a lot of fun doing the opening ceremony and quickly learned why Olympic commentators always have that particular timbre when they're broadcasting the openings. It's because nothing about the ceremony actually makes sense to them, but they get this big document from the choreographers telling them what the symbolism means. So, you've really only got half an eye on the show and the rest you spend reading this document pretending you knew this pretentious crap all along. It's not commentary as much as it's a book reading.

Once the games started, the Matt Heath and Mike Lane hosted show offered hitherto unheard insights into some of the more arcane Commonwealth Games events and bylaws.

HEATH: If I remember rightly, Wells was part of the opening ceremony broadcast and was meant to be involved in *The Moment* as well, but maybe he could see the writing on the wall and in the end it was just left to me and G-Lane.

The Moment was mine and Lane's chance to shine on live TV, to stand up as a sports talk duo, maybe to forge a new career together. Unfortunately, we were both too shagged from other commitments to put in any real effort. Instead, we based the whole thing on the theme song of the 1990 Auckland Commonwealth Games and slid into the daily live broadcast grossly underprepared. Amazingly, it had strong ratings. Things were going well. That was until Lane got bored and decided to Easter Egg the thing.

MIKE LANE: Once we learned the TVNZ legal team needed to see our scripts before every show, we knew what we needed to do. Give them a lesson in the Urban Dictionary.

HEATH: We should have been concentrating on actually writing a better script, but we got sidetracked trying to slip in words we knew the legal team would have to google.

LANE: The best was slipping 'Manhattan Flapjack' into the script and just leaving it out there for the team to read. Don't search it by the way.

HEATH: *The Moment* turned out to be a great way to sneak a lot of covert filth onto the national broadcaster. I know G-Lane is immensely proud of that aspect of the show.

LANE: Are we going to mention when we inadvertently commentated the Commonwealth Games para version of the lawn bowls?

HEATH: No.

LANE: Let's just say TVNZ had the lawyers in the starting blocks. I hear all evidence the show existed has been scrubbed from the archives.

In one segment, they dispelled rumours that triathletes attacked by a shark during the swim leg could immediately switch to the Paralympic category, citing a little-known health-and-safety clause.

At the weightlifting, Lane mentioned that he couldn't wait to see a female competitor's snatch, and they may have mocked our Paralympic athletes . . .

It's hard to know how to categorise this incident. Some have labelled it a hate crime, but the ACC have worked hard to change the narrative — mainly by attempting to shovel the blame onto someone else.

Retrospective press release on behalf of Matt Heath and G-Lane, hosts of *The Moment*

In 2018, TVNZ approached the ACC to do a nightly highlights show on their Duke channel to complement their wall-to-wall serious coverage of the Gold Coast Commonwealth Games.

Through a series of events, it ended up being just G-Lane and I, Matt Heath, who fronted the show, which was called *The Moment*.

The format saw us present a package of highlights that we would 'live' commentate over. This was quickly put in the can and the coverage would then cross to us for an in-studio chat about the various events that had caught our highly trained eyes.

It was an extremely tight turnaround and, with both Mike and I being ferociously busy men leading incredibly interesting lives, we didn't have time to write all the material and parse all the highlights ourselves.

It was left to Graham Hill of Able Tasmans, *SportsCafe* and Radio Live fame to do most of the clipping of highlights that would leave us with some relatively irreverent talking points.

I think it is fair to say the show was working well. It was rating high enough that it had been decided to simulcast the final week of *The Moment* on both Duke and the monolithic TV One.

That is until . . .

I was speaking to Graham about an hour before Mike and I were due in at TVNZ for that night's show. He mentioned it had been an extremely tough day on the Gold Coast with very little of interest happening. He did, however, think he had struck gold late in the piece when he found some lawn bowls. 'You won't believe the state of some of the athletes,' he said.

It sounded perfect. The one thing the Commonwealth Games has got going for it is these sports that would otherwise see very little air time suddenly receiving their moment in the sun. Gently mocking the sport of Baby Boomers sounded like it would slot right into our wheelhouse.

We get to the studio with not a minute to spare, as always, and cue up the highlights to start commentating. Hill is right. Almost immediately we recognise the comedic value of what's in front of us.

Technically, the bowlers seemed to have changed a lot since the halcyon days of Peter Belliss and Rowan Brassey. There were some crazy styles and actions and, although the sport has never required a huge amount of athleticism, some of the competitors seemed to be taking a lack of mobility to extremes.

One of the amazing things about humans, however, is we have an inbuilt sense of trouble. It's what triggers the fight-or-flight response. After about 30 seconds of our commentary, I could sense that G-Lane, a man with few boundaries in life, a man who had stitched his own mother up while live on radio, was starting to squirm uncomfortably. I, too, was finding it harder and harder to laugh at the spectacle. At the 45-second mark, it finally dawned upon us with a sickening thud.

'Oh my fucking god,' I thought. 'We've just committed a hate crime!'

That fight-or-flight response. I wanted both to run away and hide, and to punch Graham in the head.

I grabbed my phone and dialled up Graham to run a few expletives past him. What he had done was cut together a highlights package of Paralympic bowls. Those champions of the sport were not reinventing the technical aspects of the game for the sake of it, they were simply doing the best they had with the hand they had been dealt.

And we had spent the best part of a minute mocking them for it.

To be fair to Hill, he did say, 'Oh, that makes sense then,' when I told him what he had led us into. He said he had been combing through hours and hours of boring footage and genuinely believed he had found some funny observational material we could work our magic with.

I guess if there was one sport where this confusion might be harder to pick up on, it's bowls, but it was still a disaster.

It was either this shit show or no show at all, and no show at all was not an option. We ran with the footage and the now very clearly offensive commentary, and tried to Band-Aid it by going almost over-the-top with a thousand or so platitudes for the 'brave' para-athletes at the top and bottom of the show, but still we couldn't rinse away the stain of the highlights package.

It goes without saying that all talk of the show flipping on to TV One ceased from that moment forward.

It has been several years since that incident. I cannot speak for Lane, but I still can't walk past a bowls club, or the TVNZ building, without experiencing a cold shudder.

I know it will never make up for it, but I always donate when they have collections for wheelchair rugby outside my local supermarket.

Once more New Zealand, I apologise. We apologise.

Yours,

Matt Heath (also on behalf of Mike Lane)

P.S. For the record, it was mostly Graham Hill's fault.

CHARGE:	Hiring a stripper to perform in-studio during an ODI.
VERDICT:	Verdict: Guilty of a slightly lesser charge

GUILTY GUILTY GUILTY

NEW ZEALAND V ENGLAND
1ST ODI (PROBABLY)
Hamilton, 25 February 2018 (probably)

Mike Lane: Okay, so there are a few layers to this one but, yes, on the Sunday afternoon of an otherwise run-of-the-mill one-day international, an exotic dancer performed in the studio while we were commentating on a game of cricket.

So thoroughly has the hard drive of that particular memory been wiped, that only Mike Lane owned up to being there that day and even he can't remember what game it was. By process of elimination, however, we think it might have been the first ODI of the England series in 2018, won by New Zealand by three wickets after a Ross Taylor century helped them chase down the 285-run target.

Lane: I'm pretty sure it was a Sunday because there was hardly anybody in the building and I was getting a bit worried somebody would see her coming in or out of the building with her bag of 'toys'.

Paul Ford: If you were worried, why on earth did you hire her then?

Lane: We didn't! I didn't! That's the thing, the whole incident is so stupid and it sounds even dumber in the retelling.

Ford: Retell it then, we're all waiting.

Lane: I'll tell you, but this better not go in the book.

No chance˙.

Lane: So, we're commentating this game from the NZME studio and it's a Sunday afternoon. It's one of those days where no matter how much you love cricket, you're probably wondering if there are other things you could be doing with your family on such a beautiful summer's day.

Ford: Are you really going to drag your family into this?

Lane: So, as we're commentating, a text comes through on the machine. It says, to paraphrase, 'Hey, I own a strip club in town, should I send one of the girls over to dance for you?' As I said, we're all missing our families terribly, so without even thinking, one of us, probably not Jason Hoyte, replies, 'Yeah okay.'

---

*   No chance of it not going in the book.

Jason Hoyte: Not Lane's finest moment.

Jeremy Wells: G-Lane is a powerhouse. He brings the ACC together, he works so hard. I love him. He's a genius. But he can also be a pathological scorer of own goals.

Lane: Now this next bit is true. None of us actually expect her to show up. Bugger-all people know where we broadcast from. It's not like there's a big sign out the front saying 'The ACC Lives Here', but before we knew it, there's a rap on the door and, while I've never been one to rush to judgement, let's just say that the contents of her luggage made it pretty obvious she wasn't there to read the news and weather.

Ford: So, this would have been the perfect time to say, 'There's been a terrible misunderstanding, we apologise for wasting your time and here's a few dollars for your inconvenience, now let me just get you an Uber.'

Lane: Yes, but we didn't do that. Instead we come to an arrangement, a verbal contract of sorts, where she would dance at the front of the studio with her back to us and she would most definitely keep the lower half of her lingerie on.

Ford: Oh, great plan, I can't see how this is going to go wrong at all.

Lane: Yeah, well, she didn't stick to the plan.

Ford: What did she do?

Lane: She went off-script. She danced topless over the top of a table full of one of our key sponsor's products. Someone saw this on the livestream and notified the sponsors.

Ford: How did the sponsor take this?

Lane: Not that well. The CEO got involved.

Jason Winstanley (NZME GM talk radio): There's pushing the boundaries, and then there's letting a stripper perform in the studio. It's inappropriate, and we made it crystal clear that it was not to happen again. However, I wouldn't say this to Lane or the team, but if they're not pushing the boundaries, they're probably not doing their job properly. I've probably only ever spoken to them really seriously six or seven times.

Lane: I'm not brilliant at backing down or admitting I stuffed up, but that is one of the decisions I got horribly wrong and am very keen for it to stay out of the book. I should never have trusted her to keep to the script.

You can trust me, though.

Winstanley: Mike's not a young man anymore — he's got responsibilities of his own and understands the business environment we all work in.

Lane: Yeah, it goes without saying that when I hire dancers, I don't get them to come into work anymore.

2019

THE YEAR THAT DARE NOT SPEAK ITS NAME

No one likes to talk about 2019. If you try to speak about this year with a member of the ACC, they might respond to you in a brusque or even rude way.

It was suggested that the name of the year would be written at the top of this page followed by a blank space for you to draw whatever you like on the rest.
Here's what G-Lane chose to draw.

You are welcome to choose your own image.

It is, however, important not to forget that 2019 saw the Silver Ferns pull off perhaps their greatest-ever World Cup triumph, rising like a phoenix from the ashes of a disastrous Commonwealth Games campaign on the Gold Coast to beat Australia 52–51 in the final in Liverpool, England.

Not long before the tournament, the Ferns had won just six of 18 games, including 11 straight losses to Australia. They suffered embarrassing losses to Jamaica, which was almost excusable, and Malawi, which was inexcusable. In the minds of most people, of the three major New Zealand teams competing in World Cups in 2019, the Silver Ferns would have ranked third-most likely to bring home the bacon.

Which brings us, briefly, to the other campaigns.

There was a suspicion that the All Blacks had peaked in 2015, after legends Richie McCaw and Dan Carter had led them to consecutive world titles in front of a wonderfully inebriated ACC team, and that the four years through to 2019 had seen a slow diminishing of their status.

The disappointing drawn series against the Lions was strong evidence of that theory, yet popular wisdom still suggested that the All Blacks had enough talent — in Kieran Read, Brodie Retallick and Beauden Barrett (twice), they had three World Rugby players of the year — in the ranks to eke out another win.

MIKE LANE: I was sitting at the pub one afternoon with Joe Durie and Matt Heath, working out whether we'd had our fourth or fifth Liberty Knife Party, 7.1 per cent ABV by the way, when a message popped up on my phone: 'G-Lane — Eye Sockets Read here. Give me a call when you can.'

JOSEPH DURIE: It was definitely five Knife Parties.

LANE: I am naturally a suspicious man. I have stitched up far too many people to believe the All Blacks' captain would send me a random text. So I ignored it.

DURIE: Curiosity got the better of us and we double-checked with the one man that would know if this was legit — Scotty J Stevenson.

LANE: Scotty confirmed he'd passed on my number . . . shit. Kieran Read is tracking me down to kill me.

SCOTTY J STEVENSON: I thought long and hard about passing on that number to Kieran.

MATT HEATH: Admittedly, Lane has committed plenty of atrocities, so I wasn't surprised to hear Eye Sockets wanted to have a word. But, as it turned out, it was the start of a beautiful, consensual relationship.

LANE: So after a couple more Knife Parties I rang the number. He had a simple request: 'Can you please email me *all* of the nicknames you have for the current ABs? We're having an end-of-season session and I want to get them printed on the back of some shirts.'

HEATH: We had some pretty spicy nicknames and knew some players probably wouldn't appreciate them plastered across their backs, so we asked if he wanted to change any.

LANE: Eye Sockets replied: 'You don't get to choose your own nicknames. Send them all through.' So I did.

HEATH: We love Eye Sockets. What a great New Zealander.

The All Blacks worked their way out of a tough pool unbeaten, defeating old foe South Africa comfortably enough in their opening match, which set up a blockbuster quarter-final against Josef Schmidt's Ireland, who had emerged as one of the tournament favourites.

The All Blacks dominated from the opening whistle, led 22–0 at halftime and scored seven tries on the way to a 46–14 slaughter.

HEATH: Where were we for this?

LANE: I believe we had a section at Dr Rudi's rooftop bar in the Auckland Viaduct, which is where we did all the commentary from for the Japan World Cup. A vape company sponsored us and we had a VIP area with audience winners.

HEATH: I can't even remember this World Cup, but I can recall taking up vaping.

With just a semifinal against a limited England side and a final against either South Africa, who they had easily defeated in pool play, or Wales, who hadn't beaten the All Blacks since 1953, awaiting, a fourth Webb Ellis Cup was as good as won – right?

Wrong. The scoreboard read just 19–7, but England bullied the All Blacks from pillar to post, with old mate Eddie Jones pulling off his finest heist since his Wallabies beat the All Blacks in the 2003 World Cup semifinals. On both occasions, his teams went on to lose the final, with the Springboks winning the Cup to equal the All Blacks' record of three titles.

HEATH: That result didn't sit well with our team. We refused to acknowledge it.

LANE: It never happened. It's fake news. Next.

It was a miserable way to end the sporting year, but it didn't come close to the pain endured by the Black Caps and their supporters. If ever there was the need for a Black Caps Supporters Support Group, it was on the morning of 15 July.

The official result of the match was a tie.

Before we get to THAT final, though, let's look back at the sunnier days that saw New Zealand qualify. It was a different campaign to 2015, which was the year of the blunt instrument. Back then, Brendon McCullum was captain and opening batter and the approach was blitzkrieg. When batting, he bashed, and, when Baz wasn't bashing, Martin Guptill — in a slightly more refined, long-levered way — was. Or Corey Anderson.

JASON HOYTE: I'd almost forgotten about Corey Anderson. What were his stats, Leigh?

LEIGH HART: Who?

It was so weird and so wonderful that this little platoon of lunacy could combine with the amazing cricket being played by the Black Caps and get Kiwis excited about the game.

HOYTE: Never mind.

HEATH: How can you forget [to tune of 'Karma Chameleon'] 'Corey, Corey, Corey, Corey, Corey, Corey, An-der-son, he bats and bowls, he bowls and bats'?

LANE: The 2015 World Cup spawned so many great moments, the nicknames, the T-shirts and the songs. We have the Corey Anderson tune, the Hairy Jav song, the Sexy Camel and the Lovely Trenty chant. And, against all odds, Kiwis sung them loud and proud.

PAUL FORD: I remember the surreal feeling of walking into bars like the old Loaded Hog in Hamilton (House on Hood I think it's now called), or the Cherry Tree Hotel in Cremorne, Melbourne, or arriving via a commandeered public bus at the waterfront bars in Wellington. People would see us in our stupid commentary suits, matching shorts and Birkenstocks, and just spontaneously burst into song. The ACC cult really helped New Zealanders find their voices, and it was so weird and so wonderful that this little platoon

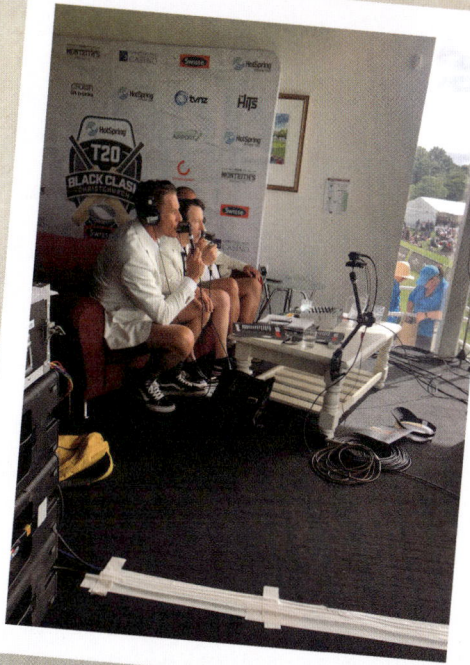

of lunacy could combine with the amazing cricket being played by the Black Caps and get Kiwis excited about the game. Cricket was cool again.

LANE: I have a very fond memory of walking into a bar after a game during that World Cup, and there were all these people singing the Corey Anderson song. I think that was the moment I realised that the ACC was doing something more than just annoying Wads and his mates. It was an extremely moving experience.

The aim in 2015 was to always have someone boofing it. When bowling and fielding, McCullum would stack the cordon, have attacking fields, use up his best bowlers early to get wickets and crash into boundary hoardings to save runs. Great New Zealanders and the ACC alike loved it because it reminded them in many ways of club cricket.

The Black Caps' play-hard-and-with-a-smile-on-your-face ethos was there for all to see.

In England four years later, McCullum was gone and in his place was Kane Williamson — more of a genius than McCullum, but without the sheer force of personality. While they both played with a smile, with slightly different personnel and the tournament being played in England, Williamson had to learn how to skin this cat slightly differently.

Leigh Hart's 6-Step Guide to
SKINNING ANIMALS

1. Make sure the animal is dead. This step is always important for ethical reasons, but even more so for the health and safety of the skinner if the animal is of the non-domesticated variety.

2. If working on a freezer-stored or snap-frozen animal, thaw before skinning. This step requires fine balance and intuition. An 'over-thawed' animal will provide a rancid canvas from which to practise this ancient art. Different animals thaw at different rates. In my experience, for example, a bison thaws much slower than an ocelot or meerkat. At different latitudes and altitudes, these times will also subtly change. As the old saying goes, 'Never try to skin a polar bear south of the Tropic of Cancer.'

3. Wherever possible, use a sharp, non-serrated knife or adze. Experienced trappers and skinners like myself can complete the entire process, including catching the animal, using only a 33-function Victorinox Swiss Army knife,

but this is not for the faint of heart. If you're just starting out in the game, have someone catch and clean your beast for you, or, alternatively, ask your local butcher to leave a little of the hide on a side of lamb or something similar. They are always happy to help and may even throw in a few sausage links (Hellers, of course) for your troubles.

4. Always skin your animal after 5.30pm. The head should always point due north if working in the southern hemisphere and vice versa if in the north. Always cut with the grain and for particularly tough hides you may want to first shave the beast and then rub in a coat of lanolin with a chamois (never use an anti-static screen cloth or wet wipe). It is sometimes written off as an old trapper's wives' tale, but nevertheless most of us still heed the advice not to skin an animal within a five-mile radius of a Native American Indian burial ground or a nuclear reactor.

5. If you haven't already, collect all the offal and sweetbreads into a vacuum-packed bag and seal it. These can be used later for tasty soups and stews, often using no other ingredients than a cup of water, one beef-flavoured Oxo cube, a sprig of rosemary and a diced carrot. Mmmm, delicious. The carcass can be left on site. It is, after all, all part of the life cycle.

6. Rinse and repeat.

New Zealand enjoyed a soft start to the 2019 tournament, thrashing Sri Lanka by 10 wickets, with Matt 'Mr Darcy' Henry and Lockie 'The Whakamana Express' Ferguson each taking three cheap wickets, and the Dead Shark Eyes of Martin Guptill and Colin 'The Stance' Munro knocking off the runs with haste. Mr Darcy took another four against Bangladesh and, even though New Zealand wobbled late (they collapsed from 160 for 2 to 238 for 8), another win was in the books.

HOYTE: He's an underrated sort of bowler is Matt Henry, including by myself. What I've never underestimated, though, is those classic English public-school-educated good looks. You can imagine following him over the trenches at the Somme, even if it meant certain death.

Afghanistan were easily accounted for, with the Little Lamb Neesham (some say he looks like an alpaca) taking five wickets and the Steadier of Ships an unbeaten 79. Three from three and then the tournament started to get interesting. The round-robin match against India in Nottingham was abandoned without a ball being bowled, which might have helped the Black Caps' cause.

South Africa followed and Steady the Ship played one of the all-time great knocks (106 not out) to get his team to the target of 242 by hitting a six and a four off consecutive balls to win with three deliveries to spare at Edgbaston. A few days later, the little genius was at it again, scoring 148 and then watching on as some Carlos Brathwaite heroics got the Windies to within five runs of a stunning victory. Played six, won five, one abandoned. Home and hosed into the semifinals it seemed.

Then the ship came off its moorings. Despite Williamson's consistency, New Zealand's World Cup bogey team Pakistan crushed them by six wickets. Then Australia and England thrashed them by 86 and 119 runs respectively.

New Zealand scraped into the semifinals in fourth, where they had to face an unbeaten India at Old Trafford with nobody giving them a snowball's chance in hell. What followed was one of the more low-key brilliant performances in Black Caps' history.

WELLS: I recall giving everyone a really good talk about how New Zealand were going to win this World Cup. Everyone was nervous, everyone had PTSD from all the other World Cup semis we had limped out of. I just knew something was different about this team.

WELLS, FROM THE PULPIT, TALKING DIRECTLY TO G-LANE AND HEATH: You guys, seriously. You guys should be ashamed of yourselves, you should be ashamed.

I don't say this often, but how dare you, how fucking dare you suggest that we shouldn't fucking be in the semifinals of the World Cup? We deserve to be there. We've had some good luck. Have there been rain-affected games? Yes, there was a rain-affected game and, yes, we had the best draw out of everyone, but how fucking dare you not back us into the semifinals?

What's going to happen? This is what is going to happen.

LANE: What's going to happen?

WELLS: New Zealand is going to qualify fourth and we're going to play Australia in a knockout game and we're going to beat those fucking c***s. England are going to play India and they're going to beat them because India beat them in the round-robin.

We are going to play England in the World Cup final and we are going to kill those c***s.

LANE (STANDING ON DESK): Oh captain, my captain. Oh captain, my captain.

Well said, Jerry. Wells' speech, delivered on *The Agenda* podcast, proved dangerously accurate if you're willing to ignore the semifinal opponent and the end result of the tournament. Still, it was bloody stirring stuff.

HART: If I remember correctly, a bit of despondency had set in with the ACC team and I saw it as my role to give them all a lift, letting them all know that I thought our Black Caps were going to beat India. It was we-will-fight-them-on-the-beaches Churchillian stuff. Everyone walked out of the pub feeling ten feet tall.

LANE: I'd have to go back over the rosters, but I'm not sure Leigh was even there. I think what's probably happened there is he's confused by his commentary team drinks. I have seen him hanging out with the likes of Quinny, P-Willy [Peter Williams] and John McBeth quite a lot.

At Old Trafford, with rain in the air, Williamson won the toss and, surprisingly to many, chose to bat. Guptill fell early, Henry 'Hairy Nips' Nicholls, in for the out-of-form Munro, struggled through to a slow 28 before falling to the spin of Ravi Jadeja. That brought New Zealand's two greatest white-ball batters together, and their big brains decided that 250 was going to be a very competitive target on a tricky surface under grey Manchester skies.

Williamson scored 67, Sir Lingus 74, and the rainy first day ended with New

Zealand on 211 for 5 after 46.1 overs, with the reserve day brought into play.

The Black Caps squirted to 239 after their 50 overs and, although it was a little shy of ideal, it was something they felt they could defend if they took early wickets.

LANE: We commentated this game from The Export Beer Garden Studio at ACC HQ. Shit, it was an emotional rollercoaster. The punishing hours, the two-day nature of it, the fear of falling short again.

HOYTE: The hours of these games were problematic. I usually require a minimum nine hours' sleep a night, with one break for a durrie about 3am.

HEATH: What was more problematic was that I had a breakfast radio show on Hauraki that started at 6am. But Lane told me to grow a pair — 'This is a one-off!' he said. Then it went for two nights. I can't remember either of those breakfast shows. I thought about filing a complaint to HR.

LANE: Heath came to the studio, but slept through both nights.

WELLS: The Black Caps do well when odd things happen to disrupt the flow of a game. Look at the Eden Park semifinal in 2015 — the rain came and ruined South Africa's momentum just when we needed it. It was a stroke of luck that changed the course of history. And when this semifinal went into the second day due to rain, I had that feeling again that this wasn't going to go well for the Indian team.

LANE: I think we jokingly said pre-match on the second night that if we can rip their top order a new one and get rid of Rahul, Sharma and Kohli then we'll be in with a sniff.

BOOMFAH! Rohit Sharma nicks Henry to Tom Latham for 1.

BOOMFAH! Virat Kohli leg before to Trent Boult for 1.

BOOMFAH! KL Rahul nicks Henry to Latham for 1.

HEATH: I didn't quite expect us to rip them quite as large a one as they did — from then on they were on the back foot. Everything just worked really well. As soon as they got those three wickets, the whole vibe of the team changed.

HART: I don't remember this game. What time of night was it?

BOOMFAH! The Little Lamb Neesham (some say he looks like an alpaca) takes a one-handed speccie at backward point to dismiss Dinesh Karthik for 6.

HEATH: I was thinking, 'What have we just fucking seen there!?'

LANE: If that's what Heath reckons, we'll have to take his word for it, though I'm pretty sure all he saw was the back of his eyelids.

India slump to 32 for 4, but they bat all the way down to Jadeja at number eight so this is far from over. Slowly but surely they bat their way back into the game and then Jadeja joins the great finisher, MS Dhoni, for the decisive partnership.

From 92 for 6, they take the score to 208 before Jadeja, on 77, hits a skyer. Williamson pouches the catch nonchalantly at long off and with 17 balls left India need 32 runs.

Eight runs and four balls later, the game is as good as dead when Guptill sensationally runs out Dhoni with little more than one stump to aim at.

LANE: That run out was the stuff of legend. Dead Shark Eyes had endured

NEW ZEALAND VS INDIA, WORLD CUP SEMIFINAL
MANCHESTER, ENGLAND, 9–10 JULY 2019
New Zealand won by 18 runs

New Zealand		R	BF
M Guptill	c Kohli b Bumrah	1	(14)
H Nicholls	b Jadeja	28	(51)
K Williamson	c Jadeja b Chahal	67	(95)
R Taylor	run out (Jadeja)	74	(90)
J Neesham	c Karthik b Pandya	12	(18)
C de Grandhomme	c Dhoni b Kumar	16	(10)
T Latham	c Jadeja b Kumar	10	(11)
M Santner	not out	9	(6)
M Henry	c Kohli b Kumar	1	(2)
T Boult	not out	3	(3)
Extras		18	
Total		239-8	

Bowling	O	M	R	W
B Kumar	10	1	43	3
J Bumrah	10	1	39	1
H Pandya	10	0	55	1
R Jadeja	10	0	34	1
Y Chahal	10	0	63	1

a difficult World Cup, but that throw sent us into the final . . . and I then needed to break some terrible news to my wife.

At the start of the tournament, I mentioned to my long-suffering life partner that if New Zealand makes the final at Lord's I will have to go. It was one of those things that may and probably will never happen again in my lifetime — seeing New Zealand play in the World Cup final at the Home of Cricket.

Her response was, 'Sure, I totally understand.' That rocked me slightly as I think she dismissed the fact we would ever make the final, and to a degree so had I. However, at 2am on 11 July, while still sitting at the commentary desk of ACC HQ, I was booking return flights to London. No accommodation. No match tickets. No sleep. Fuck yeah.

I got home and tried to sneak into bed, but woke up my wife and then

India		R	BF
KL Rahul	c Latham b Henry	1	(7)
R Sharma	c Latham b Henry	1	(4)
V Kohli	lbw Boult	1	(6)
R Pant	c de Grandhomme b Santner	32	(56)
D Karthik	c Neesham b Henry	6	(25)
H Pandya	c Williamson b Santner	32	(62)
MS Dhoni	run out (Guptill)	50	(72)
R Jadeja	c Williamson b Boult	77	(59)
B Kumar	b Ferguson	0	(1)
Y Chahal	c Latham b Neesham	5	(5)
J Bumrah	not out	0	(0)
Extras		16	
Total		221 (49.3 overs)	

Bowling	O	M	R	W
T Boult	10	2	42	2
M Henry	10	1	37	3
L Ferguson	10	0	43	1
C de Grandhomme	2	0	13	0
J Neesham	7.3	0	49	1
M Santner	10	2	34	2

said: 'Do you want the good news or the bad news?' She mumbled, 'Good?'

'We WON!'

'And the bad?'

'I fly to London in sixteen hours.'

She rolled over and went back to sleep.

WELLS: Didn't G-Lane have some ticketing fiasco to negotiate?

LANE: I managed to talk two mates into joining me on my escapade — one from Auckland and one who lived in Singapore. Jobs were assigned. Singapore-based Zippy was in charge of accommodation; Muzza was on entertainment/social functions. I was lumped with procurement of tickets. I had the most pressure: this was a final at Lord's, whose capacity of 24,000 served a city of eight million. And England were in the final! Jesus wept.

The scramble began. I fired off more social media DMs than a horny nineteen-year-old on a Saturday night. I hit up current players like Tim

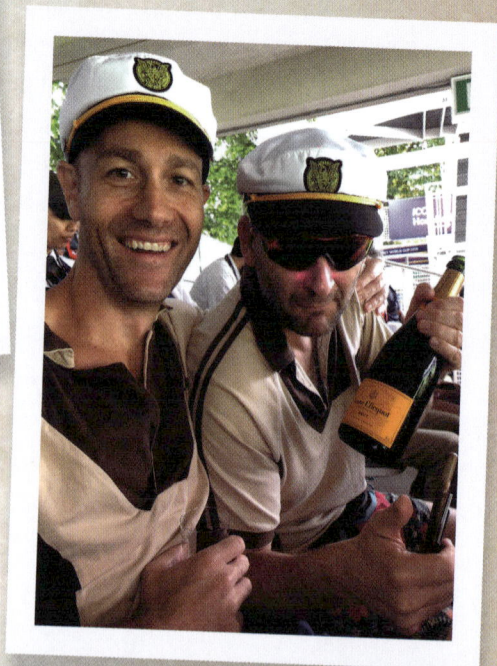

We had received so many requests for the ACC Steady the Ship hats from expats, so I got a massive suitcase and rammed 200 of them into it.

Southee, who was polite enough to say, 'Will see what I can do.' I hit up former players like Dan Vettori and Brendon McCullum, who I knew were working at the World Cup — crickets ensued.

I got hold of my old ticket-scalping contact, Paul 'The Saffer', from my Beige Brigade tour days in London. He came back with, 'I can do £1200 a ticket — guaranteed.' At the time, the exchange rate put that at about $2500 each. But what choice did we have? We were boarding a plane bound for London.

We shrugged our shoulders and thought, 'We've come this far, we can't not go.' I fired off a few more DMs on Instagram before we took off — thank god I did.

We landed in Singapore resigned to the fact we were already $2500 in the hole, then just as we were about to board the final leg to London a message popped up on my Insta, 'Hey mate — happy to help, you guys have given us so much support over the years. How many do you need?'

The three of us flew that last leg like we had just won $7500. We finally passed out somewhere over the Middle East, I think. God bless you, former Black Caps manager Mike Sandle.

WELLS: I believe Lane also got caught smuggling something into the United Kingdom. That man shouldn't be allowed to leave New Zealand; he's a massive liability, not only to himself but also the reputation of our country.

LANE: That's rich coming from the Teflon Don of media. We had received so many requests for the ACC Steady the Ship hats from expats, so I got a massive suitcase and rammed 200 of them into it. I joked to my mates that if somebody opened the suitcase it would explode like a jack-in-the-box, it was that rammed. Well, it turns out someone did open it. Customs in London thought it was mildly suspicious that 200 hats were squished into a suitcase, and they pinged me for not declaring products that were most likely going to be on-sold. We were actually giving them away, but I was way too hungover — we had celebrated the ticket windfall excessively — to argue.

WELLS: Then the Grim Lane curse went to work. We lost a World Cup final that was ours.

LANE: Because of this bullshit, I can't go to any sporting event without being accused of ruining it. I love live sport, but the abuse is starting to eat away at my soul.

WELLS: Lane has no soul and the 2019 final result lies squarely at the feet of the most cursed sports fan in New Zealand.

LANE: I don't want to talk about it. I still go down the rabbit hole: the Lovely Trenty LBW in the first over, his boundary catch that wasn't, the overthrows, the incorrect call following that . . . there, I've gone and fallen down it again. The flight home was the longest and most depressing twenty-eight hours of my life.

It was a match of middling scores and wild extremes. The craziest cricket match in history — one the ACC couldn't have scripted for their fantasy Super League.

So much of it came down to luck, and all of it went against New Zealand.

- Ross Taylor is given out leg before for 15. The ball was missing the stumps, but New Zealand has already used their review.
- Jason Roy is given not out first ball of the England innings. Looks plumb.

NEW ZEALAND VS ENGLAND, WORLD CUP FINAL
LONDON, ENGLAND, 14 JULY 2019
Match tied

New Zealand	241-8	England	241
(plus Super Over 15-1)		(plus Super Over 15-0)	
H Nicholls	55	B Stokes	84*
T Latham	47	J Buttler	59
C Woakes	3-37	J Neesham	3-43
L Plunkett	3-42	L Ferguson	3-50

New Zealand review and, although it is hitting leg stump pretty hard, under the old protocols the decision remains 'umpire's call'.

• The normally sure-handed Colin de Grandhomme, in the midst of a fantastic 10-over spell, drops a straightforward caught and bowled chance off Jonny Bairstow when he has just 18 runs.

LANE: At the ground we were still confident. We were singing. We were playing well, but there was always Ben Stokes, the Gay Avenger, threatening. Then it all started to go mental.

Neesham bowls the penultimate over, 24 are needed. It goes single, single, then he gets the wicket of Liam Plunkett, caught by Boult on the boundary. Twenty-two off nine with Stokes on strike. He slogs to long on and Boult catches it, Guptill can be seen screaming at him to toss it inside, but it is too late. Boult stands on the rope and the critical wicket becomes a critical six.

LANE: Fuck.

Fifteen needed off Boult's last over. Dot, dot, six and then Stokes scuffs one to deep midwicket. Guptill throws the ball as the batters turn for two. Stokes dives. The ball deflects off his bat to the boundary for four overthrows.

It gets ruled as six runs, but it should have been five. The umpires screwed up.

Off the penultimate ball, Stokes slips as he hits to long off. It's a simple run out at either end but Mitchell Santner goes to the bowler's end and, although they get the run out, it leaves Stokes on strike with two needed. Stokes manages a single, with Mark Wood run out coming back for two, which sends the match into a Super Over.

In the Super Over, New Zealand requires two off the final ball. Martin Guptill,

who hasn't faced a ball since early that morning, finds himself on strike. He squirts it into the leg side and, crucially, slips slightly on taking off. He is run out with the scores tied, again.

England is awarded the trophy on the little-known, never-to-be-seen again boundary-countback rule.

LANE: Fuck . . . what had I just seen?

JASON HOYTE: As soon as I heard Lane was flying over I knew we were going to lose. He lost that for us. He's the black cloud that hovers above us.

To close a miserable year in fitting fashion, the Black Caps embarked on a long-awaited test tour of Australia, including the momentous opportunity to play a Boxing Day test for the first time since the '80s. We don't talk about those tests either.

Then in late December, Jason Hoyte* is spotted on CCTV in a number of different locations around the world, with a mouse-eared bat on his shoulder and wearing an unzipped fanny-pack that looked like it contained several small vials.

The world, or the next few years at least, would never be the same again.

---

*   Possibly not Hoyte.

LANE: There's not a day goes by that I don't think about the travesty of that final, and as head of the ACC I felt it was important we made our voices heard. So before the England tour of 2020, we collectively prepared a letter demanding shared custody of the Cricket World Cup on behalf of the nation. I felt our terms were very reasonable.

WELLS: We spent days crafting that letter, then took out a full-page ad in the *New Zealand Herald* in the hope of getting the England team's attention — and also to remind Kiwi cricket fans that we hadn't moved on.

The ACC also prepared an alternative to the traditional 4 and 6 signs held up by fans at international fixtures.

LANE: Along with the *Herald* ad, we also printed the letter onto A3 cards for people to take into the ground in search of Eoin Morgan's signature. We decided to put '5' on the reverse side of the cards as a small dig at the infamous overthrow decision. NZC put a stop to that pretty quickly. We were told that a sponsor 'owned the in-ground run moment'. It felt like they didn't quite get the irony.

New Zealand
Bottom of the South Pacific

England (& Wales)
Next to (but not part of) Europe

HEATH, HART, WELLS, LANE,
BAKER, FORD, MCONIE,
STEVENSON, HOYTE
& SONS

November 2019

SUBJECT: SHARED CUSTODY REQUEST – URGENT

Dear England (& Wales),

We wish to put you on notice of our intention to apply for shared custody of the Cricket World Cup.

On the date of 14th of July 2019 a brief but passionate relationship was entered into at Lord's Cricket Ground that resulted in full custody of the Cricket World Cup being granted to you.

The dubious circumstances around you being granted full custody is the basis for our application for shared custody.

> These circumstances include, *inter alia*;
> - match - drawn
> - super over - drawn
> - misrepresentation of over throws/figures

In addition, you already have full custody of Benjamin Stokes which, as a sign of good faith, we will not be challenging.

Our initial offer is to have the Cricket World Cup every second weekend and the first week of every school holiday (except the winter holidays, as that's when we have rugby).

We believe this is a more than generous offer given the rather unfortunate circumstances you left us in. The signing of this document will be formal acceptance of the terms above.

We request your urgent response. We reserve all rights in respect of the above should we not reach an agreement.

Yours faithfully,

Jeremy Wells
On behalf of NEW ZEALAND

Eoin Morgan
On behalf of ENGLAND (& Wales)

SIGN HERE

Jason Hoyte's Guide to
UMPIRING

I'm often approached by people on the street who want to know how I've managed to combine a successful acting, commentary, DJing, podcasting and comedy career. Imagine the look of surprise on their little, awestruck faces when I tell them that not only that, for a while there I was also one of New Zealand's most promising umpires.

There was very little standing in the way of me taking my dreaded raised finger from the suburban fields of Auckland to the hallowed grounds of Lord's and Edgbaston. As an umpire, I had it all: an encyclopaedic knowledge of the MCC Laws of Cricket (for example, Law 31.3 states that for an appeal to be valid, it must be made before the bowler next begins their run-up); a showman's flair for the dramatic; and one of those clickers to make sure I counted the balls in each over correctly.

I guess if there was one thing I could have improved upon it would have been decision-making, but in many ways that is secondary to the umpire's main role, which is to keep the players off the pitch when it's raining.

So, here's my five-point guide to becoming a first-class umpire:

1. Don't sweat the small stuff. A caught behind missed here, a dodgy leg-before there, it doesn't matter. What counts is making sure you get the vibe right. A batter will forgive a bad decision as long as it's given with a certain élan.

2. You're not just an umpire out there, but a surrogate coach. If you notice a batter is playing at balls outside their eyeline, make sure you tell them that when they get to the non-striker's end. Regale them with tales of some of your better knocks to lend your technical advice a certain credibility. Let a bowler know when they're not getting through their action properly. Tell a captain if they're wasting their time with a deep square leg. All the unsolicited advice bolsters your mana as an umpire, particularly in women's cricket, I'm told, where the one thing they can never get enough of is advice from middle-aged men.

3. Get one of those optometrist's eye charts, memorise the bottom line, pin it up on the wall of whatever clubrooms you're umpiring at and make a big show of acing it before you take the field. Once it is established that you have impeccable eyesight, few will think to argue with you. Chris Gaffaney taught me this trick.

4. Learn a few 'nothing to see here' phrases to quickly quell any controversy. 'Just sliding down' or 'Was doing too much' are always good for those never-ending leg-before shouts. The great Steve Dunne was a big fan of the latter, while Doug Cowie preferred the classic 'Not out, too far forward'. Sometimes, honesty is the best policy. As long as you're sincere, nobody will complain if you simply say, 'Sorry, mate, I was daydreaming and didn't see it'. This usually happened during run outs when standing at square leg. It's such a boring job, it's inevitable that you'll find yourself occasionally transported to an imaginary world of hobbits and elves.

5. Find a healthy outlet for all the stresses you accumulate during a typical day's play. It's not easy being on your feet for eight hours trying to work out why half the Takapuna team keeps referring to you as 'dom klein mannetjie'. There was a time when some of my early mentors like Peter P-Dub would retire to a leather club off St Kevins Arcade to unwind, but that all fell apart around 1989, so now you're more likely to find us enjoying a game of cribbage and a mimosa round at my old mate Billy Bowden's place.

I know what you're thinking, why quit when I had the world at my fingertips. You'll have to talk to G-Lane about that. Time and again, I requested Saturdays off to pursue my umpiring, but every time it was refused. That would be my final tip, not just for umpiring, but for life: Never sign a contract with Lane without having a KC run over the fine print. Otherwise you might as well cut out the middleman and just shackle yourself to a life of bondage (and not the kind that Peter P-Dub enjoyed, either).

Ridiculous commentators ruin cricket

My husband and I are avid cricket fans but we are superannuitants so cannot afford Sky TV where most cricket games are broadcast. We were very pleased to discover that TVNZ 1 was going to show the *T20 Black Clash*, Cricket v Rugby game and looked forward to seeing this. Unfortunately, the game was ruined by the inane and ridiculous commentary by an inept bunch. It consisted mostly of sledging Leigh Hart who was supposed to be providing "the colour", then complaining when he didn't quite hit the mark as well as talking about Jason Hoyte's snoring and other unrelated rubbish. Jason was the only one who provided any actual cricket commentary but he was let down by all the others around him, except for Scotty Stevenson. Could TVNZ 1 please find some decent

commentators for next year's game so it is not ruined by these individuals. Sorry to be a whiner and I really am grateful that we were treated to a game of cricket on free-to-air TV. Long may it continue.

**Cricket fan
(Ngaruawahia)**

Leigh Hart

It was good that TVNZ 1 showed the Rugby v Cricket, *T20 Black Clash* game live. The annoying thing for me was the continued "waffling" from the commentators, as well as Leigh Hart who was doing interviews and seemed to think he was a comedian, but certainly is not in my opinion. All this distraction tended to take the focus away from the game. I then turned the sound down and enjoyed the game.

Roley (North Shore)

2020

LOCKDOWN

There was still one miserable test to play in Australia when the new decade rolled around. The Ship got sick and missed the SCG mauling, which followed the MCG mauling, which followed the pounding in Perth. To compound matters, India was heading to New Zealand licking its chops at the prospect of facing a beaten-up Black Caps.

The new concept developed to give test cricket more context — the World Test Championship — was off to an awful start and was poised to get worse.

Not so fast.

Tim Southee and Trent Boult had a series for the ages and New Zealand, with the ACC in raptures, beat the might of India by 10 wickets in Wellington and seven in Christchurch. Combined with a 3–0 win in the ODIs, it was a heady start to 2020, but there was a bit going on in the background.

Between the first and second tests, the first case of a novel coronavirus was recorded in Auckland. During the second test, another case, stemming from a woman who had recently returned from Italy, was announced.

A series of lockdowns were instigated.

Around the world, sport basically stopped. The Tokyo Olympics were postponed and rugby looked very different, with the All Blacks playing just six tests — two at home and four in Australia. The games weren't even that fun to watch, including a draw and a loss to an average Wallabies side in Wellington and Brisbane respectively and, most shockingly, a first-test loss to Argentina 15–25 in neutral Sydney.

It was a curious time for the ACC. In February, parent company NZME announced it would not be renewing its audio rights contract with New Zealand Cricket after failing to come to terms with the national body. The company had been running cricket broadcasts at a significant loss for some time, something Jason Winstanley, general manager of talk radio, said it was no longer prepared to wear.

It was a portent. When Covid effectively shut down both global and domestic sport, the vulnerability of Radio Sport, whose predecessor *Sports Roundup*

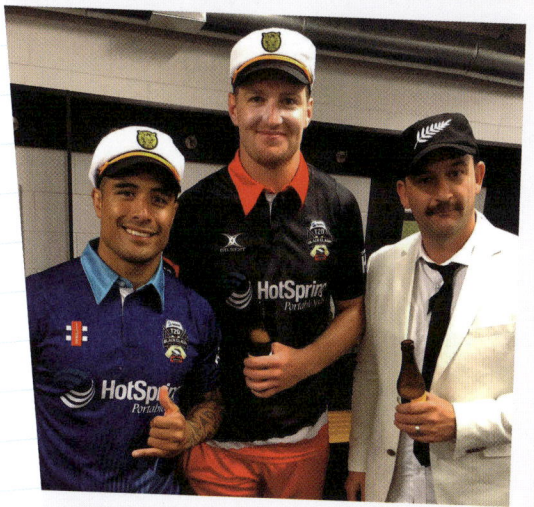

COMMENTARY AGENDA

* The box anchor
* Kiwi ice cream XI
* Steyn to Elliott — Daniel Vettori's reaction
* Broadcasting from Lovely Trenty's house

had been built upon cricket commentary, was exposed. The station was unceremoniously and immediately switched off at 1pm on 30 March 2020.

This left the ACC, which worked to a different commercial imperative, suddenly standing alone as NZME's only dedicated sports brand. A responsibility they took very seriously with their coverage of the ACC Super Seven Championship, a completely made-up rugby competition between 1st XVs of actors, superheroes, rock stars, politicians, celebrity chefs, cartoon characters and hip-hop and R'n'B artists.

MATT HEATH: We were quite proud to be the first commentary team to cover any sport during the Covid-19 crisis with the Super Seven.

MIKE LANE: We were a sports commentary team with nothing to do, so we were desperate. We'd proven the concept with the ACC Super League, so we did what we had to — create the only rugby competition that was going on in *the world,* albeit completely fake and somewhat ludicrous.

HEATH: Seven rugby teams made up of some of the biggest global superstars going around. We are talking Marvel superheroes, celebrity chefs, cartoon characters, rock stars. It was a who's who of entertainers.

LANE: We have done some cerebral shit in our time, but this one took the cake. We had SpongeBob SquarePants coming up against Nigella Lawson and Gordon Ramsay. Batman running it up the guts to be tackled by Winston Churchill. We even got a government exemption to come into work and 'commentate' the games.

HEATH: Pretty sure it was the only sport happening on Earth at that time. It was groundbreaking and hilarious. I was personally super proud of the Cartoon XV, they showed real ticker against opposition who were substantially larger than them.

LANE: The Actors XV had some real big hitters, like John Candy and Chris Farley, but then you had the likes of Notorious BIG in the Hip Hop XV and Gerry Brownlee in the Politicians XV — that's some serious units.

The grand final at Carlaw Park was a close-fought affair between the ultra-consistent Cartoon XV and the 1st XV of Rock, the overwhelming favourites. The match was always likely to be spiteful after Jon Toogood was suspended for four weeks following their round-three clash after he cynically took out SpongeBob SquarePants.

Mickey Mouse captained the cartoons and Dave Grohl led out rock. The anthems were the theme tune to *The Simpsons*, along with 'Stairway to Heaven'.

Perhaps inevitably, Speedy Gonzales opened the scoring when he was put into space. Rock replied when Shihad songwriter and guitarist Toogood fended off SquarePants, but, with just 20 minutes remaining, Rock was clinging to a three-point lead. Mick Jagger scored after some great lead-up work from Kurt Cobain and, although the conversion was missed, Grohl made up for it with a penalty after Homer Simpson was caught flopping at a ruck.

The final score was 18–7 to Rock.

LANE: What a tournament. Full of drama and controversy from the opening round. To date, there has not been a second season.

It was a VERY quiet sporting year.

However, in September, something quite momentous re-happened. *The BYC*, New Zealand's best-loved and longest-running specialty cricket podcast, was reignited starring Paul Ford, Jason Hoyte and Dylan Cleaver.

PAUL FORD: Like many good ideas, *The BYC* podcast was dreamt up over a few beers on Wellington's Featherston Street, when Ponting and Dravid,

Murali and Warne, Fleming and Bond were in their pomp and George W Bush was the leader of the Free World.

KEVIN SINNOTT: My flatmate Jed 'Jedi' Thian had seen *The Ricky Gervais Show* take off in the UK, so he started up his rugby union-focused podcast, *The Rugby Roundtable*. This took off pretty quickly and I thought cricket was an obvious angle to take here in New Zealand, so our *BYC* podcast follies followed on from there. It was also an obvious move to have a chat with the Beige Brigade boys to see if we could make something happen by the fans and for the fans.

FORD: It was on brand for the Beige Brigade to get involved as we knew there was a group of people — a small one initially — who were gagging for some not-too-life-and-death chat about cricket.

And so on Sunday 25 June 2006, the first episode of *The BYC* was recorded.

FORD: The upshot was that every Sunday evening, after dinner, a bunch of Beige Brigade rascals, reprobates, friends and affiliates gathered in a studio on Cuba Street to chew the fat about things cricket and vaguely cricket-related. Among us was the one-man minstrel and orchestra Blair 'Woman Slayer' Sayer (a deeply ironic nickname), Kev as our resident redhead and quick-witted compère, unbeaten kickboxer Jason 'Off-White Thunder' Willis, and me masquerading as the Godfather of the Beige Brigade. Our inaugural producer James 'FLOM' Irwin owned a radio-training school on Cuba Street that was pretty useful, and we also had the great pleasure of one of his radio students, Reece 'Brian' Witters, on the production crew in the early days. After ninety minutes of talking nonsense, Blair making a song from scratch, and intense hilarity, the initial Beige Brigade podcasts found their way out into the RSS feeds and eardrums of Kiwi cricket fans around the world.

The show opened up to 'The BYC Tonight', a shameless rip-off of 'Afternoon Delight' by the Starland Vocal Band, which in turn was made famous again by Ron Burgundy's news team in *Anchorman*.

BLAIR SAYER: It was definitely not a politically correct homage, but it has some sweet ukulele and some stellar lines in it about cricket umpires in dire situations and so on. Arguably tasteless, but brilliant for a cricket podcast operating outside the mainstream audience.

FORD: We doled out cricket news (together with a ruse to be outed), and dealt with correspondence that trickled and then gushed in. We occasionally confronted serious topics, like why New Zealand was rubbish at cricket (this was the bad old days!), reminisced about the halcyon days and gazed into our crystal balls to predict what lay ahead for the game of willow on leather.

DYLAN CLEAVER: Paul or Kevin must have sent me a file with one of the early shows so I could promote it in 'Quick Singles', which was a weekly cricket column I wrote for the *Herald on Sunday*. I distinctly remember having three strong and competing thoughts about it:

1. Who in their right mind is going to download an audio file of a few beered-up blokes talking shit about cricket in their spare time;
2. There's a few potentially libellous statements being thrown around willy-nilly here (mostly by Kev);
3. Damn, it sounds like great fun to make and I'm insanely jealous.

FORD: We had a couple of international contributors who got in touch most weeks, including former Kiwi wicketkeeper and raconteur Tony 'T-Bone' Blain writing a 'Letter from Whitby' in the UK (we suspect it was actually written in suburban Bradford, but seaside Whitby sounded more bucolic) and the aptly named Regular Correspondent, a stats fiend with a day job as a highly regarded Wairarapa accountant. We had a Coca-Cola rep who drove to the studio and celebrated our 100th episode in person with us — and brought a homemade trophy for us as well. We also had a female fan from Boston get in the mix when she visited Aotearoa, a cracking lady who was *The BYC* version of Mel from *Flight of the Conchords*, but way cooler and a lot more normal.

It was never about the money, which was probably just as well.

JASON WILLIS: We had an early foray into sponsorship at an Indian restaurant called Tulsi on Cuba Street. As far as commercial agreements go, it wasn't set up on the soundest footing. We'd record the podcast up the back, accompanied by what we thought were bottomless Kingfisher Strongs (7.2%) and food. However, a misunderstanding emerged and then we were 'topping up' the tab to the tune of a few hundred dollars at the end of shows, and even dropping home kitchen staff around the city.

SAYER: I'm no Warren Buffett, but after a while I could see who was getting the better end of this deal, so we eased off the pedal when it came to the Kingfishers and kormas.

WILLIS: After two weeks of not exceeding the cost of the bar tab, boom, the relationship was over.

Over the years, the line-up changed and evolved as people's lives waxed and waned through geographical changes, the demands of work and family, and as people succumbed to the daily grind.

FORD: I like to think of it as being a bit like the Lashings cricket club in Maidstone, where terrific people come and go over time.

One crucial iteration was sparked up by G-Lane when he was at Radio Hauraki, but in the pre-Alternative Commentary Collective era, alongside Wells and Cleaver, who was at that point in history *The New Zealand Herald's* head of sport.

CLEAVER: We used to meet at the shitty old TRN building on the corner of Cook and Nelson streets. I hated my full-time job with a passion. Middle management is no place to be when you have zero clout with those above you and zero respect from those below you. But I digress from my point, which was that *The BYC* was my little hour of joy every week. My only regret is that I couldn't fully commit to the show's sensibilities, as I could never quite remove my 'serious journalist' hat.

MIKE LANE: You could occasionally see Cleaver flinch when Jerry would strongly endorse match-fixing as a legitimate part of the game, or suggest that umpires might have unnatural fetishes.

The Hoyte–Ford–Cleaver unholy trinity version of *The BYC*, with key contributions from G-Lane off the bench, has shown real staying power.

JASON HOYTE: I still don't really know what a podcast is. I've never listened to one in my life.

FORD: I'm proud of what Kevin and the 2006 crew created. It is truly, madly, deeply, bloody magnificent that this little slice of Kiwi cricketing shenanigans is still going strong. I like to think we played a small part in helping carve out a niche for the ACC to take its now entrenched place in the Kiwi sporting milieu. If you have ever listened, told a mate to listen, sent us an email, laughed or cried with us on your work commute, and maybe, just maybe, learned a thing about cricket from us — thank you for being part of the little accident that is *The BYC*.

James McOnie's Guide to
WRITING A
PARODY SONG

The original *BYC*'s reworking of 'Afternoon Delight' remains a treasure, but if there is one great New Zealander who needs to be listened to when it comes to creating songs, it's the man who created 'Fat Bottomed Props', James McOnie.

With great parody, comes great responsibility. Remember, you are taking someone's precious, sometimes genius, work of art — something that may be considered untouchable — but you have a job to do: butchering it for lols.

A song parody may seem like something you could whip up overnight (and you'd be right about that), but once you release it into the world, it is your work of art now. You are piggybacking on the original artist like Yoda on Luke Skywalker in the Dagobah system, but with less expertise and wisdom. So, not really like Yoda. More like a parasite. Hey, maybe that's why it's called a parody?! I didn't realise writing this would be so educational.

Here are my five keys to writing a truly great song parody:

1. Song choice

This usually happens in reverse. So, the name Southee lends itself to 'Zombie'. Conway becomes 'Convoy'. And names like Akira Ioane and Asafo Aumua nicely replace the place names in the Beach Boys song 'Kokomo'.

But the key is that the song needs to be able to be sung easily. There's no point choosing a song that's too hard to sing, or too tricky to understand or recognise.

Admittedly, my 2022 'Bachelor's Handbag' remix of Kate Bush's 'Wuthering Heights' was ill-advised and sent me into a downward spiral wondering if I'd ever parody again. It's hard to dive into Bush. But after some soul-searching, I made a comeback with 'Mana's In The Air' when the Chiefs made the 2023 Super Rugby final.

It didn't help the Chiefs win that final, and quite possibly was a needless distraction, but, hey, I was back.

2. Lyrics

In a perfect world, the lyrics write themselves and, thankfully, that world has been created by ChatGPT.

While I haven't yet resorted to AI, I sometimes wish I had. Some lyrics still feel clunky (e.g., 'Hoskins Sotutu/I wanna do you too-too' in that 'Kokomo' cover), but there's no going back after the fact. Song parody is an art form that's always seeking fresh pastures.

In the case of 'Southee'/'Zombie', I knew I had to capture the Cranberries' gravitas as the song builds towards its climax:

> *Another ball swings so slightly, a catch is neatly taken.*
> *It's quite violent and it's silent, like a fart that's escaping . . .*
> *But you see young Lockie, and there's Lovely Trenty.*
> *In your head, in your head, balls are rising . . .*

Black Caps opening batter Devon Conway was in a rich vein of form leading into the World Test Championship final in 2021, so in 'Conway'/'Convoy', the trucker speaking on the CB radio ended up like this:

> *Now down at the show, Bumrah's good to go, and Kohli's lickin' his lips.*
> *Ishant Sharma is like a snake charmer, as the new ball seams and dips.*
> *At two for 69, Steady's on the line, sayin': 'This could be your last BJ.'*
> *So get the Sexy Camel and any other mammal, and let's have ourselves a*
> *Threeway.*

I feel like these lyrics captured the enormity of the task ahead of the Black Caps and the pressure of facing world-class opposition, much like engaging in a threesome.

3. Timing

Striking while the iron's hot is ideal. Caleb Clarke burst onto the scene in 2020 with an impressively powerful derrière. Sir Mix-A-Lot was the perfect fit: 'I like Clarke's butt and I cannot lie . . .'

But if you miss the window, songs can end up on the cutting-room floor. When Jason Hoyte exposed his man boobs when the Black Caps won that World Test Championship final in Hampshire, I wrote the parody 'Get Your Baps Out, Get Your Baps Out Hoytey' to Primal Scream's 'Rocks'. But life got in the way, the moment passed and instead I sang a duet with Trent Boult to the tune of 'April Sun In Cuba'.

> *We're tired of the white-ball life, Devon's getting runs.*
> *Colin's mullet is so long, it glistens in the sun.*
> *So don't tell us we can't bat, we're here to play for Kane.*
> *Dukes ball swinging twice as nice, and we got to bowl today . . .*
> *Take me to the World Test Champs in Hampshire, Oh-oh-oh . . .*

However, the recent 2023–24 cricket season was one of lost opportunities. I toyed with the idea of 'Kane' to the tune of 'Fame' as well as 'Part-time Spinner' sung to Stevie Wonder's 'Part-time Lover' in honour of the work done by Glenn Phillips and Rachin Ravindra.

And where was my tribute to retiring pace bowler Neil Wagner? To be honest, the line from 'Ignition' 'Bounce, bounce, bounce, bounce, bounce' would have been ideal, but using an R Kelly song is problematic, even by ACC standards.

4. Simplicity

Sometimes you just need a hook and nothing else. Perhaps the catchiest ACC song parody is the shortest. The reggae style of 'Dillon Hunt Hunt Hunt' (instead of 'Feeling hot hot hot') kept on giving long after Dillon retired in 2021 . . . well, it transferred to Mitchell Hunt.

Take the lyric 'Akira Ioane, so cold in the Cake Tin tonight' to the tune of '80s Kiwi synth pop hit 'Sierra Leone' by Coconut Rough. Ioane only plays in the Cake Tin once or maybe twice a season . . . but who gives a shit, it works. Don't @ me.

Many of the songs are penned as love letters, like the Earth, Wind & Fire classic 'September', which I rebooted in honour of the Chiefs.

> *Do you remember, Sam Cane is the best defender.*
> *He's always tackling those pretenders, and chasing the Blues away.*
> *Our props were mauling, and the moves that Cruden was calling.*
> *As we beat Razor's boys, remember, how Boshier stole the ball away . . .*

So, think of your subject. What do they do? What did they do? Do be do be do.

5. Longevity

The dream for any song parodist is for their song to live on and even replace the original in some people's minds. The OG, Weird Al Yankovic, is the master and his parodies approach immortality, such as his Michael Jackson covers 'Fat' and 'Eat It', his Madonna parody 'Like a Surgeon' and the Huey Lewis and the News reboot 'I Want a New Duck'.

Of my parodies, 'Fat Bottomed Props' (the 2015 Rugby World Cup song I did for *The Crowd Goes Wild*) is the only one that went viral. My Shakira cover of 'Waka Waka', again written for *CGW*, probably covered the most ground (or water), with every single Kiwi medallist in the Tokyo Olympics getting a mention.

A law protecting parodies in many countries allows these songs to be twisted and mangled by people like me, but sometimes they disappear from social media if music companies flex their copyright muscle. Other times the songs or the lyrics can be found in the seediest backwaters of the internet, like the dark web, community Facebook groups and the ACC 3236 text line.

But no matter what happens to your carefully crafted works of art, it's better to have sung and lost than to have never sung at all.

The year had a bit of a kicker to it as well, when Mike Lane, the man who has never come across something he can't laugh with or at, had a big hole cut in his head.

LANE: I had a wee lump in the middle of my forehead that wouldn't go away. Not a mole, so not visible on the skin. Just a small lump. It had probably been there for two years.

LEIGH HART: Did we notice it? Yeah, you could hardly miss it. Massive.

LANE: My GP thought it was probably a cyst. My daughter, who was five, reckoned it was the start of a unicorn horn. I found that quite amusing at the time, then all of a sudden it wasn't quite as funny.

His GP popped some local anaesthetic around the area and proceeded to cut the offending protrusion out. Halfway through he stopped and said, 'That's a bit weird,' stitched up the hole and sent some samples off for testing.

LANE: In the back of my mind I knew there wouldn't be this much fuss over a harmless little bump — the tone of the GP's voice said it all. Ten days later my phone rang, followed by my doctor 'inviting' me in to see him. A classic bad news scenario.

Lane had a one-in-a-million type of skin cancer called dermatofibrosarcoma protuberans. He was told it was incredibly rare and normally found on the torsos of African-Americans.

LANE: You have this movie-scene idea about what it must be like to receive the news you have cancer, but for me it was just so matter-of-fact — maybe because I could see it coming. My only words to the doctor were: 'How do I get rid of this motherfucker?'

MATT HEATH: This feels like a real opportunity for the rest of us at the ACC to say something quite heartfelt.

HART: We should probably get Ford to do that. He's known him the longest. I'm not saying I wouldn't miss Lane, just not as much as Paul.

PAUL FORD: I've known Mike since we were teenagers and it really freaked me out when he got struck down with that female African-American cancer.

He's such a force of nature, a magnificent friend, an amazingly magnetic person and it just felt horrendously unfair.

HART: Paul was the right choice.

LEE BAKER: When I heard Mike had a weird lump on his forehead that would need to be operated on, my first thought was, 'Okay, what cricket match can he commentate while the surgical procedure is carried out?' It worked great that summer of 2017 when he called a game between New Zealand and Australia while getting the snip on his downstairs operation. The guy's a specialist.

FORD: Behind all the alpha bravado and nonsense is a wonderful mate, a kind son, a doting father, a high-voltage husband and a guy who works his arse off to make great things happen. It was unfathomable that this cancer might mean he might not be around.

Lane was lucky that the cancer mutated slowly, did not often metastasise and was caught before its tentacle-like structure burrowed into his eye-socket. The bad news was that it would have to be cut out of his skull while he was awake initially and it would leave a divot in his bonce as if Rory McIlroy had just hit a well-struck eight iron off his forehead.

LANE: I had two days of ever-increasing circles being cut out of my forehead under local. It was unpleasant. You could hear them scraping away on my skull. They got most, but not all of it, so two days later I was in hospital having surgery under general.

The resultant wound was spectacular.

LANE: My normally stoic wife had to take a moment for herself in another room when a compression bandage was stapled to my head. Peak heinousness occurred when ooze from a leaking bandage dripped over my dinner plate one night.

DYLAN CLEAVER: NZME, being a news organisation as well as a house for entertainment brands, decided to make the most of Lane's personal crisis and I was tasked with writing his cancer story. We retired to a taphouse on the North Shore and had several beers, which gave me confidence he was bouncing back. Probably not the most professional environment for an interview, but he had some great lines, like when his oldest son, who had taken to calling his dad Cherry Piehead, would notice people staring at him because he was wearing a bandanna.

LANE: Ralph was a real icebreaker. People would look at me and he would shout: 'He's got CANCER! He's got a MASSIVE HOLE IN HIS HEAD! Wanna see it?'

Ralph wasn't embellishing it by much. Under the bandage, Lane had a bovine lattice upon which flesh granulated to partially fill the gap. The wound had to remain open for three months over summer before getting a skin graft from his groin to close it up.

JASON HOYTE: That was purely so he could keep some skin from beside his balls near his brain.

A full forehead reconstruction would follow, but first he needed to stretch the skin on his forehead so he could create a flap for the surgeons to work with as they patched up the hole in his head.

HEATH: It was full on. We do actually love each other and we were all super worried about Lane.

LANE: If they were worried, they sure went about expressing it in an unique way. Heath and Wells called me 'Tits Lane' for those months when I had tissue expanders in my forehead. Mainly on the radio and commentary to hundreds of thousands of people.

HEATH: It was a compliment. He had an enormous set of boobs on his forehead.

JEREMY WELLS: They were a great set of tits. I recall someone doing something terrible off those tits. I think there is a photo somewhere.

Tits Lane is cancer-free now.

LANE: It was a four-year journey from diagnosis to full reconstruction and, if I can be serious for one second, it did have one positive side effect and that was that my mates started going to have check-ups. If in doubt, check it out. You might get a set of tits for your own head.

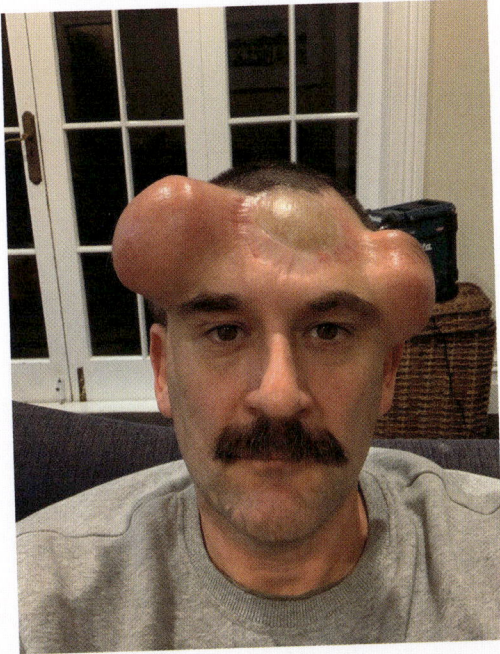

It did have one positive side effect and that was that my mates started going to have check-ups. If in doubt, check it out.

ALTERNATIVE
COMMENTARY
COLLECTIVE

RADIO
HAURAKI

ALTERNATIVE
MACE TOUR

WHEREVER YOU WANT IT.
WHENEVER YOU WANT IT.

HEAD TO HAURAKI.CO.NZ & THEACCNZ.COM FOR MORE DETAILS

2021

THE MOUNTAINTOP

No Sleep 'til Test Champions!

BLACKCAPS VS INDIA
FROM 10PM, TONIGHT

ICC WORLD TEST CHAMPIONSHIP

LISTEN ON iHeart RADIO SEARCH ALTCOMMVE

ALTERNATIVE COMMENTARY COLLECTIVE

SIMULCAST ON RADIO HAURAKI

With the world slowly waking in staggered fashion from a global pandemic, a lot happened in 2021, but it's time to ignore whatever memories you might be having and head straight to the ACC studios to relive THE SINGLE GREATEST MOMENT IN ACC SPORTS HISTORY — the closing stages of 'No Sleeps 'Til Victory'.

Kane Williamson, fast establishing himself in the eyes of the ACC and all those who listen as the Greatest Living New Zealander, has just pulled a ball to the square-leg boundary to bring up his half century, which nicely complements the 49 he scored in the first innings. Chasing just 139 to win, he and Ross Taylor, for so long the stalwarts of New Zealand batting efforts, are getting very close.

MATT HEATH: Kane Williamson, what a great New Zealander. Just six runs to win. Jason Hoyte, start loosening that tie.

New Zealand needs just six more runs to beat India in the final of the World Test Championship at the Rose Bowl, Southampton, with eight wickets in hand. If New Zealand can complete the mighty upset, Jason Hoyte has agreed to get his man-baps out.

MIKE LANE: Start to work those nipples up.

JASON HOYTE: Turn that video off.

HEATH: Can we get him some ice to rub around those nipples to make them pert?

HOYTE: Six more runs to win. Sharma to Taylor, down the leg side. No run.

HEATH: They'll be disappointed, India, they had them thirty-three for two.

[*It was actually 33 for 1 and 44 for 2*]. They needed early wickets.

HOYTE: It's a hiding, really.

LANE: Oh yeah.

HOYTE: We wanted ten wickets.

LANE: I'll take eight.

HEATH: We're not going to send an eight-wicket win back, but ten would have been a real statement. But how good is this? We came to England, we beat England, so everybody who said we could only win at home can get stuffed. When and if we win this game, the whole world can suck it. Is that good sportsmanship?

HOYTE: You're a good winner, Matt. Sharma bowls to Taylor who drives back to the bowler. It ricochets off him, but there is no run.

HEATH: I've never seen so many texts come through, Jase.

LANE: If you don't do it, I'm going to give out your home address.

HEATH: You're going to dox him.

Sharma is injured while trying to field off his own bowling.

LANE: Yeah, it's your fingernail, mate.

HEATH: You've got a sore finger, that's the difference. Okay, mate.

LANE: Get out.

HOYTE: Yeah, get off.

HEATH: Are you hoping for rain are you? Get out. Six more runs to win it.

HOYTE: Oooh, ouch.

LANE: Yeah, that would have hurt. All the best to him and his family.

HEATH: Thoughts and prayers, bless, bless, bless. Who's going to finish his over?

LANE: Virat Kohli hopefully.

HOYTE: So we can launch it into the stadium for six.

LANE: Jasprit Bumrah's going to finish Snake Sharma's over. He's gone off with a broken fingernail.

HEATH: Do you know how I said I didn't think it was possible for me to love Kane Williamson any more? Well, it's happened. I've found a new area in my heart to fill.

HOYTE: Bumrah now to Taylor. Short, and he opens the face and runs it down to third man.

LANE: Two there.

HOYTE: They get a couple.

LANE: Here we go, finish it with one shot.

HEATH: Come on New Zealand.

HOYTE: It's been a great knock from Taylor, too. He's been under pressure and he's answered his critics.

The camera pans to a small pocket of New Zealand fans who have undoubtedly ventured down from Hammersmith, Clapham and Acton for the day.

HEATH: Has there ever been a greater advertisement for New Zealand than that grey-haired man with his shirt off?

LANE: Are there any women there?

HEATH: No women. That's not how we roll.

LANE: He's got a good rig . . . Oh yeah, the pūkana.

HEATH: Four runs to win the World Test Championship.

HOYTE: Bumrah up to Taylor and ooh, he nearly chops it on. Dearie me.

HEATH: Can we do it in one shot? Can we do it in this over? Have we done the per capita maths on this, or when we win do you not need to do that? You just take the win?

HOYTE: You do.

HEATH: Let's just say there's 1.4 billion of them and five million of us, and the population of South Africa. Let's just say that.

LANE: Come on Taylor, come on Ross Taylor.

HOYTE: Bumrah to Taylor again. He turns this off his pads to the man at midwicket and there's no run.

HEATH: I'm starting to believe, boys. And girls. I'm starting to believe, with four more runs to win. How are you feeling, Mike Lane?

LANE: So much relief. After the heartbreak of Melbourne and the agony of Lord's in 2019, this is going to be emotional.

HOYTE: Bumrah again to Taylor and ooh, that's a good, sharp delivery that Taylor leaves through to the keeper. He's going to leave it to the skipper to blaze one through the covers to take us home.

LANE: Wouldn't that be good, Jason Hoyte. How fitting. Well, it's been an eventful six days. It has had pretty much everything.

HEATH: Can I just say as a person who wasn't here the whole time, just a big round of applause for you guys for coming in every night.

LANE: I didn't come in every night.

HEATH: Just take the applause, Jesus.

LANE: It was actually more Joe Shuker and Joe Durie, Tom Harper.

HOYTE: The support team.

HEATH: I normally don't like showing support to the support team, but good on ya.

HOYTE: Rightio . . .

LANE: Come on New Zealand, let's go. Come on Kane.

HOYTE: Shami bowls to Williamson and he defends and there's no run.

HEATH: You think about it and, G-Lane, I need to ask you how you're feeling because you bum-rushed the show to Lord's in 2019, you just packed up, you caused major ructions in your domestic life, grabbed ten grand out of the bank and headed over to England. Then we got the World Cup stolen from us with some terrible officiating and some bad luck.

HOYTE: Shami again and oh, Williamson tries to slice him fine down to third man and makes no contact.

HEATH: So, for you is this going to be worth it because test cricket, that's the one you want because it's test cricket where you truly find out who's the best in the world?

LANE: It's a world championship. That's all I care about . . . we're going to be world champions. We are going to be world champions. The only thing we've ever won was the Champions Trophy, which was a bit of a diddle of a tournament, but this is the big show.

HOYTE: Shami to Williamson again, who defends and they scamper through for a quick single.

A quick and slightly unbecoming debate briefly flares as to whether a small whimper emanated from the studio or the ground-effects mic. The cameras again pan to a shirtless crowd.

HEATH: There's baps out there and there'll soon be baps out here as that plethora of baps will soon be joined by Jason Hoyte.

HOYTE: Shami again to Taylor, who lets it go and there's no run.

HEATH: Believe in the leave. Three runs to get, Williamson fifty-two, Taylor forty-three and New Zealand 156 for two.

HOYTE: Shami with the chamois again to Taylor, whips it off his pads . . .

LANE AND HEATH: Yeeeeaaaaahhhhhhh!

HOYTE: And it's going to go for six I think.

While the commentator would like a recall on that, it went for four, the rest he stands by . . .

HOYTE: After so much heartache, after so much pain, after so much suffering, the New Zealand cricketers are now CHAMPIONS. OF. THE. WORLD. Magnificent.

LANE AND HEATH: World Champions! World. Fucking. Champions!

HOYTE: What a magnificent performance from New Zealand. They have been the best team in the world for the past year. So many people doubted their ability and their pedigree but they've proved their critics wrong and now they stand atop the mountain — champions of the world.

ICC **WORLD TEST CHAMPIONSHIP FINAL 2021**

CHAMPIONS

Nº	BATSMAN		HOW OUT		BOWLER	R	B	4
1	R.G. SHARMA	c SOUTHEE	Third slip held thick edge low to his right		JAMIESON	34	68	6
2	S. GILL	c † WATLING	Drawn into nibbling at one angled across him		WAGNER	28	64	3
3	C.A. PUJARA	LBW	Swung back in and hit both pads on leg stump		BOULT	8	54	2
4	V. KOHLI *	LBW	Futile review to off-cutter hitting top of middle		JAMIESON	44	132	1
5	A.M. RAHANE	c LATHAM	Flapped a pull at a shorter ball · to square leg		WAGNER	49	117	5
6	R.R. PANT †	c LATHAM	Over-eager drive at wider one · to second slip		JAMIESON	4	22	1
7	R.A. JADEJA	c † WATLING	Strangled down leg trying to glance off his hip		BOULT	15	53	2
8	R. ASHWIN	c LATHAM	Snicked a tempting outswinger to second slip		SOUTHEE	22	27	3
9	I. SHARMA	c TAYLOR	Fenced at lifter outside off · first slip held it		JAMIESON	4	16	·
10	J.J. BUMRAH	LBW	Pinned in front first ball by inducking yorker		JAMIESON	0	1	·
11	M. SHAMI	NOT OUT				4	1	1

INDIA — 1ST INNINGS — TOSS WON BY NEW ZEALAND

BYES	·	
LEG BYES	111	3
WIDE BALLS		·
NO BALLS	11	2

EXTRAS 5 · 217 · 10 WICKETS · RUN RATE 2.35 · 92.1 OVERS

PARTNERSHIPS

W	T	R	B	OUT		NOT	
1ST	62	62	121	R SHARMA	34	GILL	27
2ND	63	1	26	GILL	1	PUJARA	0
3RD	88	25	95	PUJARA	8	KOHLI	17
4TH	149	61	165	KOHLI	27	RAHANE	32
5TH	156	7	37	PANT	4	RAHANE	1
6TH	182	26	30	RAHANE	16	JADEJA	10
7TH	205	23	43	ASHWIN	22	JADEJA	1
8TH	213	8	35	I SHARMA	4	JADEJA	4
9TH	213	0	1	BUMRAH	0	JADEJA	0
10TH	217	4	2	JADEJA	0	SHAMI	4

BOWLING

BOWLER	O	M	R	W	wb/nb	E
SOUTHEE	22	6	64	1	·	2.90
BOULT	21.1	4	47	2	·	2.22
JAMIESON	22	12	31	5	1	1.40
DE GRANDHOMME	12	6	32	0	·	2.66
WAGNER	15	5	40	2		2.66
TOTALS	92.1	33	214	10	2	2.35

New Zealand were nearly not in the final at all. Four defeats in their first five games, all away from home, put them among the ranks of the also-rans. Then came the coronavirus pandemic, and amid cancellations here and curtailments there, three planets aligned for the Black Caps. First, they enjoyed a run of seven consecutive home games in the course of 12 months, and won them all at a canter. Then Australia, in pole position to reach the final, withdrew from a series in South Africa they surely would have won. Finally, Australia were docked four points for a slow over rate in Melbourne; but for this deduction, they would have pipped New Zealand to the wire. Still, after their disappointment in the 2019 World Cup final, not a soul in world cricket begrudged the 'nice guys of cricket' their fortune.

PLAYED AT THE HAMPSHIRE BOWL · ENGLAND

NEW ZEALAND — 1ST INNINGS — FOLLOW-ON IMPOSSIBLE

Nº	BATSMAN		HOW OUT		BOWLER	R	B	4/6
1	T.W.M. LATHAM	c KOHLI	Reached for ball and drove to short extra cover		ASHWIN	30	104	3
2	D.P. CONWAY	c SHAMI	Chipped a clip to leg · good grab to mid on's left		I. SHARMA	54	153	6
3	K.S. WILLIAMSON *	c KOHLI	Thick-edged forcing shot to very wide second slip		I. SHARMA	49	177	6
4	L.R.P.L. TAYLOR	c GILL	Drove on the up · brilliant dive by short cover		SHAMI	11	37	2
5	H.M. NICHOLLS	c R. SHARMA	Groped outside off and first slip held off edge		I. SHARMA	7	23	1
6	B.J. WATLING †	BOWLED	Full in-seamer burst through tentative defensive		SHAMI	1	3	·
7	C. DE GRANDHOMME	LBW	Off-cutter hit him just on the line of off stump		SHAMI	13	30	1
8	K.A. JAMIESON	c BUMRAH	Fetched off-side bouncer with hook to long leg		SHAMI	21	16	/1
9	T.G. SOUTHEE	BOWLED	Played on making room to hit flatter dart on leg		JADEJA	30	46	1/2
10	N. WAGNER	c RAHANE	Second attempt at slip · ball leaped to take edge		ASHWIN	0	5	·
11	T.A. BOULT	NOT OUT				7	8	1

BYES	4	4	
LEG BYES	1 1 1 1 4 1 4 1 1	16	EXTRAS 26
WIDE BALLS		·	
NO BALLS	1 1 1 1 1 1	6	RUN RATE 2.50

249 — 10 WICKETS — 99.2 OVERS

PARTNERSHIPS

W	T	R	B	OUT		NOT	
1ST	70	70	206	LATHAM	30	CONWAY	38
2ND	101	31	88	CONWAY	16	WILLIAMSON	12
3RD	117	16	88	TAYLOR	11	WILLIAMSON	2
4TH	134	17	39	NICHOLLS	7	WILLIAMSON	5
5TH	135	1	5	WATLING	1	WILLIAMSON	0
6TH	162	27	72	DE GRANDHOMME	13	WILLIAMSON	9
7TH	192	30	29	JAMIESON	21	WILLIAMSON	9
8TH	221	29	42	WILLIAMSON	12	SOUTHEE	10
9TH	234	13	15	WAGNER	0	SOUTHEE	13
10TH	249	15	18	SOUTHEE	7	BOULT	7

BOWLING

BOWLER	O	M	R	W	wb/nb	E
I. SHARMA	25	9	48	3	·	1.92
BUMRAH	26	9	57	0	/3	2.19
SHAMI	26	8	76	4	·	2.92
ASHWIN	15	5	28	2	/1	1.86
JADEJA	7.2	2	20	1	/2	2.72
TOTALS	99.2	33	229	10	/6	2.50

UMPIRES

MICHAEL GOUGH   RICHARD KETTLEBOROUGH

RICHARD ILLINGWORTH (REPLAYS)

MATCH REFEREE · CHRIS BROAD

NEW ZEALAND'S ROUTE TO THE FINAL

AUG 2019 v SRI LANKA
GALLE
LOST BY SIX WICKETS
PATEL 5-89

COLOMBO
WON BY AN INNINGS & 65 RUNS
LATHAM 154

DEC 2019 v AUSTRALIA
PERTH
LOST BY 296 RUNS
SOUTHEE 5-69

MELBOURNE
LOST BY 247 RUNS
BLUNDELL 121

SYDNEY
JAN 2020
LOST BY 279 RUNS
PHILLIPS 52

FEB 2020 v INDIA
WELLINGTON
WON BY 10 WICKETS
SOUTHEE 5-61

MAR 2020
CHRISTCHURCH
WON BY SEVEN WICKETS
JAMIESON 5-45

DEC 2020 v WEST INDIES
HAMILTON
WON BY AN INNINGS & 134 RUNS
WILLIAMSON 251

WELLINGTON
WON BY AN INNINGS & 12 RUNS
NICHOLLS 174

JAN 2021 CHRISTCHURCH
WON BY AN INNINGS & 176 RUNS
WILLIAMSON 238
JAMIESON 6-48

v PAKISTAN
MOUNT MAUNGANUI
WON BY 101 RUNS
WILLIAMSON 129

18 (NO PLAY) · 19 · 20 · 21 (NO PLAY) · 22 · 23 JUNE 2021

INDIA			2ND INNINGS		32 BEHIND				
Nº	BATSMAN		HOW OUT		BOWLER		R	B	4
1	R.G. SHARMA	LBW	Shouldered arms to inswinger heading for off peg		SOUTHEE		30	81	2
2	S. GILL	LBW	Attempted on-side flick but missed fuller ball		SOUTHEE		8	33	·
3	C.A. PUJARA	c	TAYLOR	Had to play at one angled in · nicked to first	JAMIESON		15	80	2
4	V. KOHLI *	c †	WATLING	Wafted inadvisedly at length ball in the channel	JAMIESON		13	29	·
5	A.M. RAHANE	c †	WATLING	Gloved a fairly harmless leg side ball behind	BOULT		15	40	1
6	R.R. PANT †	c	NICHOLLS	Recklessly advanced and skied to running gully	BOULT		41	88	4
7	R.A. JADEJA	c †	WATLING	Snicked an excellent ball seaming across him	WAGNER		16	49	2
8	R. ASHWIN	c	TAYLOR	Chased a full · wide sucker ball to solitary slip	BOULT		7	19	·
9	M. SHAMI	c	LATHAM	Top edged massive heave to well-placed fly slip	SOUTHEE		13	10	3
10	I. SHARMA	NOT OUT					1	6	·
11	J.J. BUMRAH	c	LATHAM	Nicked defensive prod low to second slip's left	SOUTHEE		0	4	·

BYES	1		1					
LEG BYES	4121		8	EXTRAS	11	170	10	WICKETS
WIDE BALLS	1		1					
NO BALLS	1		1	RUN RATE	2.32		73	OVERS

PARTNERSHIPS							BOWLING						
W	T	R	B	OUT		NOT		BOWLER	O	M	R	W	wb/nb	E
1ST	24	24	65	GILL	8	R. SHARMA	15	SOUTHEE	19	4	48	4	·	2.52
2ND	51	27	97	R. SHARMA	15	PUJARA	12	BOULT	15	2	39	3	·	2.60
3RD	71	20	54	KOHLI	13	PUJARA	2	JAMIESON	24	10	30	2	1/1	1.25
4TH	72	1	10	PUJARA	1	RAHANE	0							
5TH	109	37	75	RAHANE	15	PANT	21							
6TH	142	33	77	JADEJA	16	PANT	13							
7TH	156	14	39	PANT	7	ASHWIN	7							
8TH	156	0	2	ASHWIN	0	SHAMI	0	WAGNER	15	2	44	1	·	2.93
9TH	170	14	16	SHAMI	13	! SHARMA	1	TOTALS	73	18	161	10	1/1	2.32
10TH	170	0	4	BUMRAH	0	! SHARMA	0	* PANT dropped by SOUTHEE at second slip on 5 (8)						

WHAT THE EXPERTS SAID

A ONE OFF AND INCREDIBLY IMPORTANT GAME SHOULD NOT BE PLAYED IN THE UK
KEVIN PIETERSEN

LOOKS LIKE THE WTC FINAL WILL BE A DRAW
W. V. RAMAN

A SADLY PREDICTABLE DISASTER
FOX CRICKET

IT'S VERY SAD FOR THE FANS. ICC DID NOT GET ITS RULES RIGHT. ALL IN ALL, YOU WANT A CHAMPION.

V·V·S LAXMAN

TO HAVE THE FINAL IN ENGLAND WAS NOT THE SMARTEST CALL
SUNIL GAVASKAR

ICC GOT THE TIMING WRONG
VIRENDER SEHWAG

WAS ICC WRONG IN HOSTING WTC FINAL IN SOUTHAMPTON? ... OR WAS IT PURE BAD LUCK?
FREE PRESS JOURNAL INDIA

IT HAS TO BE BEST OF 3
VIRAT KOHLI RAVI SHASTRI

INDIA SHOULD HAVE HOSTED THE FINAL
AAKASH CHOPRA

PLAYER OF THE MATCH · KYLE JAMIESON

N°	BATSMAN	HOW OUT		BOWLER	R	B	4
	NEW ZEALAND	**2ND INNINGS**	**TARGET 139 FROM 53 OVERS**				
1	T.W.M.LATHAM	st † PANT	Danced down pitch and missed shorter off break	ASHWIN	9	41	.
2	D.P.CONWAY	LBW	Came well forward but played all round front pad	ASHWIN	19	47	4
3	K.S.WILLIAMSON *	NOT OUT			52	89	8
4	L.P.R.L.TAYLOR	NOT OUT			47	100	6
5	H.M.NICHOLLS						
6	B.J.WATLING †						
7	C.DE GRANDHOMME						
8	K.A.JAMIESON						
9	T.G.SOUTHEE						
10	N.WAGNER						
11	T.A.BOULT						

					EXTRAS				WICKETS
BYES		.			13	**140**	2		
LEG BYES	41141	11							
WIDE BALLS		.	RUN RATE	3.05			45.5		OVERS
NO BALLS	11	2							

PARTNERSHIPS

W	T	R	B	OUT		NOT	
1ST	33	33	81	LATHAM	9	CONWAY	14
2ND	44	11	23	CONWAY	5	WILLIAMSON	6
3RD	140	96	173	TAYLOR	47	WILLIAMSON	46
4TH							
5TH							
6TH							
7TH							
8TH							
9TH							
10TH							

BOWLING

BOWLER	O	M	R	W	wb / nb	E
I SHARMA	6.2	2	21	0	.	3.31
SHAMI	10.5	3	31	0	.	2.86
BUMRAH	10.4	2	35	0	.	3.28
ASHWIN	10	5	17	2	.	1.70
JADEJA	8	1	25	0	/ 2	3.12
TOTALS	45.5	13	129	2	/ 2	3.05

CLOSE OF PLAY " SCORES

DAY 1	RAINED OFF
DAY 2	INDIA 1ST 146-3 KOHLI 44 · RAHANE 29
DAY 3	NZ 1ST 101-2 WILLIAMSON 12 · TAYLOR 0
DAY 4	RAINED OFF
DAY 5	INDIA 2ND 64-2 PUJARA 12 · KOHLI 8

The teams approached the game in different ways. New Zealand played, and won, a tough two-Test series against England, unbeaten at home since 2014. India eschewed match preparation and instead opted to practise at the ground for three weeks. Though India selected two spinners, the pitch and weather were obviously going to be perfect for seam bowling, and there followed a high-quality exhibition of the craft from both teams' world-class attacks which rendered batting incredibly demanding. Above them all rose Kyle Jamieson who had, during the IPL, refused Virat Kohli's request to bowl at him with the Dukes ball in the Bangalore nets. India went into the final day 32 ahead with eight wickets in hand. They, like the public, fully anticipated a draw. New Zealand had other ideas.

NEW ZEALAND WON BY EIGHT WICKETS

Slightly later . . .

HOYTE: Was it a six by the way?

LANE: I'm not sure.

HEATH: Who cares.

In so many respects, the World Test Championship victory wasn't just validation of the Black Caps, but also of the ACC's obsession with a sport that seems in so many ways to be stuck out of time. The ACC love cricket more than any other sport because of its inherent weirdness, and here was the weirdest thing of all: New Zealand, stuck down the bottom of the world in a time zone that makes it incredibly hard to sell a daytime sports product; typically enduring soaking-wet spring months that make it almost impossible to produce decent conditions for kids to play cricket in; and with a population that is dwarfed three times over by the city of Delhi, was somehow world champion in the least random, most treasured and traditional format of them all.

WELLS: I mean, you can picture the Black Caps sneaking a T20 title somewhere by stringing a few big games together and, my god, they've been close in ODI World Cups, but tests! Bloody hell, that's weird. Bloody hell, cricket's weird. Bloody hell, the success of the ACC is deeply weird. The Black Caps are weird and 2021 was when all that weirdness coalesced into something beautiful and magnificent.

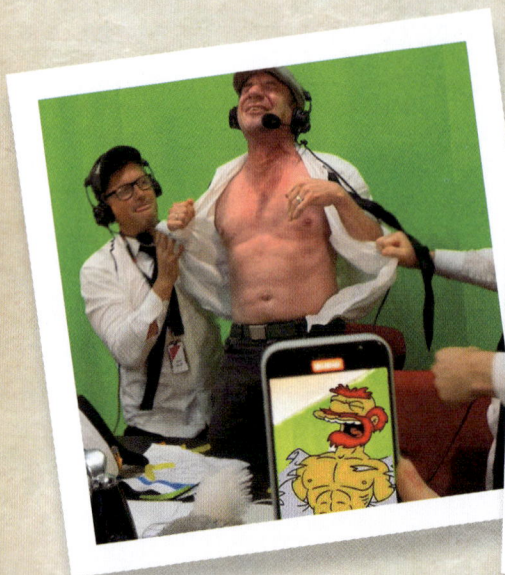

LEE BAKER: I absolutely love cricket. I don't think you'll find many people who genuinely love cricket but didn't play the game. It doesn't matter what level. Even intermediate school. If you play the game, you appreciate its beauty. You don't have to be a first-class cricketer for that to happen, to love the quirks and subtleties.

It's so rich in idiosyncrasies, in magic and intrigue . . . and psychology. In that respect I think cricket is a really healthy environment, especially for young men, when growing up. It's got its dark side — everybody who's played senior club cricket will know that — but the camaraderie is great and it's such a beautiful game.

Nowhere was that beauty and camaraderie more richly ingrained into the fabric of New Zealand sport than in the moment Ross Taylor shuffled down the wicket to the brilliant Mohammed Shami and flicked an arrow-straight delivery over square leg for four. Yes, Jason Hoyte got his baps out and, while they were magnificent in their own right, the scenes on the balcony of the New Zealand changing sheds were even more wholesome, as was the slightly awkward, aw-shucks hug between Williamson and Taylor, New Zealand's batting bulwarks for more than a decade, as they met in the middle.

So, now that we've all experienced that hug, let's go back to how we got there.

The World Test Championship was a new concept, designed to give context to bilateral test cricket that, outside the marquee series like The Ashes or the Border–Gavaskar Trophy, was struggling to keep a toehold in an increasingly T20 world.

After the disastrous tour to Australia (mentioned earlier in passing), New Zealand needed to both play out of their skins and have a few other things go their way. They beat India 2–0 at home, the West Indies 2–0 at home and, when a combination of a slow over-rate penalty and their Covid-enforced cancellation of a South African tour meant Australia couldn't accumulate enough points to automatically qualify, it left New Zealand needing to beat Pakistan 2–0 at home to win through.

On paper it looks like this was achieved comfortably enough, with wins by 101 runs and an innings and 176 runs respectively, but the first test at Bay Oval was actually a bit of a thriller, with Neil Wagner emerging as a special kind of ACC hero by bowling through the pain of broken toes.

WELLS: I always thought Lane commentating while receiving a vasectomy would be the bravest thing I ever saw in cricket, but Wags' effort at Mount Maunganui has to be right up there alongside it.

New Zealand accumulated a formidable first innings of 431, thanks in large part to Williamson's 24th test century and 50s from Ross Taylor, Henry Nicholls and BJ Watling.

Pakistan replied with 239, with Kyle Jamieson's 3-35 the best return. New Zealand slapped 180 for 5 declared, with two Toms, Latham and Blundell, hitting half centuries, and when Pakistan ended day four on 71 for 3, the target of 373 looked hopelessly out of reach.

But when New Zealand took just two wickets in the first two sessions of day five, there was good reason for concern as Fawad Alam (102) and Mohammad Rizwan (60) put on 165 for the fifth wicket in 63 painstaking overs.

Up stepped the courageous Wagner to blast a couple out on eight working toes and a large shot of painkiller, but with less than five overs remaining in the day, Pakistan's last-wicket stand was frustrating the hosts. Thankfully, Mitchell 'Santa's Little Helper' Santner delivered at the crucial moment, grabbing a leaping one-handed return catch to winkle out Naseem Shah. He didn't know it at the time, but as Williamson piled on more runs at Christchurch and Jamieson ran through the visitors' batting for a crushing victory in game two of the series, Santner's 'Hand of God' had effectively sent New Zealand to the World Test Championship final.

FORD: The thing that added piquancy to New Zealand making the final was the hand Australia played in it by being penalised for slow over rates. They've crushed our cricket dreams plenty of times, so it was nice that they kept this one alive.

Before the Black Caps arrived in Southampton for the ultimate test, a new hero emerged. Like others before him, Devon Conway came from that hotbed of 100 per cent genuine Kiwi talent: Soufrica, just west of Taranaki.

In a two-test series against England in the lead-up to the final, Conway, aka Threeway, scored a double century on test debut at Lord's, bringing up three figures with a spectacular 'flamingo' shot, and went from 194 to 200 with a pulled and slightly top-edged six.

That test ended in a draw, but a crushing eight-wicket win at Edgbaston in the second test, where there were contributions from players like Will Young (82), Matt

NEW ZEALAND VS PAKISTAN, 1ST TEST
MOUNT MAUNGANUI, 26–30 DECEMBER 2020
New Zealand won by 101 runs

New Zealand	431
K Williamson	129
BJ Watling	73
R Taylor	70
S Afridi	4-109

Pakistan	239
F Ashraf	91
K Jamieson	3-35

New Zealand	180-5 dec
T Blundell	64
T Latham	53
N Shah	3-55

Pakistan	271
F Alam	102
M Santner	2-52
N Wagner	2-55

NEW ZEALAND VS PAKISTAN, 2ND TEST
CHRISTCHURCH, 3–6 JANUARY 2021
New Zealand won by an innings and 176 runs

Pakistan	297
A Ali	93
K Jamieson	5-69

New Zealand	659-6 dec
K Williamson	238
H Nicholls	157
D Mitchell	102*

Pakistan	186
K Jamieson	6-48
T Boult	3-43

NEW ZEALAND VS ENGLAND, 2ND TEST
BIRMINGHAM, ENGLAND, 10–13 JUNE 2021
New Zealand won by 8 wickets

England	303
D Lawrence	81*
R Burns	81
T Boult	4-85
M Henry	3-78

New Zealand	388
W Young	82
D Conway	80
R Taylor	80
S Broad	4-48

England	122
N Wagner	3-18
M Henry	3-36

New Zealand	41-2
T Latham	23*

Henry (six wickets) and Ajaz Patel (four wickets) who weren't even likely to play in the final, put New Zealand in a great frame of mind as they headed down the M3 towards increasingly leaden skies.

HOYTE: There's nothing quite as niggly for world-class commentators like ourselves as potentially wet weather in the UK time zone. Being dedicated professionals, we can't just doze off in anticipation of there being no play. We have to be 100 per cent on our game and ready to spring into action at any time. I can't speak for the others, but I know I had a bunch of stats sheets to pore over during the inevitable breaks.

Chosen not because of its prestige, but because the hotel on site meant it was easy to create a relatively Covid-safe environment, the Rose Bowl was a curious venue for such an auspicious occasion. Both teams went through the formalities of naming highly predictable elevens.

The first day was completely lost to rain. No worries, the ICC had cleverly scheduled a reserve day in case the English summer intervened.

When play finally did begin, New Zealand won the toss and inserted India on the second morning. The day ended in a rain-affected stalemate, as India progressed to

New Zealand	India
Tom Latham	Rohit Sharma
Devon Conway	Shubman Gill
Kane Williamson (c)	Cheteshwar Pujara
Ross Taylor	Virat Kohli (c)
Henry Nicholls	Ajinkya Rahane
BJ Watling	Rishabh Pant
Colin de Grandhomme	Ravindra Jadeja
Kyle Jamieson	Ravichandran Ashwin
Tim Southee	Ishant Sharma
Neil Wagner	Mohammed Shami
Trent Boult	Jasprit Bumrah

146 for 3 in the 65 overs possible, with Virat Kohli looking dangerous on 44. There was another delayed start to day three, but as soon as they resumed Kyle Jamieson had Kohli out leg before.

FORD: That was such a great subplot. Jamieson had been signed for big money by the Royal Challengers Bangalore, and Virat had tried to get Jamieson to bowl to him in the nets using a red Dukes ball but he refused. I'm not saying New Zealand wouldn't have won if he had succumbed to the pressure, but in a match where the weather put it on a knife edge, Kohli's wicket was critical.

India folded to be all out for 217, with Jamieson taking five wickets, and at the end of day three New Zealand were 101 for 2 — Conway's impressive start to his career continuing with a half century.

Rain prevented any play on day four and delayed the start on day five. When India finished the day 64 for 2, leading overall by 32, a draw seemed to be the only realistic result.

HEATH: I'm not sure anybody was aggressively putting their hand up to do

the last day. It was a bit of a short-straw situation. Still, if you're going to be up watching it play out to a draw anyway, you might as well be doing it with your mates in the ACC studios.

Although few people realised it at the time, the stage was actually set for New Zealand's greatest day in 91 years of test cricket. Jamieson mowed down Kohli, India's talisman, again; Henry 'Hairy Nipples' Nicholls took a great catch running back from point to get rid of the dangerous Rishabh Pant, and a few hours later Jason Hoyte had his baps out.

No one can be quite sure what heaven looks like in a world governed by the ACC, but it would be filled with days like that.

HOYTE: When you're a kid you dream about winning games of cricket for New Zealand. That dream ended for me when I stopped growing at eight. This was the next best thing for me.

LANE: A bloody long six nights. A lot of rain and a lot of time spent thinking that sharing a trophy wouldn't be the worst thing that could happen, especially after what we'd been through two years earlier at Lord's.

HEATH: That is a great philosophical question: would you be happy to retrospectively share the 2021 WTC if it meant you could share the 2019 CWC as well?

World Cup Morning Glory

FROM 3AM, MONDAY FINAL

LIVE WATCH ALONG COVERAGE ON 📘 ▶️ (((♥))) iHeart

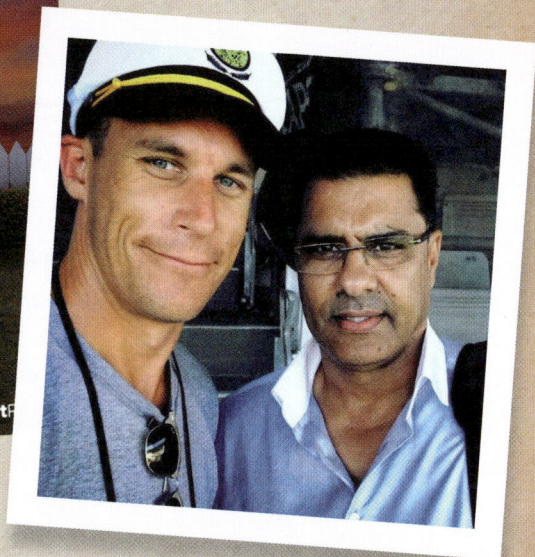

NEW ZEALAND VS AUSTRALIA, T20 WORLD CUP FINAL
DUBAI, 14 NOV 2021
Australia won by 8 wickets

New Zealand 172-4	Australia 173-2 (18.5 overs)
K Williamson 85 (48)	M Marsh 77* (50)
J Hazlewood 4-0-16-3	T Boult 4-0-18-2

FORD: Yes, 100 per cent.

Not long after that great moment, the Black Caps had a chance to get their hands on another ICC trophy. As has become the norm for New Zealand in recent times, they also made their way into the final of the biannual T20 World Cup, with Daryl 'Son of a Mitch' Mitchell pulverising England in the semifinal.

In the final in Dubai, Kane Williamson showed his all-format brilliance with 85 off 48 in setting up New Zealand's competitive 172 for 4 against the nemesis from across the Tasman. Guttingly, Davey Dumb-Dumb and Mitch Marsh batted superbly to lead Australia to a convincing eight-wicket win with seven balls in hand.

Bugger.

Joseph Durie's Guide to
ONLINE NOTORIETY

A great man once said, 'Get busy living or get busy dying.' Andy Dufresne may not have been active on Instagram, but he beautifully foreshadowed the world of social media. You're either all in or you're dead. You can't be half-pregnant; you're at the third trimester with every meme. You're either blind drunk on homerism (a devotee whose judgement is clouded by their love for a particular team) and the link between a fan's brain and your keyboard, or you're just another piece of wallpaper on the social media living room of sports coverage.

Make as many enemies as fans and, if you're good enough, some of those enemies become reluctant fans . . . and sometimes 1.4 billion Indians will insist that your mum enjoys sex with dogs. Usually all you need is a good Kane Williamson > Virat Kohli post. At other times, the requirements are slightly more nuanced. Anyway, lock up your mums and follow these steps if you want to have some fun and gain online cachet (or if cachet remains elusive, at the very least, some followers).

Get busy . . .

You're a fan, so act like it

We're not journalists. We're not award-winning media pundits writing a thesis on the social impact of the media on athletes. We're fans. We cheer, and if we're not cheering then we're probably crying and swearing at every terrible, horrible, no-good cheating call by the ref. We can be as biased as we want.

When we first started the ACC social presence, we took/stole a massive amount of inspiration from the social media accounts of the NHL's Los Angeles Kings. Back in 2012, the Kings' team of Dewayne Hankins and Pat Donahue changed how team accounts behaved forever — and for the better. No more 'Hooray, sport was the winner' or 'Good luck to the other team'. It was all-in or get out. In this vein, we celebrated any New Zealand victory no matter how big or small and shoved it in the face of the opposition and their fans — just like you would do on the couch, at the pub and at the ground.

Punch up, always

Never ever did I think creating stupid images about sport would see me subjected to death threats. Not just one or two, but hundreds. And not just me, but also my mother. Christine Durie has never been one for social media — except for sending adorable 'What family means' Facebook status updates once a year — and thankfully so. If she had been dropping GRWM reels* and making sure the entire world was updated on mindfulness and breath work, then the month of June 2021, the month the mighty Black Caps from a country of five million people humiliated Kohli's 1.4 billion Indians, would not have been good for her manifestation of positive energy.

You plan and God laughs

In my world there is no God, but this is a good way to think about whatever higher power is controlling the latest edition of the simulation we're living in. No matter what you think will happen and whatever you've got planned, it doesn't count for shit when the unexpected happens. In a world of streaming subscriptions and on-demand viewing, sport remains the Neo — the remainder of an otherwise perfect mathematical equation creating an algorithm to predict your next content consumption.

You MUST watch sports live. Don't schedule anything, or you might just curse something. You believe in bad ju-ju, right?

---

* Get Ready With Me

Your rugby commentary <u>tonight</u> was appalling, distasteful, disrespectful and offensive..! The disrespect to our National Anthem was disgusting and the coarse derogatory nicknames for our Allback team members and their opposition was crude and disrespectful. You knew little about the rules and at times unable to provide professional opinion on key moments in the game. You did the game of Rugby a great dishonour.

The customer is always right . . . and smarter, and funnier

Basically, everything good to come out of the ACC social channels has been created by a listener, or a viewer or user. The ACC audience is incredible. Ask and they will deliver. In spades. From teeing off from a mate's butthole, to a cricketing mangina, to nicknames, to songs, to memes. We're the outlet for anything that happens in sports, as soon as it happens. It's a wonderful and cursed realm to exist in. During its time in operation, the 0221 CURLY 6 phone was both a script of God and potential evidence in a criminal case.

In late 2015, while the Black Caps played Bangladesh in Nelson, we decided to ask listeners to send in brown-eyes for every boundary hit by Neil Broom during the run chase. It seemed like a harmless idea. After all, Broom had played 23 one-day internationals to that point. He was averaging 17.75. He had scored six ducks. He had accumulated a sum total of 29 boundaries at a rate of 1.26 boundaries per innings. We were on safe ground. Except we were not.

Broom scored an unbeaten 109. He hit eight fours and three sixes. And we saw at least 100 buttholes. It was a haunting insight into the breadth, and dark, hairy depth, of the audience we were dealing with. That sim card needs to be fired into the sun. Some things should be read out live on radio without any screening and then never heard again.

No regerts

There have only been a few cases that we've had to delete posts. Not because of our own moral compass, but mostly because an old guy jerking off to the virtual-reality version of his departed wife was too spicy for a client. Who'd have thought? (Don't worry, it was AI special effects.)

If you think you're going to have issues looking at your horrific meme in the cold, sober light of the day, don't send it. Otherwise, never delete. No regrets and no surrender.

Sports should be fun. Sports media should be fun. David Warner is a cheat.

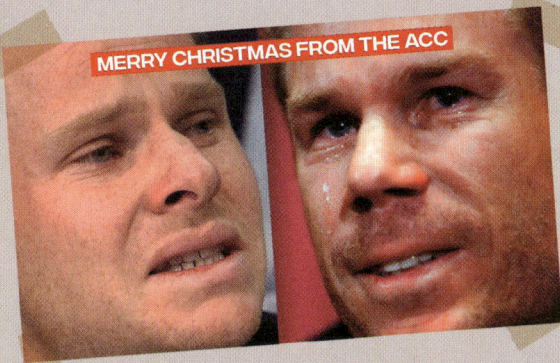

MERRY CHRISTMAS FROM THE ACC

TOKYO 2020 (TOOK PLACE IN 2021)

COUNTRY	GOLD	SILVER	BRONZE	TOTAL
New Zealand	7	6	7	20

Quite aside from these magnificent cricketing odysseys, 2021 was a bloody big year of sportsing.

Holding the Olympics in 2021 and still calling them the 2020 Summer Olympics sounds exactly like the sort of thing Leigh Hart would have done in *Olympico*, the show also starring Jeremy Wells and Jason Hoyte that took London by storm in 2012.

Nine years later, it was in Tokyo where New Zealand's seven golds won became their second-highest number ever behind the eight won in the boycott-hit games of 1984. The overall medal total of 20 was a record.

Gold in the women's rugby sevens provided great excitement and joy, but again it was water-skimming vehicles that proved the most efficient way of travelling around Tokyo. There were golds for Kerri Gowler and Grace Prendergast in the women's coxless pair, and Emma Twigg in the single sculls, while Lisa Carrington got really greedy and brought home three — the K1 200m and 500m, plus the K2 500m with Caitlin Regal. The biggest shock came in the men's eight, where the Hamish Bond-inspired crew pulled off an unexpected victory.

LEIGH HART: When you think about Olympic sports, nothing girds your loins and points to a nation's ideals of uncomplicated manhood quite like the men's eight. You're right to ask, is there any more manly sport on earth than the rowing eight?

The women's eight also won silver, as did Brooke Donoghue and Hannah Osborne in the double sculls.

Silvers were also returned in the men's rugby sevens, the sailing 49ers and two at the track cycling, with sprint sensation Ellesse Andrews finishing runner-up in the keirin and Campbell Stewart the same in the omnium.

The variety of sports represented by bronze was perhaps the most surprising and pleasing aspect of the games.

Lydia Ko added bronze to her 2016 silver in golf.

MATT HEATH: Really? Is golf an Olympic sport?

Dylan Schmidt finished third in trampoline.

MIKE LANE: All those hours trying to double-bounce your cousins off the tramp at Christmas finally paying off.

Marcus Daniell and Michael Venus won bronze in tennis doubles.

JASON HOYTE: Now I know you're taking the piss.

Add in Hayden Wilde restoring some pride in New Zealand's triathlon stocks, Tom Walsh and evergreen Valerie Adams throwing the shot put a long way, and David Nyika, the good-looking heavyweight boxer, securing bronze and the result was a great Olympics for New Zealand.

There are three bits of ACC business that need acknowledging before we close the book on this seminal year.

1) The ACC XI took on the Dulux Tradies XI in what has become an annual T20 cricket match. Held in a bucolic, back-country Hawke's Bay setting, the Tradies proved too strong, though much of the commentary attention focused on the efforts of opening batter Jason Hoyte.

'He's just so weak,' Heath said after Hoyte swung and missed his first ball. The statement turned out to be grotesquely unfair when Hoyte cut his fourth delivery

backward of point for four. There was much mirth at the size of his pads, too, an issue that would come back to haunt him in later editions of this match.

Still, he had the last laugh, scoring a cultured 13 off 28 deliveries.

2) The ACC stunned the media world by winning the 'Best Sports Reader, Presenter or Commentator' at the NZ Radio Awards. The named recipients, in a pointer to the growing coterie of talent assembled under the banner, included: Mike Lane, Jeremy Wells, Matt Heath, James McOnie, Jason Hoyte, Scotty J Stevenson, Mike Minogue, Manaia Stewart, Chris Key, Ben Hurley, Paul Ford, Dylan Cleaver, Leigh Hart, Joseph Durie, Joseph Shuker, Tom Harper and Claire Chellew. There is some conjecture that it is the most named winner on a single entry since the awards began.

3) Matt Heath and Mike Lane endured another commentary shocker — this time due not to Paralympic bowls, but an over-reliance on the hydrating properties of gin and tonic while broadcasting the closing moments of the America's Cup. It prompted another detailed explanation from Heath.

MATT HEATH: As I understand it, we had the radio broadcast rights for the America's Cup. It was quite the set-up, though. We had all the monitors, the effects mics and about seven or eight support crew. It was a semi-professional set-up and we were broadcasting live from the Viaduct — more specifically, from upstairs at Saint Alice, a bar and restaurant.

We knew the owners, great New Zealanders, and they kept sending G&Ts over. The jocularity started early, especially among the support crew.

They became very loud and in some cases obnoxious and, although they'll dispute this, I'm quite happy to shift the blame.

Lost in all the noise and carry-on was the news that racing had been delayed. We didn't get that, what turned out to be in hindsight quite vital, information.

You've got to remember that if Team New Zealand won that day, if they beat Luna Rossa, then we would retain the America's Cup, so this was a high-stakes, knife-edge situation. Team NZ were leading six to three and it was first to seven. With so much on the line, I expected a bit more from the people we employed to help us.

This was a Wednesday, if I recall, and as the race on our screens started, either Mike or I noted how uncannily it appeared to be unfolding just like Tuesday. Not once did we click, however, that it was unfolding uncannily like Tuesday's race because it was, in fact, Tuesday's race.

We were so geed up, slightly plastered on G&Ts and ready to trumpet New Zealand's invincibility on the high seas, their mastery of the foiling monohulls, when somebody came over and pulled the rug out from under us.

'Why are you getting so excited about a replay?' they asked.

We turned to our crew: 'Is this true? What the fuck are you guys doing?'

Joseph Durie, three sheets to the wind, looked a bit sheepish and said that they all thought it was part of our act. That we were doing a 'bit'.

Another said they weren't even watching it.

Two were discovered off in another part of the bar trying to chat up some girls.

To this day, whenever the incident comes up, and it comes up quite often, G-Lane and I will say: 'Where was our support?'

No, we weren't completely innocent on the G&T front, but nor did we deserve to be left marooned in a shipwreck not of our own making.

As it turned out, it might be the last day of America's Cup sailing in New Zealand in our lifetimes, so why not commentate two races instead of one?

2022

THE RUN OUT

In 2020, a large portion of cricket coverage in New Zealand had moved to Spark Sport, the short-lived alternative to Sky Sport, and 2022 marked the first time you could stream the ACC commentary on an app.

This meant the ACC found themselves starting their working year on New Year's Day when the Black Caps took to the field at Bay Oval for a test against Bangladesh without a guy who had become the third player in test history to take all 10 wickets in an innings . . . in the previous match.

Ajaz 'Jazz Hands' Patel produced the stunning figures of 10-119 at Wankhede Stadium, Mumbai, the city of his birth, in December 2021, but found himself surplus to requirements when the home test summer kicked off.

The match ended with a humiliating first loss at home in any format to Bangladesh. The previous year, the mountaintop had been scaled. People started to wonder if the slide down the other side might be steep.

The second match in the series saw the team commentating Ross Taylor's final test — against the same opposition, in Christchurch — a game that ended in the most inapt way, with Taylor's filthy offspin taking the final Bangladesh wicket in a crushing innings win.

A series against South Africa followed, with the spoils also shared, and in the winter a rare opportunity for a three-test series presented itself in England.

Under the brand-new regime of great New Zealanders Brendon McCullum and Ben Stokes, England decided to begin reinventing test cricket and the stuck-in-neutral Black Caps were their first victims, falling 0–3 in a series that could have just as easily been 3–0 in their favour.

That series would prove to be the test swansongs for two more WTC legends, Lovely Trenty Boult and the Minute Piece, Colin de Grandhomme. The dominoes were falling.

The test year ended in Karachi under the captaincy of Tim Southee, after Steady the Ship stood down to ease his commitments, but Williamson proved that, despite

NEW ZEALAND VS INDIA, 2ND TEST
MUMBAI, 3–6 DECEMBER 2021

India

M Agarwal	c Blundell b Patel	150
S Gill	c Taylor b Patel	44
C Pujara	b Patel	0
V Kohli	lbw Patel	0
S Iyer	c Blundell b Patel	18
W Saha	lbw Patel	27
R Ashwin	b Patel	0
A Patel	lbw Patel	52
J Yadav	c Ravindra b Patel	12
U Yadav	not out	0
M Siraj	c Ravindra b Patel	4
Extras		18
Total		**325**

Bowling	O	M	R	W
T Southee	22	6	43	0
K Jamieson	12	3	36	0
A Patel	47.5	12	119	10
W Somerville	19	0	80	0
R Ravindra	4	0	20	0
D Mitchell	5	3	9	0

the changing environment, some things remained constant, by scoring an epic unbeaten 200.

The white-ball format saw the emergence of a hard-hitting opener called Finn Allen, Fineous Slog, who had a big role to play as the Black Caps enjoyed a crushing and totally unexpected 89-run win against hosts Australia in the opener of the T20 World Cup after Covid had created a situation of back-to-back tournaments. It was fun while it lasted, but New Zealand eventually bowed out to Pakistan — a team they cannot beat in ICC white-ball tournaments — in the semifinals.

Women's cricket returned to the Commonwealth Games held in Birmingham, with the White Ferns securing a bronze medal on the back of captain Sophie Devine's unbeaten half century against England in the third-place playoff.

BIRMINGHAM 2022

COUNTRY	GOLD	SILVER	BRONZE	TOTAL
New Zealand	20	12	17	49

The ups and downs of the international game in 2022 paled into insignificance when placed alongside the biggest, and most replayed, cricket story of the year: Jason Hoyte run out for a duck in the ACC's match against the Tradies XI.

Here's how Jason Hoyte described the incident on *The BYC* podcast in the immediate aftermath of the event:

'Live from the Export Beer Garden Studios, you're listening to *The BYC*. It's often said that cricket can be a cruel game. On Friday, the fourth of November 2022, at the beautiful Bay Oval in Tauranga for the annual Dulux Tradies eleven versus the ACC eleven, the cricketing world witnessed an act that reverberated around the globe; an act so callous, so horrific that cricket lovers everywhere could only shake their heads in disbelief and disgust. Being run out is one of the more unfortunate ways to be dismissed, but even worse is to be run out in circumstances that bring shame and forever blight the reputation of the guilty party. For that travesty to be caught on camera only exacerbates the situation.

'I have in the last few days received tearful apologies from my *BYC* colleague Dylan Cleaver, whose extraordinary act of self-preservation, his blatant disregard for his partner, has seen him inundated with abuse online. I cannot stand for this. The fallout from the Dulux Tradies event has hit him hard. I have dug deep to forgive him and so must you. The fact it was probably the worst example of sawing off your partner is by the by and, besides, we have more important things to focus on, like the semifinals of the T20 World Cup.'

DYLAN CLEAVER: This was my first Tradies match. I'd padded up for the ACC a couple of times for games on the Eden Park Outer Oval, but never under the red-hot glare of the cameras.

JASON HOYTE: I'd played the year before at Clifton and was just moving through the gears in that match when I smashed one off the middle of the bat and midwicket took a screamer.

CLEAVER: I'd watched the 'highlights' of the year before and the one thing that struck me was how Hoyte needed youth pads because he couldn't run in full-sized gear.

HOYTE: I was looking forward to batting on Bay Oval. At Clifton I don't think the conditions necessarily played to my strengths, but in test conditions I was confident of a big score.

CLEAVER: I wasn't quite as confident. My eyesight isn't what it once was and I've never been able to rig up my glasses to stay on my head or stop fogging up. Anyway, I watched Jase block a couple and then got a couple of nudges away. Nothing to set the world on fire, but solid enough.

HOYTE: I was seeing it like a beach ball and knew I needed to farm the strike.

CLEAVER: I've seen what happened next enough times to be reasonably confident in its accuracy. I received a gentle ball on leg stump and flicked it off my thigh straight to backward square. No run.

HOYTE: It's behind square, it's my call. I've called 'yes' and taken off.

CLEAVER: I wasn't wearing my hearing aids. Didn't hear him call, didn't see him coming and assumed he wasn't. You can clearly see me raise my arm in the air — the universal signal of no run.

HOYTE: I forgot that Cleaver is basically deaf. So, I slammed on the brakes and started haring back to the non-striker's end.

MIKE LANE: There are two things I'll never forget about that run out. One is Cleaver's bowl haircut —that's pure Lloyd Christmas straight out of *Dumb and Dumber* . . .

CLEAVER: I experimented with a helmet for one ball and when I discarded it I left my hair as it was. Bad look . . . no two ways about it.

LANE: The second was, as Jase is trying to scramble back, his pads start to fall off.

HOYTE: I suffered a bit of a gear malfunction.

CLEAVER: I didn't know whether to cry about the miscommunication or laugh about the state of Jase and his gear. I took the laugh option.

LANE: Who can't put a pair of pads with Velcro straps on properly?

HOYTE: I'm trying to muster whatever dignity I have left and I look up and Joe Durie's got a camera in my face for the social media channels.

DURIE: I take my job pretty seriously and it was clear that this was a pivotal moment in history that needed recording.

MATT HEATH: A captain of a team has never been more happy to see their opening batter run out than G-Lane watching on. Being run out for nought is bad enough, but a massive gear failure just added to the shame.

HOYTE: That's what makes Lane such a good leader. He always has your back.

CLEAVER: The funny thing is, the night before when we were doing a bit of team bonding at the pub, one of the ACC bigwigs sidled up to me to tell me I was opening with Hoyte and to give him a short leash before running him out, because they didn't want another 'Clifton situation'. It was a genuine cock-up, though. I did feel bad about it and I was getting some deserved grief on socials. I momentarily feared for my safety.

HOYTE: My fans were understandably not happy. Another big score nipped in the bud.

CLEAVER: It's probably time to acknowledge the truth: the run out was 70 per cent my fault. I sold poor old Jase down the river. But, Christ, it was funny.

The rugby highlight of 2022 was undoubtedly the Black Ferns' World Cup win against England in front of a record crowd at Eden Park.

HEATH: That was a mindwarp of a fortnight, from the drama of the end of the semifinal against France [Caroline Drouin missed a kick at the death that preserved the Black Ferns' 25–24 lead] to one of the greatest sporting finals ever played. It felt like a big moment for the country, too, a celebration of women's sport on a scale that might have been unthinkable a generation or two ago.

Some late Stacey Waaka magic led to a second try for Ayesha Leti-I'iga, which led to a 34–31 victory and Ruby Tui leading a 40,000-strong rendition of 'Tūtira Mai Ngā Iwi' after the final whistle. It was a campaign that captured the nation and completed an incredible turnaround for a team that had lost four consecutive matches on the previous year's European tour.

For the All Blacks, it was the year of the Great Coaching Debate, or Really Tedious Coaching Debate depending on your view of the world. The team started the year so badly that it appeared a racing certainty that Ian Foster was about to get the heave-ho for Scott Robertson, who had seven Super Rugby titles on his CV.

The All Blacks won their first test of the year against Ireland in Auckland, then went on a horror run, losing to the same opposition twice and then being easily turned over by the Springboks in Mbombela. That made it five losses in six tests, and in the background Razor Robertson was instructed to send a Telex and assemble his coaching team.

On cue, the All Blacks pulled off a spirited win in Johannesburg and Razor was told to hastily disassemble that coaching team and to stay quiet about it. Foster was 'backed' through to the end of the 2023 World Cup, and the team, the majority of the senior players having publicly supported the coach, celebrated that announcement by losing to Argentina in Christchurch.

As a halfway-house solution, New Zealand Rugby then started the appointment process for the next coach and Robertson won the job, leaving Foster as a lame duck for the next 12 months.

James McOnie

"Quick txt here from the Rangiora Golf Club... can confirm the keys are now in the bowl!"

UNMISSABLE

LEIGH HART: And another thing, it's probably not on topic, but what the hell is going on with this whole Foster–Robertson thing? New Zealand Rugby needs its head read. It's got so confusing I wouldn't be surprised if both showed up to the next Rugby World Cup. Maybe that wouldn't be a bad thing.

So, of course, at the peak of the will-he-stay-or-will-he-go shemozzle, Foster's All Blacks started playing well again.

HART: And don't get me started on the board. What are they doing about grassroots rugby? When is that money going to start to filter down? And don't get me started on Pacific rugby and how we've hung the Tongans, the Samoans, the Niueans and the Tokelauans out to dry. And don't get me started on what they've done to the NPC . . .

Unfortunately, we had to cut Leigh off as he was five pints of Knife Party deep and started threatening to phone Murray Deaker to get some things off his chest.

Take it as read that the coaching crisis was an unholy shambles.

COMMENTARY AGENDA

* Shoot/Shag/Marry — Sameer from the ANZ ads, David Warner, Kevin Pietersen
* Best Sporting Gullivers
* Big Units XI
* Lee Baker's gender reassignment

IF ONLY WE'D BEEN THERE

An alternative history project, by Lee Baker

As a long-time history buff — I graduated from Auckland University with a Master of Arts in History and Art History, achieving first-class honours, not to mention a first-class ticket to nowhere — I've often wondered how great moments in New Zealand sporting history may have benefitted from commentary by the ACC. If only the ACC team had been there, in the caravan, on the scene and on the mic with the official call. How might our unique lens have changed the way Kiwis think about themselves?

They say history is written by the victors. Actually, it's written by historians, and as commentators we are the first historians on the scene, calling it as we see it — writing the story of New Zealand as we go.

A story that might have been quite different. Consider, if you will . . .

1953

ED HILLARY AND TENZING NORGAY CONQUER EVEREST

Jason Hoyte: Good evening New Zealand, you join us at the top of Mount Everest and the news from out in the middle is that it is absolutely sheeting down up here.

Mike Lane: But at least it's not raining, Jase.

Hoyte: Indeed, it's more of a blizzard.

Lane: Which means play can continue. The surface, while not ideal for cricket, is a reasonable track by mountaineering standards — hard and fast, slippery as hell.

Jeremy Wells: It won't be anything these climbers haven't seen before, as we await the first members of this British expedition to conquer Everest. Will it be the affable New Zealander, Edmund Hillary — a humble bee-fancier from Auckland — and his often forgotten Sherpa companion, Tenzing Norgay?

Hoyte: Perhaps I'm snow blind but to me the top of the mountain looks like one huge, glorious test-cricket sightscreen — white, featureless, a blank canvas awaiting the brush of history to be dragged across it, writing a new chapter in the story of our young nation.

Wells: Beautifully put, Jase. Who's that emerging from the mist? Is that a yeti?

Leigh Hart: Did someone say yeti?

Lane: No, it's the Kiwi pair, steaming in now from the China end . . . what a partnership this has been, Paul Ford.

Paul Ford: It's a record partnership, Mike, now worth almost 29,000 feet and counting.

Hoyte: Here they come, Hillary and Tenzing — Tenzing the local lad, what a great moment for him in front of his home crowd, even if they are languishing in a godforsaken valley kilometres below us.

Wells: Good to see Hillary using his feet, albeit slowly.

Hoyte: He's inching towards the summit. I feel like I'm watching the slow-motion replay, but I'm assured that this is live, if only just.

Lane: Looks like he's going to come around the summit, no, beg your pardon, he's going to come over the summit.

Hart: Yes, that's the point. If they go around, they'll surely come up short.

Hoyte: Hillary, squinting into the gale-force wind now, like a man about to receive some chin music from Jack 'The Bull' Cowie.

Wells: Just a few more steps.

Hoyte: Hillary, on the front foot now, lurching forward, rock-solid technique and — wait for it . . . Yes, there it is. There it is! A New Zealander's boot has set foot on the world's tallest summit, what a moment! The first man on top of Everest, and he's a Kiwi.

Wells: Hang on!

Hoyte: Oh no, wait a minute. Wait a minute.

Lane: We're just taking a look at that again, hang on.

Ford: Actually, I think part of his foot is just short of the line there.

Hart: This could be one short.

Hoyte: Surely, they won't review this? Surely?!

Ford: Nonetheless, I think we may need to go upstairs here.

Hart: Upstairs? We're literally on top of the world, it would be downstairs if anything.

Hoyte: It doesn't matter, he's planted the flagpole and Tenzing is taking the photo. There it is, the crucial proof of this great moment.

New Zealand will not be denied.

Matt Heath: A photo? Is that all we get?

Hart: I would have done this at sea level, in a studio with a wind machine and half a tonne of polystyrene balls, could have saved a lot of time and money.

Hoyte: Be that as it may, history has been made here, New Zealand. A beekeeper from Auckland, Edmund Percival Hillary, has become the first man to stand atop the world's highest peak.

Heath: What a day for the sport of . . . for the sport of . . . what is this sport? Is this even a sport?

Hoyte: It's mountaineering, Matt, yes it's a sport, well, it is now. We'll take it, thank you very much.

Heath: I wouldn't be surprised if we dine out on this for years, seizing on this singular achievement to define our tiny, pathetic, often overlooked islands at the bottom of the world.

Hoyte: Perhaps, but he's got to get down first.

Ford: Speaking of which, get down off me, Lane.

Lane: We knocked the . . .

Ford: Bugger off, Lane!!!

1955

NEW ZEALAND
ALL OUT FOR 26

Wells: Welcome back to Eden Park where New Zealand are in all sorts of trouble against England here at twenty-six for nine, and we've only had twenty-six overs.

Lane: We have been absolutely pumped by our former colonial masters, Jerry . . . If England is the mother country, then this is some kind of unholy incest.

Manaia Stewart: Beautifully put, Lane.

Wells: Settle down, Mike. Believe it or not, we are on the cusp of history here.

Heath: What the hell are you talking about, Jerry?

Wells: Stats man, Leigh Hart, what is the current record for the lowest test score in an innings?

Hart: Hard to say, Jerry, I haven't actually been born yet, but if I was to take a guess . . . I'd say . . . it's more than twenty-six — this is a chance for New Zealand to rewrite the history books.

Ford: Come on New Zealand, this is a golden opportunity for us to set a world record for the lowest test score. I can tell you Leigh Hart and Jeremy, that South Africa currently hold the record. Twice they were dismissed for thirty against England, once at Port Elizabeth in 1896 and also in 1924 at Birmingham. At twenty-six we currently hold it, just one more wicket and history will be made.

Hart: Thanks Paul, great facts there.

Lane: I've got more caravan thickness than usual, but this feels weird.

Ford: Hayes is on zero, so far three New Zealand batsmen have been dismissed for a duck.

Stewart: Can he become the fourth?

Wells: Hayes, facing Statham, the number eleven. In comes Statham, bowled him! Out! Clean bowled. New Zealand are all out for twenty-six! It's a world record.

Ford: Absolutely brilliant from New Zealand, they've done it — a world record set in world-record time.

Lane: They said it couldn't be done, but they found a way.

Stewart: Absolutely fucking brilliant. Again, New Zealand dumbfounds its critics. Twenty-six all out!

Wells: Twenty-six runs that will live in infamy . . .

Hart: Twenty-six — I've scored more Miss New Zealands than that.

Stewart: And the sad thing is, I think if you'd offered that to them this morning, they would have taken it.

Heath: We can put a man on Everest but we can't score thirty fucking runs in a test-match innings? Jesus.

Wells: It really is brilliant. This will go down as one of the all-time great, appalling cricketing efforts from New Zealand.

Lane: What a triumph! Hear that? Do you hear that sound?

Stewart: What sound?

Lane: That is the sound of the history books being rewritten.

Wells: Well, I'm sure we won't have the ignominy of holding this record for long.

1980

COLIN CROFT VS FRED GOODALL

Lane: Welcome back to Lancaster Park in Christchurch as we watch Paddles, Richard Hadlee, and Jeremy Coney continue. They're just a few more bad umpiring decisions away from securing their maiden test centuries here.

Heath: I've got to say, there's a lot of tension in the air. It's almost as though the West Indians don't think our completely biased New Zealand umpires are being fair.

Lane: Here's Croft to Hadlee, wide of the crease, it's another bouncer and Hadlee tries to hook. It brushes the glove, Deryck Murray takes the catch down the leg side and all the West Indians go up as one. It's a huge appeal, but 'not out' says Fred Goodall.

Wells: The West Indians are not happy. They've had more refusals than a huntaway cross trying to split the sheep on *A Dog's Show*.

Heath: It's almost as though the West Indians expect a batsman being caught off his glove to be given out. Well, we do things differently down here. Welcome to New Zealand.

Lane: Words are being exchanged. Goodall, our most experienced test umpire, is standing in his fiftieth first-class match, not that you'd know it. Steve Woodward comes in from square leg.

Wells: The umpires are approaching West Indian captain Clive Lloyd, who hasn't moved a muscle from his position at first slip. Goodall is having words, but this is like watching a ventriloquist's dummy talking to the guy with his hand up its arse. What's the punchline? One wonders.

Lane: He's folding his arms, Lloyd, as, like some Guyanese Gulliver, he peers down at the Kiwi umpires. Who knows what they're saying, but I can tell you the body language is all four-letter words right now.

Heath: Who can blame the West Indians? They've been sent to the bottom of the world, they don't like the food, they don't like the three-star motels, they don't like the weather and they don't like the officiating. Not only that, they find themselves in Christchurch.

Hart: Sausages and beans, Matt.

Heath: Sausages and beans what, Leigh?

Hart: That's what they've been fed at every break, Matt, and even at this relatively nutrition-naive point in history, I think we can see the high-performance shortcomings of that offering.

Lane: Fred has reluctantly returned to his position behind the stumps. Here's Croft coming in again to Hadlee. And that's another bouncer and this time a no-ball is called. Colin Croft doesn't like it. That's the eleventh time he has been called.

[LOUD BOOS FROM THE CROWD]

Ford: Do you see what he's done there? He tipped the bails off with his fingers as he walked past Goodall, who has left it to Coney to pick up and place them atop the stumps once more.

Lane: Croft is fuming. Here he comes again, steaming in from the Christchurch Civic Creche end.

Heath: He's coming in hot, look at that angle.

[MUFFLED GRUNT ON THE EFFECTS MIC]

Lane: And whack, he's gone straight into the umpire and Fred Goodall has fallen away to his right, clutching his left arm like a wounded soldier.

Wells: Beautiful action, Colin Croft . . . reminds me of the whirling dervishes.

Lane: Push has literally come to shove here at Lancaster Park.

Wells: Hard to tell if that was a genuine accident, a poorly timed come-on, or an aggravated assault, but one thing I can tell you is that is a no-ball.

Hart: It might be a dead ball, Jerry. It's definitely a dead arm for Fred.

Ford: He's certainly put the striker back into 'non-striker's' end, Colin Croft.

Lane: Let's have a look at the replay. Matt Heath, talk us through it.

Heath: Colin Croft, off his long run, lovely rhythm . . . beautiful fluid wind-up, arms high and whack! Straight into the umpire. Perfect technique, you have to say, that is not a ball he bowls often.

Lane: Absolutely bang on. I thought he was coming over the wicket, but I much prefer this through-the-umpire approach.

Wells: Fred doesn't like it. He has convinced the square-leg umpire, Woodward, to come with him for another chat with Lloyd. I wonder what he's saying to Woodward.

Lane: He's saying: 'What is the sanction for a bowler mugging the umpire and how do I signal it?'

Hart: Woodward, smartly, remains at least a step or two behind Goodall as they approach Lloyd, who once again seems fairly blasé about the whole show.

Ford: Fred is still clutching his left arm. Fortunately that's not the arm that raises the finger, so it won't stop him firing West Indian batsmen at will.

1992

SPINNING RHOMBUS
JUMPS FOR GOLD

Hoyte: Hello and welcome to the ACC's continued coverage of the Games of the twenty-fifth Olympiad, live from Barcelona, Spain. If you're huddled around the screen at this early hour of the morning, grab that cup of Bournvita, chuck a few more Carbonettes on the fire and get Mum to throw together some cheese and Marmite on toast. And if none of that warms the cockles, this might: the New Zealand three-day eventing team is poised to win gold after a stunning cross-country performance yesterday and a great start to the showjumping today.

Lane: You're spot on, Jase. What a comeback this has been, after Mark Todd's mount got into trouble with a few too many rails going down yesterday and was eliminated. Leigh Hart, too many rails has been the difference.

Hart: Absolutely, Mike. I probably should have stopped after four or five last night.

Lane: I'm talking about the rails on the equestrian course. The horses. There were a few refusals causing problems out there, talk us through it.

Hart: It's true, I think her name was Juanita. She was a definite 'no', I probably should have checked if she was married, to be fair.

Lane: I'm talking about the refusals on the course, Mark Todd's mount Welton Greylag refused at a few of the jumps, that was all it took. But the good news is we're in with a chance here today in the showjumping, Matt Heath.

Heath: Welton Greylag sounds like a character in an Agatha Christie novel to me, perhaps it's for the best Mark Todd was eliminated. I think our horses need to have confidence-inspiring names, names that sound like winners. Think Phar Lap, think Charisma. Who are we rooting for today, anyway?

Lane: Spinning Rhombus.

Heath: Spinning what?

Lane: Rhombus.

Heath: What the hell is a rhombus?

Hoyte: It's a quadrilateral, Matt Heath. A quadrilateral whose four sides are of equal length.

Heath: I take from that this horse has four legs and they are all the same length — that has to be a good thing.

Hoyte: Of course a horse is only as good as their rider, Matt Heath. Andrew Nicholson is under a lot of pressure, but spirits are high in the New Zealand team, Paul Ford.

Ford: That's one way of putting it, Jase. Toddy's on a real high, as are most followers of this powerhouse New Zealand team. After his sensational cross-country run yesterday, Blyth Tait has taken Messiah out and jumped a clear round. He was followed by Victoria Latta and Chief, who dropped just the one rail.

Hart: Just one rail? I admire her restraint.

Hoyte: Play is about to get under way here at the magnificent Real Club de Polo de Barcelona venue. Stats man Leigh Hart, do you have any idea how this sport is scored?

Hart: I don't to be honest, Jase. I just know too many rails can get you in trouble.

Ford: Precisely, Leigh Hart, it's five points down for a rail. New Zealand has forty-two points up its sleeve over Australia, so Nicholson can afford to drop eight rails over the eleven fences on the course and gold will still be ours.

Lane: In other words, Spinning Rhombus would need to spin completely out of control for us to lose from here. I can feel a gold rush coming on.

Hoyte: Just finally, Leigh Hart, as Nicholson readies to make his entrance, the eternal question: man or beast?

Hart: Are we playing shoot, shag or marry?

Hoyte: No, man or beast? Which is most important in equestrian?

Hart: I'd say beast, as in beast-mode.

Ford: Rider, no doubt, Jase. These are brilliant athletes and technicians — think Hadlee, Crowe and Michael Jones rolled into one — they can take the equestrian equivalent of a Hillman Hunter and turn it into a Ferrari for a day.

Hoyte: Ferrari For A Day sounds like a great name for a horse. The kind you'd put a few hundred on. Righto, New Zealand, brace yourself, the flag has dropped and we're under way here. Spinning Rhombus approaches the first fence and, oooh, he looked a bit hesitant clearing that, but that's one safely completed.

Lane: We can't beat Australia at cricket, surely we can beat them at forcing animals to jump on demand. Nicholson says jump, Spinning Rhombus says how high, am I right?

Hoyte: If only it were that simple, Lane. He's clipped the second fence, this is a wobbly start, as he approaches the third.

[LOUD CRASH]

Lane: Shit the bed, Spinning Rhombus has knocked down his first rail.

Heath: That was a full-frontal assault. This is not looking good.

[ANOTHER RATTLE FOLLOWED CLOSELY BY ANOTHER]

Hoyte: Jesus Christ, Nicholson has knocked down three in a row.

Hart: This would make a great drinking game — sink one for every rail dropped — but I'm not sure anyone could drink this fast.

[MORE CRASHES AND RATTLES]

Heath: What he did to that last fence was a hate crime. Is it possible Spinning Rhombus has somehow been radicalised by more sinister horses in the stable?

Lane: What in god's name am I watching here? This is starting to look more like a rodeo in formal wear.

Heath: Spinning Rhombus is behaving more like a circus elephant gone AWOL. Call the police.

Ford: I'm hearing we could have a ketamine situation here . . . a lowly stable-hand might have put some of the tranquilliser in Spinning Rhombus's oats.

Hart: Of course, Special-K. I've seen this sort of thing before and I can tell you that Spinning Rhombus is showing all the telltale signs of having fallen down a K-hole.

[CRASH]

Lane: There goes the eighth fence crashing to the ground.

Hoyte: One more mistake and it's all over . . . He's just gotta guide Spinning Rhombus over a few more jumps for god's sake, just a few more rails to clear. It all comes down to this for Andrew Nicholson. All those punishing early-morning starts at the local pony club, all those Saturday afternoons coming home smelling like a horseshit and equine liniment, all those mocking, sneering teenage girls from pony club teasing young Andrew about his horse's ill-timed erections knocking over the rails and embarrassing all those incredibly MILFy, oh-so-fine Remuera mums in their Land Rovers and Jaguars, all those saddle sores and strained thighs and stupid bow ties, it all comes down to this . . .

[CRASHING SOUND]

Lane: There it goes, that's the ninth rail!

Hoyte: And like sand through the hourglass, gold has slipped through New Zealand's fingers here in Barcelona today . . .

Lane: Gold turns to silver in the worst kind of alchemy.

Hoyte: That's right, Lane. Forget gold, it's silver, New Zealand, but it might as well be bronze, or lead or even tin as far as I'm concerned. Gold has gone begging and it was gold or nothing for me. Do we even deserve a medal? It might as well be a piece of soggy balsa wood for all I care. After a performance like that, it might as well be steam, just a cloud of steam, that's how empty this whole thing feels. A puff of steam once was hopeful water, turning to vapour, evaporating in the Barcelona heat, like our gold-medal hopes.

Lane: Great call, Jase. I think this is why I only follow horses that run around in reliable circles.

Ford: And have slightly less ridiculous names.

Heath: Spinning Rhombus, I'm sure that was the name of a useless Dunedin student band I used to see at university. I may have even slept with the bass player. Spinning Rhombus, I never want to hear that name again.

Hart: Spinning Rhombus can spin off to the glue factory as far as I'm concerned.

Lane: What a disaster. This has been like watching a super-slow-motion nine-car pile-up on the Northern Motorway . . .

Ford: Involving Hillman Hunters.

Heath: Hillman Hunter, great name for a horse.

2003

AMERICA'S CUP
— RACE FOUR

Hoyte: Good afternoon New Zealand, you join us on the sparkling waters of the Hauraki Gulf for race four of nine in the America's Cup. Here come the boats, beating away to windward . . . like two demented swans.

Lane: Conditions today best described as wet, Leigh Hart. How much is that likely to be a factor?

Hart: Not much, to be honest, Mike. It's wet above and below right now, that's pretty much the idea with sailing.

Lane: There's Alinghi, helmed by former Team New Zealand skipper Russell Coutts. Some call him a traitor, but the truth is he's being paid millions to cock his head to one side like an inquisitive poodle and say nothing, and right now he's doing a brilliant job of it.

Hoyte: Alinghi, in the grey and red, is leading Team New Zealand in black, not that you could possibly tell. This has all the spectacle of a pair of spectacles.

Heath: Hard to believe we're being schooled in sailing by a challenge from a landlocked country. I'm surprised their boat can even operate in salt water.

Hart: You might be interested to know, Matt, that Lake Geneva covers 580 square kilometres and in 1827 it was used to test the speed of sound. Plenty of room to sail a boat around there, which I believe the likes of Charlie Chaplin, Audrey Hepburn and even that great New Zealander Freddie Mercury used to do in their spare time. But you're right, it is a freshwater lake.

Hoyte: Well, the salt water doesn't seem to be bothering Alinghi — apparently they're slightly in front, not that you can tell looking at this wide shot of open water. And people say test cricket is boring.

Wells: But there's something wonderfully pure about this sport. It's just man versus the elements — and a few hundred million bucks belonging to faceless billionaires.

Lane: People say America's Cup racing is just a rich man's sport. I don't think that's fair. I'm not sure you can call this a sport. But it's a great pissing contest.

Hart: And just to make it more interesting, they're pissing into the wind. We're four minutes away from the top mark . . . if that helps.

Hoyte: It doesn't. But we'll let you know if absolutely anything happens in this extremely wet, paint-drying spectacle off the coast of Auckland.

[LONG PAUSE. SILENCE]

Hoyte: Not much to say here, to be honest. This is about as exciting as the opening credits to the 1970s British maritime drama *The Onedin Line.*

Lane: What this sport needs is more action. Or any action. Perhaps a whale sighting, or even a Hector's dolphin — the yachting equivalent of a streaker. Anything!

[A LOUD BANG]

Hoyte: Wait a minute, wait a minute! Either Team New Zealand has just unveiled a radical new collapsible mast design or their mast has just snapped like a twig. Spectacular!

Heath: Looks like a rapid unscheduled mast-reduction event to me. Or it's a sensational bluff.

Hoyte: Oh dear, oh dear. A mighty tōtara has fallen.

Heath: It's more like carbon fibre I think, Jase.

Hoyte: Shards of carbon fibre are showering down on the crew like some kind of sick confetti, except they won't be celebrating a win today.

Wells: Suddenly *NZL 82* looks like some dismal piece of origami that's been left in the rain . . .

Heath: Normally you wait until the race has finished before you take the mast down, this is highly unconventional from TNZ . . .

Ford: Hopefully the mast is still under warranty.

Wells: I know middle-aged men can have trouble hoisting the mainsail, but this is a whole new world of humiliation.

Hart: Dean Barker is on the walkie talkie . . . Who's he calling? The coastguard? The AA?

Hoyte: Neither will be able to help with this . . .

[SAILOR ONBOARD: 'FUCKING BOAT!']

Lane: And all the crew can do is swear like sailors . . . That's got to be the call of the day: 'Fucking boat!' indeed.

Wells: Well, there was talk they had pushed the design envelope to the limit. They were supposed to *push* the design envelope, not slice themselves open on it, leaving an entire nation to bleed to death from a paper cut.

Heath: What a humiliator!

Lane: You mixed that metaphor like a cocktail, Jeremy Wells. And now the sailors look like they are mixing one, too, as they literally bail water out of their racing yacht.

Heath: Okay, the mast snapped like a twig, and the New Zealand defence lies in tatters . . . but how about that wave? We can take a lot of pride in that wave, that was a great New Zealand wave — stoic, indestructible, not taking shit from long pieces of expensive fibreglass.

Lane: That's right, Matt, this is a victory for New Zealand's maritime conditions.

Heath: Another triumph for the mighty azure waters of the Hauraki Gulf. What a great New Zealander!

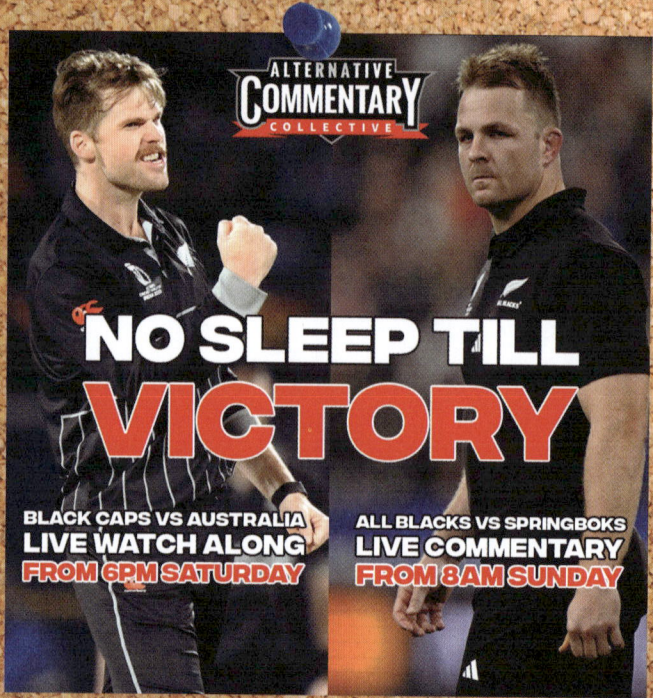

ALTERNATIVE COMMENTARY COLLECTIVE

NO SLEEP TILL
VICTORY

BLACK CAPS VS AUSTRALIA
LIVE WATCH ALONG
FROM 6PM SATURDAY

ALL BLACKS VS SPRINGBOKS
LIVE COMMENTARY
FROM 8AM SUNDAY

2023

SLEEPLESS NIGHT, WOUNDING MORNING

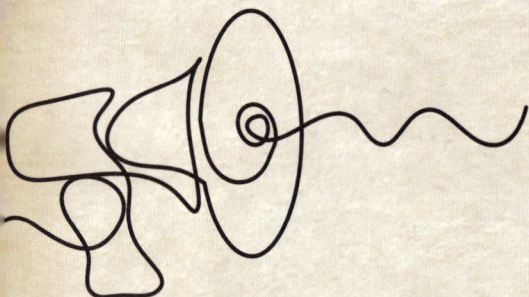

At least the Silver Ferns had bailed out the country in 2019 — what can you say about 2023 . . .

MATT HEATH: A complete shitter of a World Cup year.

PAUL FORD: Yet two of the greatest cricket tests I've ever seen were played back-to-back.

Our flagship sports teams might have been sputtering, but the ACC, however, were firing on multi-platforms, with *Champagne Rugby* transmogrifying into podcast form, led by comedian Tony Lyall.

Aural pleasure was something the ACC had become serious about, with its podcast offerings expanding and contracting by the season. *The Noob Squad*, a gaming podcast, ran for two years and more than 50 shows, while *The Benchwarmers* covered the 2022–23 NBA season.

Between Two Beers, the long-form interview podcast, was part of the ACC stable before an amicable separation when the show started evolving beyond sport. Since 2022, the racing and betting podcast *Boys Get Paid* has joined the network.

Alternative commentary of Super Rugby, the All Blacks and Warriors was all carried under the yellow button on Sky, giving the ACC the unofficial title of the most prolific calling team in New Zealand.

Adding even more strings to their bow, the ACC also commentated the Netball World Championships live from a studio in Auckland as the Ferns fell in the semifinals in South Africa.

While you could argue there was nothing as acutely agonising as the Black Caps' two-time-tie that became a boundary-countback Lord's tragedy, the one-point loss in the Rugby World Cup final was close, particularly given the wounding input from off-field match officials, who played a pivotal role in the no-sense-of-occasion red card awarded to Sam 'The Cleveland Steamer' Cane, a disallowed try and just general annoyingness.

"IT WORRIES ME HOW MUCH I ENJOY THIS COMMENTARY..."

KIERAN REA

A crap result can be lived with, but a crap result in a crap game is just that much more difficult to come to terms with. The 12–11 Springboks victory had few redeeming features, coming as it did on the back of an ACC all-nighter that saw New Zealand lose a thrilling match to Australia in Dharamshala during the round-robin stages of the Cricket World Cup (we'll get to that shortly).

Billed as another instalment of 'No Sleep 'Til Victory', this was to be a commentary double-header where no sleep was to be had.

JASON HOYTE: I feel like we curse these sorts of events with marketing like that, but who am I to argue with the genius of Mike Lane?

A couple of weeks earlier, the All Blacks met red-hot favourite Ireland in a quarter-final for the ages. Let's go back to the last 90 seconds of that match, with the men in green in possession and throwing everything they have at the All Blacks.

MIKE LANE: They maintain possession, twelve phases, the Irish. One and a half minutes left, I can't deal, I can't deal.

TONY LYALL: A penalty won't do it, they have to score a try.

LANE: Conor Murray, Sexton to Ringpiece, oh a half-break, they continue to the right-hand side.

One minute remaining, the pressure is INTENSE!

MATT HEATH: Fifteen phases, it's relentless, they've got to score.

LANE: They're just inside the All Blacks' ten-metre line, one minute remaining, the pressure is INTENSE!

This malarkey continues for some time, with the ball moving left and right, the phases stacking up, the clock running into overtime and the commentary team getting increasingly hoarse.

LANE: Time is up! Time is up on the clock. The greatest quarter-final of all time, which way is it going to go? Time is up, one mistake is all they need. Into the twenty-two . . . it's scrappy.

LYALL: It's got to be a penalty to the All Blacks!

LANE: No, they've got it, still. He [Ardie Savea] was begging for the penalty, but here come Ireland, spinning it to the left. They've got numbers out to the left.

There is a danger that the three-person team might spontaneously combust as, against all odds, Ireland are refusing to drop it and New Zealand are refusing to buckle. As the phases tick towards 30, it is fast becoming one of the great stonewall defensive displays of all time.

LANE: It's relentless. Oh my god, I'm going to have a heart attack! They're on the twenty-two, they have plenty of numbers out left.

LYALL: They just need to D up and get one mistake from Ireland.

HEATH: Come on the All Blacks!

Ireland thrust their way inside the 22, with Bundee Aki taking a short Johnny Sexton pass and almost getting his arms free in the tackle. These are desperate times, and not just for those on the field. Mike Lane sounds in desperate need of oxygen.

LANE: Ireland still have it, ten metres out. They have to score a try to make the semis.

HEATH: THIRTY-FIVE PHASES!

LANE: Kelleher . . .

HEATH: Oh, big D . . .

YYYYEEEEEESSSSSSSSSS!

LANE: Penalty to the All Blacks! And they win. Take your number-one [ranking], take your favourites tag and shove it in your . . .

Yeah, things slid a little for the next few seconds after that, with even the Cranberries unfairly dragged into Lane's orbit of angry ecstasy, but geez, what a win!

If that had been the final, rugby would have been talked about in every corner of the globe for its intensity and stupendous action. Unfortunately, the quarter-final weekend proved to be the high point of the tournament, with neither the semifinals or final coming close to replicating the magic of the first weekend of knockouts.

NEW ZEALAND VS IRELAND, WORLD CUP QUARTER-FINAL
PARIS, FRANCE, 14 OCTOBER 2023

New Zealand 28   24 Ireland

Fainga'anuku (19)	Aki (27)
Savea (33)	Gibson-Park (39)
Jordan (53)	Penalty try (64)
Conversions: Mo'unga 1/2 (21), J Barrett 1/1 (54)	Conversions: J Sexton 2/2 (29, 40)
Penalties: Mo'unga 1/1 (8), J Barrett 2/3 (14, 69)	Penalties: J Sexton 1/2 (22)

NEW ZEALAND VS SOUTH AFRICA, WORLD CUP FINAL
PARIS, FRANCE, 28 OCTOBER 2023

New Zealand 11   12 South Africa

B Barrett 58	Penalties: Pollard 4/4 (3, 13, 19, 34)
Penalties: Mo'unga 2/2 (17, 38)	

Without a shadow of a doubt, Kane Williamson has been the most dominant single figure in the first decade of the ACC's existence.

PAUL FORD: The ACC would have been successful and outrageous regardless of the Black Caps' results, but there's no doubt the smorgasbord of magic moments from Kane over the past ten years has meant the commentary has developed a built-in sense of optimism, expectation, positivity and confidence that would not have been possible in most eras of New Zealand cricket.

MATT HEATH: We released the ACC captain's hats that became ubiquitous at games before Kane even became captain. They were symbolic of his ability to heroically and skilfully weather the storm for his country. He healed weary, damaged and seasick fans; welcomed us back on board and then set a course across turbulent seas to greatness.

It stands to reason that Williamson and the ACC are inextricably linked because they mirror each other in so many respects: they're both brash, outspoken iconoclasts in their field. They court controversy as a matter of course. They're mercurial, emotional and prone to irrational outbursts. They both sprinkle their conversations and quotes with childish innuendo.

Or maybe that's just one of them.

FORD: Williamson goes about his business in an unassuming, hard-working, ego-free way —the exact opposite of the ACC — a quality that New Zealanders appreciate from their heroes. Quietly striving to stand out, steely determination, no gimmicks or bullshit, uncontroversial and fair, fleeting glimpses of emotion, and punching above his weight is the Kane way — and it's the way Kiwis like to see themselves on the global stage.

Is it any coincidence that Williamson's peak years coincided with the arrival of the ACC? Williamson's pre- and post-ACC numbers make for revealing reading. From the ACC's starting point in January 2014, Williamson's statistics have exploded to a point where correlation must surely equal causation.

At the end of 2013, Williamson had four test centuries and was averaging 35.88.

From the ACC's arrival to the end of the 2023–24 summer, he has added a further 28 centuries and is averaging 63.75 in that span.

In ODI cricket, he had posted three centuries and was averaging 35.21. Post-ACC he has 10 centuries and is averaging 53.64.

His pre-ACC T20I average was 22.9; post ACC's arrival it is 35.46.

LEIGH HART: Can we say that I drummed those stats up so I have something to take to my end-of-year review with G-Lane?

JASON HOYTE: The numbers speak for themselves, and I think Kane is on record saying we were exactly what he needed at that point of his career.

There is absolutely no record of Williamson saying this or anything even hinting at this.

HEATH: If our relationship with Kane was a sexual position it would be the sixty-niner.

Perhaps there is a better way to define the symbiosis between the ACC and New Zealand's greatest batter?

HEATH: For New Zealand cricket fans like us who struggled through the hard times of the '90s and '00s, Kane gave us hope. We had been hurt over and over again by catastrophic starts to our innings. We now had a player who could steady the ship. A calm and brilliant man who would fight back against adversity. Our fears slowly subsided.

On balance, it's a totally one-sided relationship. He has given the ACC a lot of pleasure over the years. In return, the ACC has given him a hat.

We now had a player who could steady the ship. A calm and brilliant man who would fight back against adversity. Our fears slowly subsided.

FORD: We certainly provided him with a lot of avant-garde advice and gave him a brand beyond being good at scoring tonnes of runs.

You're probably reading this and asking: 'Why all the Kane Williamson love now? He'd been brilliant for the best part of a decade, so why wait until the year 2023 of this almanack to fully give him his dues?'

Well, because towards the end of the 2022–23 summer Kane was starting to look vulnerable. He was unwanted by his Sunrisers Hyderabad Indian Premier League franchise, was starting to get injured with some regularity and had walked out to bat in the second innings against England at the Basin Reserve having passed 50 just once in his previous 12 test innings (an unbeaten 200 versus Pakistan at Karachi), and with just 10 runs in his three innings in the series to that point.

HART: Ditto re making sure I get credit for these stats.

Reinforcing the sense of desperation was the fact the Black Caps were trailing England 1–0 in the series after being destroyed in Williamson's backyard at Mount Maunganui, and here at the Basin they were following on after a disastrous opening two days.

HOYTE: I was concerned we were heading for an even more humiliating defeat than the first test.

After two days, New Zealand was a miserable 138 for 7 replying to England's blistering 435 for 8 declared. What followed was a series of events that, when pieced together, created an inexplicable finish.

FORD: I was quite emotional. I went along every day — this was just an incredible match, a jaw-dropping, electric, unforgettable, heartbreaking, pulse-racing match.

First, the skipper Tim Southee reached deep into his batting bag of tricks and smited six sixes on his way to 73. That allowed New Zealand to scrape out 209 and kept England's ageing bowlers in the field longer than they had expected.

Then the great New Zealanders Brendon McCullum and Ben Stokes chose to

enforce the follow-on, going against the grain of modern cricket trends.

That decision was soon in the spotlight as Devon Conway and Tom Latham laid a 149-run platform upon which the 'out-of-form' Williamson could build.

And build he did, refusing to even acknowledge an adoring crowd early on day four as he went past Ross Taylor's New Zealand record of 7683 test runs.

Williamson found staunch support in Daryl Mitchell (54) and Tom Blundell (90) as he made his way to a quite brilliant century.

FORD: A batting masterclass. Seven hours for 132. He was in his own little world the whole time.

What was at the time really annoying, but in hindsight very handy, was a late-innings collapse that saw England with a niggly target of 258 to win. The final day see-sawed wildly, with New Zealand on top early and then England had it well in hand at 201 for 5 — only for Neil Wagner to intervene in his usual manner. It came down to James Anderson on strike and Wagner bowling. Two to win, one wicket in hand.

MIKE LANE: Wagner to Anderson, ball down the leg side . . . he's got him!

SONIA GRAY: OH MY GOD! OH MY GOD!

LANE: New Zealand have won a historic test match as Jimmy Anderson gets strangled down the leg side. Wagner gets it and, for the fourth time in history, a team that has been forced to follow on has turned around and won the match.

It. Was. Epic.

FORD: I love the fact we won and that it was one run and all the statistical nerdery that comes with that, and just the sheer joy that erupted around the Basin when that wicket was taken. But at the heart of it was the fact it made me realise just how much I love the game, the intricacies, the weirdness, the tactics, the game management, the chaos, the unpredictability, the grind. Matches like this are what gets cricket into your bones. It really is the ultimate.

One test match like that a year would be extraordinary. Two in a fortnight defies explanation.

This time it was Sri Lanka in Christchurch, who kicked the test off with a

NEW ZEALAND VS ENGLAND, 2ND TEST
WELLINGTON, 24–28 FEB 2023
New Zealand won by 1 run

England	435-8 dec
H Brook	186
J Root	153*
M Henry	4-100

New Zealand	209
T Southee	73
S Broad	4-61

New Zealand (following on)	483
K Williamson	132
T Blundell	90
T Latham	83
J Leach	5-157

England	256
J Root	95
N Wagner	4-62
T Southee	3-45

fighting 355, despite Tim Southee's five-wicket haul. New Zealand replied with a 373 that was mainly down to Daryl Mitchell (102) and some lusty hitting from the tail, particularly Matt Henry (72).

Sri Lanka's 302 left New Zealand a daunting 285 to win, a target that appeared fanciful when the final day dawned to heavy rain and New Zealand starting on just 28 for 1.

In scarcely believable scenes, Williamson on 121 not out swung and missed at a ballooning bouncer off the day's final ball, but Neil Wagner scampered through for a bye on a torn hamstring and, although the stumps were broken at the non-striker's end, replays showed Williamson to have made his ground by millimetres.

Test cricket, eh?

The boys at *The BYC* were suitably impressed.

HOYTE: There's nothing quite like the grinding, anxiety-inducing feeling of five days of test cricket coming down to the final session, let alone the final hour, let alone the final over, let alone the final bloody ball.

DYLAN CLEAVER: Kane's Kane and we love him for it, but Daryl Mitchell, Son of a Mitch, there's a guy who bats with a chip on his shoulder and the chip says, 'Nobody thought I'd be good enough to be here but I'm not just going to show them I'm good enough, I'm going to show them that I'm better than they are and they can stick that up their arse.'

NEW ZEALAND VS SRI LANKA, 1ST TEST
CHRISTCHURCH, 9–13 MARCH 2023
New Zealand won by 2 wickets

Sri Lanka	355
K Mendis	87
T Southee	5-64
M Henry	4-80

Sri Lanka	302
A Mathews	115
B Tickner	4-100
M Henry	3-71

New Zealand	373
D Mitchell	102
M Henry	72
A Fernando	4-85

New Zealand	285-8
K Williamson	121*
D Mitchell	81
N Wagner	0* (0)
A Fernando	3-63

FORD: He's turned into a world-class player. That's not luck. It's a combination of his siege mentality and his West Australian cricket education.

One-day cricket immediately became the focus for the rest of the year. The Black Caps' campaign was eerily similar to that of four years ago. They front-loaded their wins, including a stunning victory over England in the World Cup opener.

That saw the emergence of Rachin Ravindra, the country's most exciting batting talent since, well, Kane Williamson.

HEATH: Did you know Rachin's first name is a portmanteau of Rahul and Sachin, as in Tendulkar and Dravid?

WELLS: It's entirely coincidental I believe, Matt, but that's beside the point. You just wanted the chance to show off by using a big word, didn't you?

HEATH: Affirmative.

He and Devon Conway made mincemeat out of the English, and it was just the start for Ravindra, who went on to score three centuries in the tournament, including a dazzler when New Zealand nearly mowed down Australia's 388 on the fateful night that turned into a miserable rugby morning.

NEW ZEALAND VS ENGLAND, CRICKET WORLD CUP
AHMEDABAD, INDIA, 5 OCTOBER 2023
New Zealand won by 9 wickets

England	282-9		New Zealand	283-1 (36.2 overs)
J Root	77		D Conway	152*
M Henry	3-48		R Ravindra	123*

Ravindra scored another century in a losing cause against Pakistan, but whereas in 2019 the Black Caps limped into the semis then shocked India, this time they didn't quite have enough left in their armoury to repeat the dose, despite a brilliant Daryl Mitchell century.

NEW ZEALAND VS AUSTRALIA, CRICKET WORLD CUP
DHARAMSHALA, INDIA, 28 OCTOBER 2023
Australia won by 5 runs

Australia	388		New Zealand	383-9
T Head	109 (67)		R Ravindra	116 (89)
G Phillips	3-37		J Neesham	58 (39)
			A Zampa	3-74

FORD: It was actually a bloody good tournament and Rachin lit it up, but the time zone made it a bit harder for cricket fans to fully engage. *The BYC* went absolutely gangbusters during these couple of months and, worryingly, I think a lot of New Zealanders were relying on us for our razor-sharp analysis, which of course we were happy to provide.

HART: I don't remember this tournament at all.

FORD: See what I mean?

WELLS: Unlike England in 2019 when I knew we could go all the way to the final, I feel like the semifinal was New Zealand's ceiling at this tournament, so I wasn't as gutted as I normally would be when we lost.

FORD: We just left ourselves too much to do against an annoyingly good Indian side, who then lost to an annoyingly annoying Australian side in the final. *Plus ça change.*

Given how allergic the young Kane Williamson was to self-promotion and marketing his extraordinary talent, you could make an argument that the ACC's portrayal of him as a ship's captain, with the accompanying hat and the Steady the Ship moniker, is one of the most successful pieces of sports marketing in New Zealand history. The movement was so infectious that the Labour Government's Minister of Finance Grant Robertson, a huge cricket fan, took to wearing the hat, and described his ethos when faced with the task of trying to balance the books coming out of the global pandemic as 'steadying the ship'.

Williamson's was not the only nickname to get serious traction. The Hairy Jav (Grant Elliott), Sexy Camel (Tim Southee) and Lovely Trenty (Trent Boult) quickly became part of the everyday cricket vernacular. Some, like Elliott, embraced the moniker and have come to use it as a quasi-marketing tool. Others less so.

On the rugby side, the ACC once received an impassioned plea from Aaron Smith to change his nickname from 'Dickpic', after an unfortunate photo-sharing experiment with a 'friend' found its way into the public domain. There was a brief point, too, when he was known as After David, following a toilet tryst, after which he asked for a 'sawn after David' rather than a sworn affidavit so he and a different friend could get their stories straight.

Smith, a decent keeper-batter in his days in the Feilding High School 1st XI, was playing in the first Black Clash, commentated by the ACC. On the bus on the way to the hotel after the game, during which he'd been called Dickpic by the adoring crowd, Smith found himself seated next to a sheepish Matt Heath.

'Come on, man,' Smith said to Heath. 'My mum listens to you guys.'

Scotty J Stevenson allegedly cut in with, 'Shut the fuck up, Dickpic, you don't get to choose your own nickname,' but Heath was moved by the halfback's plight and co-opted Mike Lane into the conversation.

LANE: He was such a nice guy and he had this pleading look in his eyes, so given his namesake at the Highlanders and All Blacks was Ben from Accounts, we decided he would be Aaron from Distribution. Nice and harmless . . . he still gets called Dickpic from the bank a bit, though.

It appears the nickname discussions will continue for many years to come. As the finishing touches were being put on this book, news was rolling in that Caleb Clarke, a huge *Star Wars* fan, was pitching to have his Jabba the Butt designation changed.

STEADY THE SHIP

A very steady ship.

A neck beard that results in the voice of an angel.

Captain's pipe.

Matrix of leadership.

Penchant for the film "Grandad's Bum"

Elbow: Has a tendency to bend occasionally on release.

Dangerous number of cherries in the meat of the trusty Gray-Nicolls.

@UGLY_INK

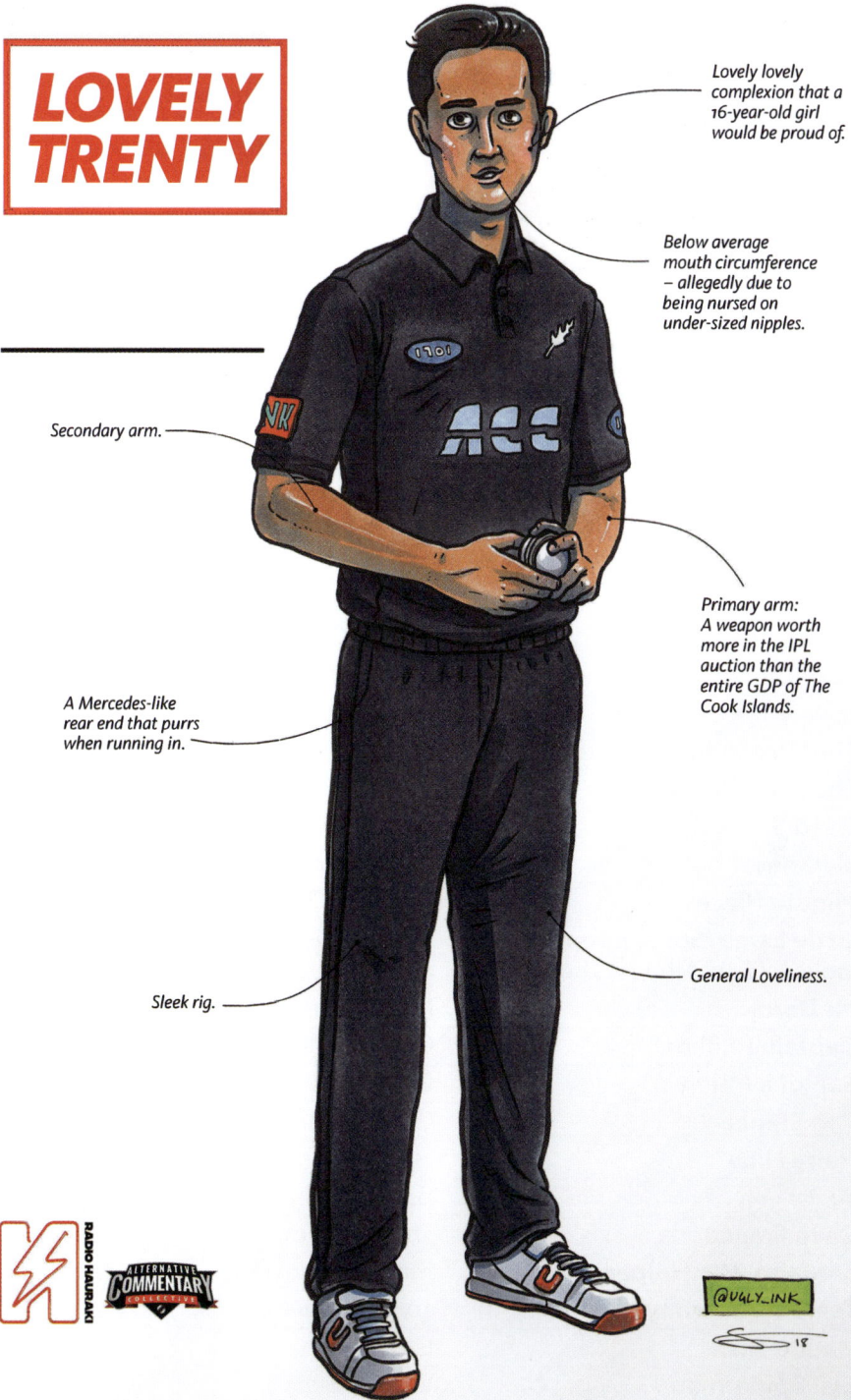

LOVELY TRENTY

Lovely lovely complexion that a 16-year-old girl would be proud of.

Below average mouth circumference – allegedly due to being nursed on under-sized nipples.

Secondary arm.

Primary arm: A weapon worth more in the IPL auction than the entire GDP of The Cook Islands.

A Mercedes-like rear end that purrs when running in.

General Loveliness.

Sleek rig.

@UGLY_INK

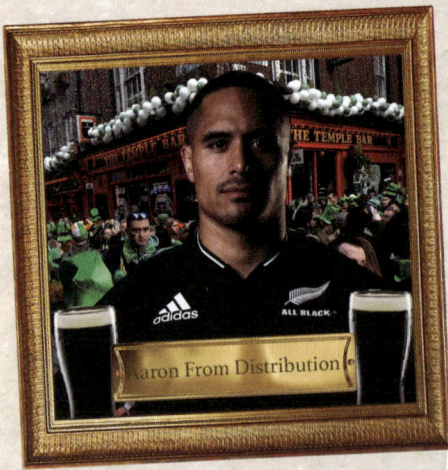

NICKNAMES: AN INCOMPLETE GLOSSARY OF SOME OLD AND NEW FAVOURITES

CRICKET

Steady the Ship	Kane Williamson
Sexy Camel	Tim Southee
Lovely Trenty	Trent Boult
The Whakamana Express	Lockie Ferguson
The Hairy Jav	Grant Elliott
Dead Shark Eyes	Martin Guptill
Sir Lingus	Ross Taylor
Minute Piece	Colin de Grandhomme
Little Lamb/Some people say he looks like an Alpaca/The Stud	James Neesham
Mr Darcy	Matt Henry
Captain Phillips	Glenn Phillips
Son of a Mitch	Daryl Mitchell
The Stance	Colin Munro
Hairy Nips	Henry Nicholls
BJ	BJ Watling
Dave Franco	Tom Latham
Santa's Little Helper	Mitchell Santner
Tea Bag/Cowboy	Tom Blundell
Ish the Dish	Ish Sodhi
Evil Spiderman	Will Young
Devon Threeway	Devon Conway
007	Neil Wagner
Gulliver	Kyle Jamieson

Davey Dumb-Dumb	David Warner
The Gay Avenger	Ben Stokes
Murder She Woakes	Chris Woakes

RUGBY

Dickpic/After David/Aaron from Distribution	Aaron Smith
Ben from Accounts	Ben Smith
Dogroll	Scott Barrett
Lurch	Brodie Retallick
Runny Bum	Dane Coles
Cody's 8%	Codie Taylor
McAwesome Hedgehog	Richie McCaw
Mad Eye Moody	Joe Moody
Cleveland Steamer	Sam Cane
Captain Caveman	Sam Whitelock
Eye Sockets	Kieran Read
Beaker	Ardie Savea
Jack Good Spew	Jack Goodhue
The Saveloy/Severed Piece	Sevu Reece
Pita-Gus Stubbie Cooler	Pita-Gus Sowakula
The Lorax	Karl Tu'inukuafe
The Hyena	Damian McKenzie
The Mother	Folau Fakatava
Anton Do Bro	Anton Lienert-Brown
Epilady Perineum	TJ Perenara
Mike Hoskins Sotutu	Hoskins Sotutu
The Seat/Jabba the Butt	Caleb Clarke
Slippery Barrett	Beauden Barrett
Cheryl Mo'unga Marie	Richie Mo'unga
The Udon Noodle	Jordie Barrett
Good Will Jordan	Will Jordan
Sierra Leone	Akira Ioane

The ACC's relationship with rugby league became supercharged in 2023, due in no small part to the Warriors becoming supercharged under the leadership of coach Andrew Webster, captain Tohu Harris and the spectacular return to form of halfback Shaun Johnson.

The high-energy *Mad Monday* podcast, which launched in 2022 and stars Chris Key, Ben Hurley, Manaia Stewart and the world's biggest league fan, Dai Henwood, became appointment listening in 2023, and the commentaries under the yellow button grew in fervour as it became obvious the Warriors were going to charge into the playoffs.

For many, a season of gratitude culminated in a playoff victory against the Newcastle Knights in front of a sold-out 26,000 screaming fans at Mount Smart Stadium, but Dai Henwood had found his moment earlier in the year.

NEW ZEALAND WARRIORS VS NEWCASTLE KNIGHTS, NRL FINALS WEEK 2
AUCKLAND, 16 SEPTEMBER 2023

Warriors 40 10 Knights

Tries: Charnze Nicoll-Klokstad (1), Addin Fonua-Blake (6), Marcelo Montoya (11), Dylan Walker (46), Rocco Berry (59), Dallin Watene-Zelezniak (63), Bayley Sironen (75)

Conversions: Adam Pompey 6/7 (8, 13, 47, 60, 65, 76)

Tries: Greg Marzhew (24), Dylan Lucas (42)
Conversions: Kalyn Ponga (43)

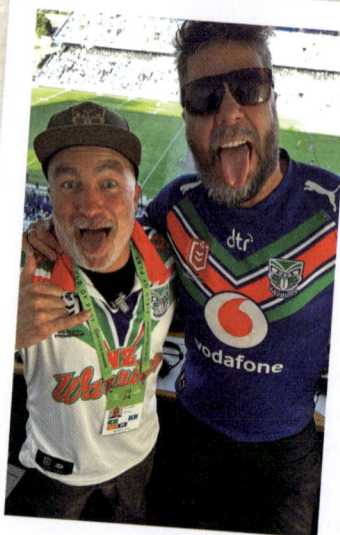

Dai's weekly 'Off The Back Fence' segment is usually reserved for an epic, topical rant, like this beauty when the All Blacks played the Springboks at Mount Smart Stadium because Eden Park was out of commission due to the FIFA Women's World Cup being held at the same time.

'Well, it sucks to be you All Blacks. Go and play at Colin Maiden, mate. Go and play up the road at Gribblehirst. Go to the Domain. Find somewhere else to play.

Don't come out to the mighty Fruit Bowl, Mount Smart Stadium, where the mana drips from the rooftops, where the rugby league taniwha guards the wonderful New Zealand Warriors. Don't come and put your nose into our honey jar . . . We'll take your 6000 extra seats, but we're not happy about it because we're going to have to spray the BORING off the pitch you left there from the night before when you got all BORED against the BORING South Africans, getting all BORING on your BORING rugby union. You can piss off.'

But in mid-July, Dai changed tack. It was beyond touching.

Off The Back Fence, 17 July 2023

'Look, this is a bit of a different one today. Normally I'm just fizzing and shouting and going crazy, but this is a gratitude "Off the Back Fence".

'I've been doing chemo for the last month or so. I'm four rounds into six rounds of this current one...it's bloody tough. I'm suffering mentally and physically. It's an absolute shambles, but I just want to say thank you to all the ACC fans that listen to the commentary. I get to come in and commentate the Warriors and the Warriors, honestly, when I'm going through chemo I watch old Warriors wins. I pore over Warriors stats.

'The New Zealand Warriors are something that is a massive highlight in my life, win, lose or draw. They just buoy me up. League as a hobby is something I absolutely love. I get to come in here and commentate the league with absolute legends in the ACC and absolute legends like you who are listening and watching. You send in texts, you fill up my bucket and you make me forget about having cancer. That is a massive thing because otherwise I think about cancer 24/7.

'So, the fact that I get to come in here and commentate the mighty One New Zealand Warriors and watch us surge into the top four this week...So, a massive thank you to the New Zealand Warriors and a massive thanks to the fans of the ACC who join us week in, week out. I bloody love you.'

The feeling is mutual.

How to Know if You're
WARRIORS HARD
A checklist, by Manaia Stewart

My love of the Warriors started the same way as most people my age:
by asking my old man why he was so angry on a Sunday afternoon.
My dad is so Warriors Hard that he considers me Warriors Medium.
Some of that is circumstance. I was only four years old in 1995, so over
several beers and a shaky wi-fi connection, I leaned on him to help me
compile the following list of signs that you, too, are Warriors Hard.

#001. Dean Bell. Alright, so that's a lame joke — but, if you don't get it, you're probably not Warriors Hard.

2. Your life partner tells everyone that the Warriors are the only thing you're optimistic about.

3. If your wife left you for Stacey Jones (or Shaun Johnson), you'd probably ask if you can still be friends.

4. At least once in your life you've sat through 60 minutes of sideways rain just to watch Shaun Johnson nail a sideline conversion to cut the deficit to 30.

5. You're still salty about the way they treated Ali Lauiti'iti.

6. You can directly link Konrad Hurrell to the Ferndale Strangler.

7. You can do the same with Buck Shelford and Chanel Harris-Tavita, but for different reasons.

8. You can name the supermarket franchise Steve Price managed*.

---

* Four Square

9. You know what car Mark Tookey drove*.

10. You can't sleep for at least an hour after watching Hitro Okesene highlights.

11. Or Sean Hoppe's daughter's highlights, for that matter.

12. You have at least one story about seeing Stacey Jones in the wild.

13. The Mad Butcher's told you to get fucked.

14. You could tell me the fellow league flyer who Lee Oudenryn beat in a 100m sprint in 1992**.

15. You can't spell Oudenryn.

16. You spent quite a bit of time thinking his surname was double-barrelled, as in, Lee Oudenryn-Dropsit.

17. You can vividly picture Clinton Toopi's iconic Cornrowhawk.

18. Your nan's favourite player was Manu Butterfly.

2024

WE'RE STILL HERE

Somewhere on Auckland's Southern Motorway, a car with an animated driver and passenger drove up alongside the ACC's ute and caravan as it was pointing south towards Mount Maunganui and the 2024 Tradies XI game. They were trying to yell something above the din of the traffic.

MIKE LANE: They were pointing back to the caravan. Maybe it had a flat, but nothing about the way it was handling suggested anything wrong. Against my better judgement, I pulled over to the hard shoulder to inspect.

As Lane suspected, when they did an inventory, there was nothing wrong with the tyres. The shell of the caravan that acts as their commentary nerve centre when they're on the road was intact.

LANE: 'Just a pair of dickheads seeing the ACC livery and thinking they're hilarious winding us up,' was what I thought as we jumped back in the ute to complete the trip.

It wasn't until the next morning, when they turned up to commentate the opening match of the weekend — a highly charged T20 encounter between two teams of Dulux tradies — that they realised they weren't being pranked. The caravan, their pride and joy, squelched under their feet the moment they stepped inside.

LANE: There was a skylight-sized square hole in the roof and my thoughts quickly changed from cursing the dickheads that tried to tell us what had gone on to hoping like hell the torn appendage hadn't created havoc on the motorway. Those things would be pretty unforgiving if they frisbeed through your windscreen at 100 kilometres per hour.

Dulux TRADIES XI VS ALTERNATIVE COMMENTARY COLLECTIVE

BAY OVAL - TAURANGA
15 MARCH 2024

WIN A SPOT FOR YOU AND A MATE IN THE ACC TEAM
TEXT DULUX TO 3236 TO ENTER

The caravan, the second they've been in charge of since using a mate's re-skinned one during their first year, would need some TLC.

This version was picked up from Taranaki. It had been sitting unused at The Radio Network in New Plymouth. Well, unused is hardly fair. It had been commandeered by a member of the homeless community and was in dire need of an airing.

The caravan was stripped out and transformed into a rudimentary, yet highly effective, commentary suite. On hot days at the cricket, it became a foetid hellhole, yet it was their foetid hellhole and they learned to love it.

In its kitted-out form, the caravan has been used as a Trojan horse for smuggling booze; as a mobile bar; and as a potential asylum house for streakers. Ministers of the Crown have entered the lair and been interviewed live on air. A lowly intern once used the caravan for a tryst with a communications professional. It has been the subject of conflict between the ACC and venue administrators. It has had food and beverages thrown at it. Underpants, too.

Once it caught fire. An intern, not the same one as mentioned above, took it to get a warrant of fitness but never released the brake. When he entered the testing station he wondered why a mechanic was running in his direction with a fire extinguisher, and he also wondered what that horrific burning smell was.

It looks a bit tired now. The skylight flying off on the motorway was as good as any indication that its structural integrity is starting to waver.

MATT HEATH: Some hard decisions probably need to be made about its future soon. It will be hard to say goodbye, though.

Could we see the ACC travelling the country in an RV, one happy family of Griswolds making a Netflix-style documentary?

LANE: It's too early to rule anything out, but we're not going anywhere in a hurry.

'We're not going anywhere in a hurry.' That could be the ACC's motto.

In 2013, they were just a loose idea. In 2014, they were discussing losing their virginity and commentating to an audience of zero from a mate's caravan. A year later, they were annoying the shit out of the ICC and wearing out the welcome mat laid down for them by New Zealand Cricket.

A decade later, they're still wearing out welcomes, still annoying the shit out of people and still commentating, only this time their audiences across their various channels and platforms extends to hundreds of thousands.

The ACC has accidentally-on-purpose morphed into one of the biggest sports media brands, if not the biggest, in the country.

They're sought after by sports as diverse as horse racing, lawn bowls and skiing. They're wanted for Super Bowl events and charity cricket matches. If they said 'yes' to everything they were asked to commentate on or appear at, they'd have about three weekends off a year.

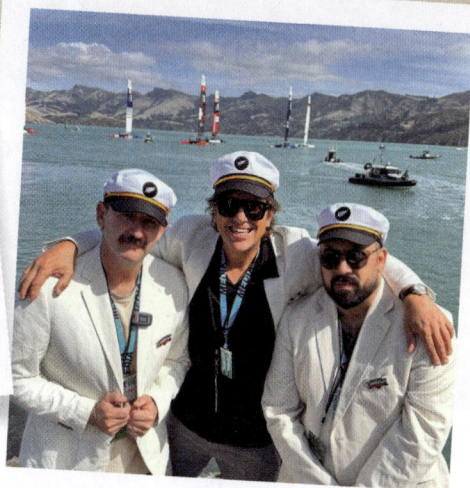

JEREMY WELLS: It's hard to know where we'll go, but we're aware we're in a balancing act. The critical letter in the ACC is the 'A'. We have to be an alternative. To be alternative there needs to be a mainstream and that mainstream cannot be us. That's the whole idea of what alternative is — a different voice.

Women's sport has proven to be a highwire they're reluctant to cross without a safety net. Their act is unashamedly blokey; their humour turns 'dangerously sexual' quite early and often.

> 'Just to let you know incase [*sic*] you weren't aware, the only people who find your commentary funny are idiot pig-headed blokes and the reason why you make them laugh is because you're idiot pig-headed blokes.'— Sandi

They have ventured into netball, but their output is overwhelmingly male sport for a male audience.

LANE: I've been approached by some White Ferns, who are keen for us to cover them, but even the nickname side of it becomes more problematic with women's sport. The ones who have spoken to us have said, 'We don't care, call us what you like, talk the same sort of shit you do with the Black Caps, we can take it,' but the problem is never the athlete. It's the people who don't even listen to us but get told by someone else who knew

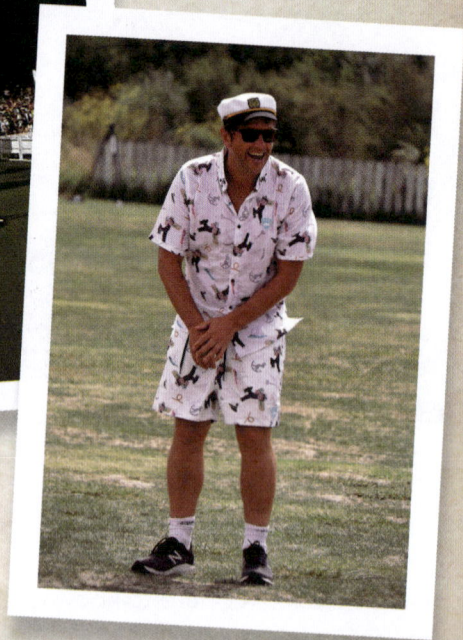

someone else that was cousins with someone who heard us. They listen back so they can get outraged on behalf of the athlete.

We'll figure it out and get there, but it will probably require some more out-of-the-box thinking . . . and, for once, that was not an attempt at a childish pun.

Cricket was their raison d'etre. For some, it still is, but with savvy recruitment and sheer good luck they've managed to find love in their hearts for other sports, particularly the national obsession.

LANE: We take callers in the middle of games, we have a talkback function where punters can leave their own piece of commentary. I'm pretty sure there is no other rugby commentary team in the world that takes live callers to air during games — because it's ludicrous and highly dangerous!

We've got to a stage now where we know who we are and how we want to cover rugby. There's no time for whimsy like there is in our cricket coverage, it's just full-noise, unfiltered, hellishly biased commentary. Nobody's taking it seriously, there are nicknames flying everywhere and we get massively over-excited.

The key to their success is their authenticity.

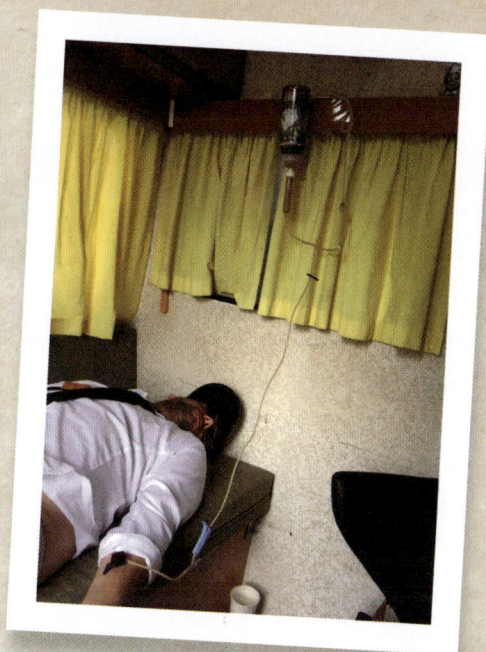

It's not contrived. It's sort of accidental, and it's sort of honest, but it's certainly real. Our audience responded to that.

LEE BAKER: It's not contrived. It's sort of accidental, and it's sort of honest, but it's certainly real. Our audience responded to that. Sure, it meant that we sometimes ended up talking about cats fucking, or something utterly banal, outrageous and offensive, but we always did it with this kind of misplaced honesty. Our mostly young, male audience picked up on that. It was kind of reassuring for them that there were people talking to them on their level, that they were indulging them and their little quirks as well. That's what we were doing, we were indulging ourselves.

Lee Baker would admit to moments of sheer regret, when words flew out of his mouth that he immediately wished hadn't.

BAKER: Fuck yeah, it happens all the time. I like to say things that can be deemed quite extreme, because it's exhilarating to do that. Often my mind goes like this: 'I shouldn't really say what I want to say . . . fuck it, I'm going to say it anyway.' That's the rock 'n' roll element of it.

Our audience is a very forgiving audience. They're unlikely to get us in trouble.

WELLS: These past eleven years have certainly given me a new appreciation for cricket, but they have also opened my eyes to the depravities of my co-commentators. I've learned more disgusting things about them and the human condition than I could ever imagine. So yes, it's been an absolute blast.

HEATH: I am so very grateful G-Lane and J-Wells invited me into the ACC all those years ago. I am not sure exactly what the last decade of my life would have been like without it. But I know I would have suffered terrible FOMO from the outside. There have been so many adventures, laughs and shocking humiliations. We have been lucky enough to be there shoulder-to-shoulder to document some of the greatest moments in New Zealand sporting history. We have met our sporting heroes. Travelled the world. Together we have achieved incredible numbers in terms of audience and incredible lows in terms of behaviour. It's a brotherhood, a cult and a scam. A way to spend time with the very best of mates while being able to claim to anyone who might complain that it's actually work (well, to be fair, it is a lot of work for Mike and Joseph). But the rest of us can claim it's hard work when it isn't and we get to go away and watch the sport we love with the friends we love. Well, to be honest, no one really believes what I do for the ACC is work, but somehow we keep getting away with it year after year. Viva la ACC!

JASON HOYTE: I have found it a very easy and liberating experience. You turn up, everything is organised for you and then you simply get to watch and talk about a sport you love. With a project like this, it doesn't even feel like you have to talk. Words just appear under your name. It's amazing.

LANE: It's a shitload of hard work bringing it together. It's a battle day in and day out. My marriage would probably be a lot healthier without it, as would my general wellbeing. But if my marriage is going to break down and my health continues to deteriorate, I wouldn't ask to do it with any other people. A band of self-destructive brothers.

LEIGH HART: Sometimes I find myself wondering about how far we have come, but most often I don't think about it at all. To cut to the chase, I thought we would have taken the whole thing a bit further than this by now. Maybe not world domination, but at least enough to afford a second-hand car. At the beginning, Jeremy talked about making a shitload of cash, but that's never happened. We're like seven middle-aged men in a covers band. We get to spend a bit of time away from the partners and have a few laughs and a few beers, not necessarily in that order. I can probably take it or leave it, to be blunt. But having come up with the idea and being the unofficial vice captain, I feel not so much a sense of responsibility but more an obligation to stick around. Still, no regrets. I look at the past eleven years and think, 'It could have been worse.'

PAUL FORD: Honestly, who would have thought this could go from being a brain fart of an idea into a mega cult for New Zealand sports fans, who are keen to get out of the missionary position of traditional broadcast teams? Who would have thought so many were ready to roll the dice with some new Kama Sutra commentary fare? It is preposterous. If you're being rude, you'd say that our point of difference revolves around a shoestring budget, a Sprite Alpine caravan made in Ōtorohanga in 1975, uninformed analysis, no former international cricketers, a plethora of obscure anecdotes and a mild scatological obsession. And you'd be right. But what I love the most is that all the crew who have been involved in the ACC are not in it for the money or the fame, but for the joy, the self-deprecation, the serendipity, the nonsense and the love of the games. Long live the caravan of love. Long live the ACC.

Which brings us to the neatest and yet messiest way to end a story about the ACC.

The single-most-complained-about piece of 'commentary'. There can only be one.

LANE: Granddad's bum.

WELLS: Baker's granddad story.

HART: Shit, good question. I still laugh every time I think about Jerry recalling the time he had sex with a woman with pleurisy, but it probably wasn't that. Was it Baker's granddad?

HEATH: It'd have to be Baker wouldn't it?

BAKER: I was responsible for one of the few broadcasting standards complaints that went quite a long way through the process. I remember this complaint was happening and Mike turned to me and said, 'That was you.' I can't remember what it was.

   If you're not standing on the edge, it's not that interesting. It will be too much like the establishment. We've got to keep shifting that line in the sand.

So, what was this line-shifting moment?

LANE: I'm not going to go into the full details, but we had been speculating that Kane Williamson had to have some demons. He couldn't be that perfect.

HEATH: He is perfect. I love him.

LANE: One of the things speculated upon was that he had a giant collection of granddad porn. All bullshit obviously, but Baker used the opportunity to tell this story about how when he was a kid, his granddad would try and fill his head with all these facts and Lee would respond, 'Tell us something we don't know, Granddad.'

   This continued on for years until one day his grandfather had enough and said: 'I'll tell you something you don't know, your grandma loves . . .'

Until the next time!

From the offices of
Scotty J Stevenson
ACC Head G-Lane
ACC Towers
Auckland
New Zealand

Dear G-Lane,

Having now been exposed to your right testicle on 23 separate
occasions, it behoves me to tender my resignation from the ACC.

Don't get me wrong. It's not just your right testicle. It's your
left one, too. Which is slightly larger than the right. And it's
the fact I know this that really concerns me.

Things started well. The Social Media Testicle was great value. I
would have quite happily sat in that dangling pink porch nut sack
all day long and answered the bewilderingly inane questions you
wrote for me. Then you had to let your mouse out of the house.

I should have never got you Wayne Barnes's actual Barnesies. He
warned me. I did not listen.

It's not me, it's you. And not just those two parts of you.
Everything you touch turns to calamity. The flying chicken-
nugget incident in Napier during which you accommodated us in a
refurbished rest home that still smelled of dead people springs to
mind. I can still recall waking up in a bed next to Lee Baker who,
half naked as he was, resembled a dead person. I thought he was
dead, in fact.

Sure, it has been fun, but the events in the immediate aftermath of
the great cricketing travesty of 2019 still haunt me. As does the
recollection of contending with an out-of-control sea lion during
a routine Black Clash getaway in Hawke's Bay. Actually, why did so
many awful things happen in Hawke's Bay? Never mind.

I love you. You know that. But ever since Hoyte took the middle
initial you gave me and pawned it off as his own, it's like a
part of me has died. Much like Joe Durie essentially did when he
passed out on the finish line of the Queenstown half marathon after
attempting to run it in full merino undergarments.

Please apologise to Matt Heath for me. I did not mean to punch a
hole in his television. I had never used VR before. Or since, for
that matter.

I like Jeremy. He seems nice.

Best for your continued exposure,
Scotty J Stevenson

THE CREW

THE ORIGINAL SEVEN

JEREMY WELLS

The host of *Seven Sharp*, formerly known as Newsboy. He is co-host of Radio Hauraki's *Matt & Jerry Show* and has numerous television credits, including *Eating Media Lunch*, *Taskmaster NZ* and *The Late Night Big Breakfast*.

MIKE LANE

Co-founder of the legendary fashion and fan group the Beige Brigade. Mike was once touted to be the next big thing in rugby, but discovered a social life and things rapidly degenerated from there. Now steadies the ship as CEO of the ACC.

PAUL FORD

Co-founder of the legendary fashion and fan group the Beige Brigade. The only qualified journalist in the group, Ford was once trespassed from the Basin Reserve for berating highly strung Australian opener Michael Slater for the 45 minutes he remained in the 90s. Is the founder and regular panellist on *The BYC*, New Zealand's oldest and favourite specialty cricket podcast.

LEE BAKER

A history graduate with an eye for esoterica and ill-conceived analogies, Baker is the unthinking man's thinking man. His television credits include *Eating Media Lunch*, *Neighbours at War*, *The Unauthorised History of New Zealand* and *Underarm: The Ball That Changed Cricket*. The born-and-bred Aucklander is a published author, having penned the bestseller *Way of the JAFA: A Guide to Surviving Auckland and Aucklanders*.

LEIGH HART

Gate-crashed his way into the nation's consciousness as That Guy on *SportsCafe*. He parlayed that into shows such as *Moon TV* and *The Late Night Big Breakfast*, before getting his big break as the stats man for the ACC.

MATT HEATH

A modern-day media polymath, Heath was guitarist and singer for cult band Deja Voodoo, and played Danny Parker on *Back of the Y Masterpiece Television*. The co-host of the *Matt & Jerry Show* wrote a weekly column for the *New Zealand Herald*, is a published author and paints Post-Impressionist-style landscapes as a hobby.

JASON HOYTE

One half of famed comedy duo Sugar & Spice, Hoyte's acting chops have landed him roles as diverse as Steve Mudgeway the guidance counsellor on *Seven Periods with Mr Gormsby* and as a barman on *The Brokenwood Mysteries*. Hoyte hosts *The BYC* podcast and is a former umpire in the Peter Plumley-Walker mould.

THE UNORIGINAL MANY

DAI HENWOOD

Henwood is New Zealand's biggest rugby league fan. He proves that on a weekly basis by watching every match of every round of the NRL, then when that is completed he will move on to the Queensland Cup. Dai has a surprisingly long run-up for his right-arm medium pacers and can be seen at Last Man Stands using a harrow bat and youth pads and gloves. A great New Zealander who hosts the league coverage and chips in with cricket.

SCOTTY J STEVENSON

Born in Northland and played rugby to Rippa level, then spent the next 17 years honing his commentary skills while training to be an early childhood teacher. He got his big break in 2010 when Tony Johnson missed a flight to Kerikeri and quickly became a go-to rugby commentator and analyst — which makes him perfect for cricket.

BEC SANDYS

Comedian, snowboarder and massive cricket tragic, Bec's greatest sporting moment came when she entered a beginners' skateboarding competition and won! It mattered little that she was 21 and the three other competitors were all under nine. Bec has written for *The Project* and *7 Days*, and has performed stand-up shows at the Melbourne International Comedy Festival.

BEN HURLEY

There's something about comedy that attracts fervent league/cricket followers, or is it vice versa? Whatever way round it goes, Ben fits the mould perfectly. The comic has probably seen more live cricket than anybody in the team due to his role as ground MC for New Zealand Cricket, a job that eventually broke him, so he sought the comforting bosom of the ACC caravan.

JAMES MCONIE

The leading sports journalist on Sky Sport, host of *The Crowd Goes Wild* and, alongside Weird Al Yankovic, one of the greatest parody songwriters of his generation. Although originally from Te Awamutu, McOnie started his career just down the road on a King Country newspaper and knows more about the Meads family than the Meads family themselves.

CHRIS KEY

A *Crowd Goes Wild* alumnus, Chris has been covering sport for a number of years and has been to more press conferences than is healthy for any one individual. Chris brings his talents to Radio Hauraki's *Big Show* and the ACC's coverage of rugby, league and basketball. He thinks his moustache makes him look smarter.

MIKE MINOGUE

The future looked blinding for Horowhenua's finest, Mike Minogue, when he won acting awards for his role in *Wellington Paranormal*. The fall into the ACC caravan has therefore been steep. He, Hoyte and Key make up Radio Hauraki's *Big Show*, where Mike's love for cricket often shines through.

BEN BOYCE

The creator of *Pulp Sport* and *Jono and Ben at Ten*. Ben commentates on cricket, has entered a party in the New Zealand general election and has previously been arrested.

TONY LYALL

Another stand-up comic, Tony has worked on *7 Days*, *The Project*, Radio Hauraki and multiple NZ International Comedy Festival galas. Tony has been a match-day MC for New Zealand Cricket and the Blues, hosts *Champagne Rugby* and is the only white man in West Auckland driving a Mazda Demio.

DYLAN CLEAVER

An award-winning journalist and occasional author who has a disturbing, maybe even unnatural, obsession with the summer game. Cleaver brings an unhealthy amount of stored (some say unnecessary) knowledge and stats to *The BYC* and cannot deal with losing to Jason Hoyte in Paul Ford's 'News or Ruse'.

MANAIA STEWART

Manaia joined the ACC in 2018 and has become a fixture across the commentary and podcast network. He is best known for being able to connect any global celebrity, dead or alive, to South Canterbury within four degrees of separation, and is highly regarded for his views on the fine art of streaking.

SONIA GRAY

Gray has made a lot of real people rich as a Lotto presenter, and a couple of make-believe men poor as a con-woman on *Shortland Street*. Once had a pint of beer poured over her head at a pub by someone who could not separate real life from fiction. Is a highly emotional cricket watcher and a much better human being than most of the ACC.

MATT WARD

Has a name so common it is pointless googling to find out anything. Was once known as the Night Wolf and can drink up to 14 standard drinks before showing even mild signs of impairment.

THE GLUE

JOSEPH DURIE

Durie is both ubiquitous and in the shadows. There is little the ACC has done, criminal or innocent, that he has not seen or recorded. Is paid as much for what he doesn't say as what he does. An ice hockey — it's just hockey to him — tragic, Durie has seen Mike Lane's nut sack several times.

Special thanks to Photosport NZ for the use of their quality sporting images on the following pages:

18, 24, 26, 27, 28 (top), 29, 43, 44, 45, 62, 77, 88, 102 (top), 112, 121, 131, 140, 145, 148 (bottom), 153, 164 (bottom), 177, 189, 211, 218, 235, 258, 261, 266.

The scoresheet featured on pages 212–15 is available as a one-sheet poster at cricketkit.org.

Additional design elements such as backgrounds, clipboards, notepads, books, photo frames, flag/jersey icons, illustrations (except Ish the Dish, Lovely Trent and Steady the Ship), plus the images on pages 12 (bottom), 13 and 245, are from stock.adobe.com

PENGUIN

UK | USA | Canada | Ireland | Australia
India | New Zealand | South Africa | China

Penguin is an imprint of the Penguin Random House group of companies,
whose addresses can be found at global.penguinrandomhouse.com.

Penguin
Random House
New Zealand

First published by Penguin Random House New Zealand, 2024

1 3 5 7 9 10 8 6 4 2

Cover design by Carla Sy and Kate Barraclough © Penguin Random House New Zealand
Text design by Kate Barraclough © Penguin Random House New Zealand
Prepress by Soar Communications Group
Printed and bound in China by RR Donnelley
Produced using vegetable-based inks.

A catalogue record for this book is available from
the National Library of New Zealand.

ISBN 978-1-77695-113-0
eISBN 978-1-77695-408-7

penguin.co.nz

FSC
www.fsc.org

MIX
Paper | Supporting
responsible forestry
FSC® C144853